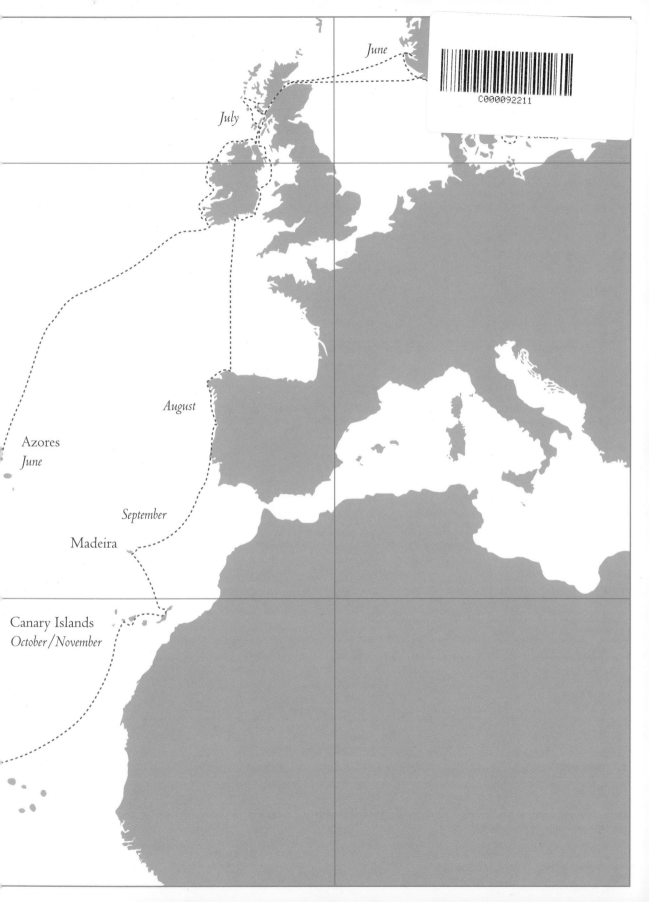

June

July

August

Azores
June

September

Madeira

Canary Islands
October / November

C000092211

To Judith

The
MISSING CENTIMETRE

[signature]

9 Jan 2010

The MIssing Centimetre
One family's Atlantic sailing adventure

First published in 2009 by

Outworn Creed Ltd
Saracens House
St Margarets Green
Ipswich
Suffolk
IP4 2BN

www.outworncreed.com
info@outworncreed.com

ISBN number: 978-0-9562762-0-9

Text © Leon Schulz
Photographs © Leon Schulz
(Page 196 Juliet Dearlove, page 257 and page 263 Daniel Gandy)

The rights of Leon Schulz to be identified as the Author of this Work
have been asserted by him in accordance with the Copyright, Designs
and Patents Act, 1988.

All rights reserved. This book is sold under the condition that no
part of it may be reproduced, copied, stored in a retrieval system
or transmitted in any form or by any means, electronic, mechanical,
photocopying, recording or otherwise without prior permission in
writing of the publisher.

A CIP catalogue record of this is available from the British Library

Editing by Tim Fenton and Martin Scudamore
Design by Eddie Ephraums, Envisagebooks.com

Printed and bound by CandC Offset Printing, China

NOTE: The material contained in this book is set out in good faith
for general guidance. No liability can be accepted for loss, injury or
expense incurred as a result of relying in particular circumstances
on statements made herein.

The
MISSING CENTIMETRE

One family's Atlantic sailing adventure

LEON
SCHULZ

Outworn
Creed Ltd

FOREWORD

Many people have written about sailing across oceans, a few about doing so with children. But none, as far I know, has succeeded in placing such an adventure in the context of the whole of life so well as Leon Schulz.

Leon and I first met in the old fishing dock that is now Darsena Deportiva Marina in La Coruña on the north-west tip of Spain. I had crossed from Falmouth and was tired but exhilarated after my first lengthy off-shore voyage. Leon, Karolina, Jessica and Jonathan had sailed south in their yacht, Regina, from Ireland. None of us said we were definitely going across the Atlantic. We were heading south and seeing how it went.

Leon was longer out of work and more relaxed than me. I was impressed by the confident way he tackled the repairs and preparatory tasks that fill the days of cruising liveaboards. It was only later, as our trip progressed, and more and more of our sea miles and nights at anchor came to be spent within VHF or even hailing range of Regina that I began to see the truly spiritual nature of Leon's voyage.

The power of his insight was confirmed for me when, a few months after we had all resumed our land-locked lives, he sent me this book's manuscript. He had written it in the third of his four or five languages and, with typical but unnecessary modesty, wanted an English journalist to read it over. I found it a revelation, a distillation of so many of the questions with which I had wrestled – questions of relevance to sailors, would-be sailors, hardened hydro-phobes or really anyone with any interest in living right.

Leon and I both know we're lucky to be among the few able to take a year or two off to relax and to think about these things. He doesn't offer answers. We all have to find our own answers. But if you want a bit of help with the questions and a delightful sparkly, spray-flecked ride along the way, then this is the book for you.

Tim Fenton

AUTHOR'S INTRODUCTION

Inspiration is infectious. It spreads from one person to another. And the medium by which it does so is that of the story. Innumerable stories had sustained and fed our dreams before we dared cast off for real. Of all those stories, I would like to mention one in particular. Ariel IV is the story of a cruise written by the Swedish couple Eric Boye & Birgitta Boye-Freudenthal, who circumnavigated with their three sons from 1998 to 2001. On its very last page, they encourage their readers to think of life as a measuring tape. As you'll see, those few sentences remained with us as a kind of guiding star, leading us into our sabbatical cruising life.

It is now time for us to try to inspire you. We wrote as we travelled. Our feelings are those we felt at the time.

If reading our story makes you think you would like to do something similar, my first piece of advice is to share that dream with your partner and crew. In Karolina, my wife, and Jessica and Jonathan, our children, I am lucky to have a crew willing to share the risks, do the work and make the dream come true. To them, I will always be grateful.

We have been blessed by the support of many people, including those who did not really understand why we wanted to do what we were doing. For keeping your doubts largely to yourselves and offering us enthusiastic and unconditional support, I am also grateful.

I would like to dedicate this book to Monika and Stephan Örn, Karolina's parents, whose support made our cruising year possible and who passed away far too early.

However great your crew, support team and dream may be, you will need an instrument with which to achieve your goals. For us this was Regina, an HR40 built by Hallberg-Rassy in Sweden. She has confidently carried us safely twice over the Atlantic, as well through calms, storms and some unforgettable nights at anchor.

It is with pride we look at our boat. It is with joy we remember our cruising year and it is with hope we look into the future, dreaming that one day we may snip off another centimetre, possibly with you doing the same.

Here's wishing you enjoyable reading!

Leon Schulz

Lista, Norway

Chapter one
In which we lose a centimetre but gain a mile

THE DREAMER

Imagine your life as a tape measure. Each centimetre represents one year of your life. For how many years or centimetres do you think your life will last? Cut there. It's not important exactly where. You don't know, anyway, do you? Then look at your life/tape carefully. How many centimetres are there left? And how do you want to fill them?

When my wife Karolina and I looked at our life/tape we saw that we had reached almost 40 cm. And we thought: what if we stole one year right there in the middle somewhere? We fetched the scissors and cut out one centimetre. We glued the two parts together. It was only one centimetre shorter. You could hardly tell the difference! It still looked pretty long to us - long enough for the life that most of us live.

The missing centimetre was lying on the table. It looked minuscule, yet it could be filled with as much experience as some whole lifetimes. If we dared!

The game of cutting measuring tapes was put aside and the missing centimetre was thrown into the drawer of my bedside table. It was soon forgotten. We had more important subjects to think of than philosophizing about the meaning of life, its length or contents or quality. We were in the middle of our lives, too busy for any diversion. We concentrated on our jobs, cared for our children, drove them to and from their numerous activities and tried to be in full swing with all our many simultaneous tasks. We lost focus on most. Every night, we found ourselves with an increasing number of unfinished jobs, no matter how skilled we tried to become in multi-tasking.

We had a good life, no doubt — a bit unexciting, maybe, but good. The daily problems, which always occur in life, we carried away like the odd stone in a field. Some issues were as big as rocks. They obstructed our path but, together, we got over them. We felt we had passed life's big climbing passages, the ones we remembered as hard when we were there. But we knew, too, that they had given us this wonderful feeling of pride and satisfaction when they were overcome. Looking forward from our position then, we tried to imagine how far our lives would grow and develop in the future. And we concluded: not much. Was this our goal in life?

Asking this question was the point at which we took our first step into the phase of Dreaming.

You see, cruising comes in four stages: Dreaming, Planning, Sailing and Readjusting. We loved the first three stages, enjoyed every one of them deeply, but had a hard time making the step from Dreaming to Planning. That's when the actual decision is made, by the way. The last phase, Readjusting, we are still in. This is the most intricate one. For us, returning has become much more challenging than we anticipated. It's still the same old track you left; what has changed is you.

During that first phase, we dreamt about doing something unusual, trying out a different life-style for a while. Not forever, but for a year or so. A radical alteration could lead you to any type of new ground. It's up to you to decide. Choose something for which you have a passion. In our family, it was sailing. And much of this book is about a sailing trip. Your passion may be different. But the most important lessons of this book will still, I hope, mean something to you. Our voyage was made with sails. But we are all on a voyage.

So, I invite you to cut out an hour or two of your busy day to relax, to join us on our adventures and to find some tranquillity. Our trip – and our new life – began the day we snipped the centimetre out of the tape measure.

This is the story of an ordinary family, with ordinary sailing experiences, an ordinary life and a quite common dream. We dreamt about doing something different, something special, something rewarding, something really memorable together. This story is about transformation, how we slowly changed and became more relaxed about big decisions, hazards, challenges and a new environment.

Maybe you are in the dreaming stage already? I guess so. Otherwise you wouldn't grab this book and start reading, right? Oh, I remember those days when I couldn't pass a chandlery bookshelf without looking for new releases about families cruising the oceans. I remember wanting to find out how they could be so brave and leave everything behind and cast off into such an adventure! I never believed it could really happen to us.

If you are like the me of a few years ago, you might believe that families like the one we are now are special, brave and fortunate. We took our kids out of school, sold our house, gave up our jobs and then just cast off and sailed away. Possibly we were adventurous and definitely we were luckier than some, but not more special or fortunate than I believe you are. Today, after meeting many other cruising families,

I know most of us have been along a similar path and have similar questions, fears and phases before and during a big life adventure.

Let me give you an example: During our Dreaming phase I remember thinking of all sorts of reasons why we could not go cruising. I loved reading about all the lucky ones who could go, and thought they lived their dreams instead of dreaming their lives, like we did. We didn't know if we could afford a year without income. We had no experience of blue-water sailing. Besides, we had good jobs and children, who went to school! They were all very good reasons for staying put.

After going to a lecture by a blue-water sailor, I said to her afterwards that I'd love to do one day what she had done. "Well", she answered, "then do it!" I thought she had missed my point. As the typical dreamer I was at that time, I stoutly believed I couldn't change my life. How stiff I was! Today, I see it very differently and would like to have the same effect on you as that lady had on me.

Reading on is, therefore, done at your own risk. Be warned: you might get infected and, one day, decide to go cruising as well. We would love to see you out there.

With hindsight, the hurdle between Dreaming and Planning was truly huge for us. It was preceded by a big battle inside us, resulting in countless thoughts and discussions. At the end, neither Karolina nor I could stand each other's pros and cons any longer. We had both heard them a million times, already. They were not very productive and really amounted to no more than "should we?" or "should we not?"

This process is very natural, and if you have already felt this battle inside yourself, don't worry, we have all suffered this way. I will try to explain: Our brain consists of two halves. One half, hosting our intelligence, is constantly blocking anything unknown by comparing new impressions with pictures stored in our subconscious. If anything new occurs, it pulls the emergency brake by using its most efficient weapon: fear! The other half of our brain hosts our feelings and intentions, encouraging us to undertake changes and test new ways; be they in art, in science or in life, itself. There is always an ongoing battle inside our brain between the two, and it is important to find a balance. Does comprehension win too often in today's intelligent, information society? Are we blocked from thinking laterally? We have evolved to understand so that we can avoid danger: the unknown might just turn out to be dangerous. But without the courage sometimes to risk doing something the consequences of which we don't fully know or understand, we would be nothing more than the product of evolution.

One night, I was looking for a pen, while lying in bed reading (guess what type of book, by the way!) Too lazy to get up, I was searching in the drawer of my bedside table. I didn't find a pen, but instead I discovered the almost-forgotten missing centimetre. It couldn't have shown up at a more appropriate moment.

All day, I had felt overwhelmed by trying to keep control of incoming e-mails. Keeping control of our own lives seemed to come a very distant second. I had questioned what this was all leading to. People around us were working on what they thought of as careers but, to me, looked more like a rat-race. We all were chasing comfort and wealth and living our lives by unthinking habit. Did I really want to carry on?

I held the snipped-out centimetre carefully by its edges between my thumb and finger and thought about our little game with the scissors. I said nothing. My brain was working on its own by now, leading a conversation with the little piece of tape in my hand.

A missing centimetre, would that be a lost centimetre? Or could it grow into something else, instead? Cutting and pasting; subtracting and adding. What would the sum be in the end?

Rather than waiting for happiness, as if it came through pure luck, we had to earn happiness by embracing problems and changes as challenges, waiting to be turned into success. Adventuring is all about finding happiness by setting a meaningful and reachable goal. You have to work through a project, allow for unexpected events, stay focused on the solution in order finally to reach life's higher altitudes.

I turned the centimetre slowly and delicately and in it I saw turquoise sea. And I thought: what if we really loved it and didn't want to return? We have a friend who once said he'd rather not try the cruising lifestyle at all. He was afraid he would love it so much, he would never be able to go back to a 9 to 5 day. "Better not to know..." he said, continuing to move papers from one pile to the other in his office. Now that I have tried it and come back, I admit he has a point.

I shook off my dreams, dropped the missing centimetre into the drawer and pushed it closed. What a crazy idea: to go cruising! Paradise is no geographical position with longitudes and latitudes, so we would not find any perfect place on earth, anyway. And it sure would be crowded, if it existed! So why try to find it?

And then I thought that life seemed to be like voltage: there must be a minus as well as a plus. I began to see what the Chinese are getting at with Yin and Yang. Not even real happiness seemed to exist without sorrow, fear, challenges and adventure. Harmony results from equilibrium between good and bad and cannot consist of positive inputs alone.

During these weeks, Karolina and I spoke a lot about our situation and future possibilities. It didn't take long until we agreed that we needed a change, even if it

Boxing up our old lives

would mean a hard time, hard work and the risk of the unknown.

Our dreams started to grow inside us and become clearer. We suddenly talked about them slightly differently. It was more like "how about if we did it this way…" than discussing all good reasons for not trying. We avoided talking about it with many others at that stage; they wouldn't understand, anyway.

One autumn day, we talked about the time we'd snipped out a centimetre from the tape measure. We laughed about how the tape was good for thinking about life and invented a new game: How would it feel, if we pinpointed a specific week sometime in the future, when we would be casting off for a year's cruise? It was still just a game.

When could it be? Well, you wouldn't want to move around with a teenager onboard, we reckoned. A youngster, who prefers to be with friends, rather than with dull parents on a boring boat on some remote spot with "nothing to do" didn't sound suitable. No, we must return before our daughter Jessica turned, say, 13? And then again, we would have so much to prepare, so it couldn't be too soon either! So we pretended – and please note: we only pretended – we would sail away when Jessica was 11 years old, returning when she'd turned 12. Our son Jonathan would be 9 years of age at the start, returning at 10.

We took the measuring tape and decided each centimetre would represent one week to go until we cast off. How many weeks would there be? The scissor went up and down the scale. At 87 cm we finally decided to cut. Ready?! One…Two… Three and CUT!

For every week that passed, we went on cutting off one centimetre. It soon became a family Sunday-evening ceremony. The tape got one centimetre shorter every week. Suddenly, it made it all feel very real and very frightening; time was passing quickly. Our tape was shrinking at an alarming speed. Life was flying by while we were just watching!

I think that is when we stopped Dreaming and started Planning.

Life suddenly had a new goal, with a fixed date. During this progress, we lived in two parallel worlds: our ordinary lives went on as usual, while our project needed more and more attention. Working on our sabbatical family-adventure project was fun, rewarding and often quite demanding. We felt we had our lives in our own hands again; we were going somewhere we wanted to go and could make our own choices as to how we got there.

We were not fleeing or running away from something, searching for paradise on a Caribbean island, when we decided to go cruising. What we wanted to do was to experience the ups and downs, storms and calms, sea and shore, as well as becoming better seamen and growing together as a family.

Spending more time with the children was a key objective. Besides, don't we owe our children the chance to see as much as possible of our world? Showing them the fact that things work differently in other countries, encouraging them to think laterally and innovatively?

If we wanted to do so, time (and the tape) was running short.

During the first phase of our adventure, Dreaming, the measuring tape was a good model for our lives. It was packed with tiny subdivisions but just went straight from top to bottom with monotonous regularity. Snipping out one little centimetre helped us start to build the confidence we needed to get off the treadmill. We used the same tape when we were Planning. Cutting off one centimetre a week helped us to see the progress we were making with our preparations and to build the belief in our hearts that we were really, truly going to go.

How did we use the tape in the third phase, Sailing? We threw it away.

The English have a saying – give them an inch and they'll take a mile. It's meant to remind people in authority that if they show any chink of willingness to allow disobedience, those in their charge will push at that chink until all authority is lost. And that is how I feel about the snipped centimetre. It gave us a tiny gap through which we could squeeze into a world measured not in tiny subdivisions but in metres and fathoms and miles and days and seasons and years. My old self would never have muddled centimetres and miles, metric and imperial measures. My new self knows that doesn't matter. The nautical mile matches a minute of latitude. There is harmony and poetry in that. The measuring tape had done its job. The little subdivisions didn't matter. The tape could go.

Throughout the entire project, we kept a very low profile. We never announced any time-frame for our cruising adventure, nor a specific destination. Too easily, it all could become interpreted as a 'fiasco', returning earlier than announced or following a shorter route than proclaimed.

If we didn't like the cruising life-style and sailed home after a couple of months, at least we would know that this was not the thing for us. We could erase these dreams from our minds with a clear conscience. This would still be better than a life spent wondering what cruising would be like, regretting that we had never tried.

We decided that we would continue sailing until any of us four family members put in a request to stop.

That request never came.

STARTING A CONVERSATION

I have written that I hope to inspire you with our story but I want also to build your confidence. The best way to do this, I believe, is to get you started in a conversation. In the early stages, you will be asking questions and learning from the answers but it won't be long before you are making your own suggestions and passing on the things that you have learned. Then your confidence will grow.

If, like me, you spend a fair amount of your leisure time strolling around marinas, always try to catch a quick word with anyone you see on board. Ask a question. It doesn't really matter what — anything that interests you. Almost all sailors will be happy to share their experiences with you. They won't tell you everything you need to know but they will tell you things based on real, hard-won experience. Combined with studying the sort of manuals and courses that provide a more structured grounding, this is the ideal way to learn.

I am going to try to start the process for you by offering, at the end of each chapter, a few tips and ideas based on our experience. These are the sort of answers I would give if you found me sitting in the cockpit of Regina. They're not complete, nor intended to teach you how to be a blue-water sailor, and some suggestions may not suit the way you want to sail. They are, however, my top tips based on our experience and the many conversations I have had with other sailors.

Read as much as you can but, remember, you will learn most by getting engaged, by giving as well as taking: by being part of the great cruising community.

Regina in Stavanger at midnight

Mollösund on the west coast of Sweden

Chapter two
In which we pack up our old lives

THE PLANNER

It was already May and the step from Planning into the actual Sailing phase was only a few weeks away. Were we in chaos? That would be an understatement! We were such good planners, surely?

What we thought would feel like organising a somewhat longer-than-usual summer holiday aboard our boat, Regina, eventually turned out to be a bigger project than we had ever thought, even after reading all those books by liveaboards and cross-questioning every blue-water sailor we ever met.

It was now two weeks before the moving company was due to empty our house, our home, and take all our possessions, every stick of furniture, bed-sheet and winter coat, book and frying pan, to a storage warehouse. Just six weeks before, we'd not even made the final decision to put the house up for sale. Planning comes with some flexibility in our family, you see.

Another family we had been in contact with had just returned home with their two girls from a three-year circumnavigation. They had asked: "Why do you want to keep your house? Why don't you sell it?" And we didn't know why not. We had thought maybe keeping the house would give us a sense of security but when we thought hard we realised that was false. And, anyway, our house was not going to be ideal for growing children. Which led us to another thought: why keep a house to which we might not wish to return? And then another thought: the world was a big place, why should we come back to the same town or region or even country, at all? With every day and every decision, our world was getting bigger.

Packing, stowing and moving on to Regina suddenly became the flipside of boxing up, stripping and moving out of our old home.

I confess: in some quiet moments I asked myself why we hadn't bought a bigger boat. Where would we stow everything? Box after box came out of our house and onto the boat and, somehow, empty boxes returned to shore. If their contents had not been dissolving in the moist marina air, they must all be onboard, somehow, somewhere. Endless lists were made, documenting where each item was now hidden inside Regina. Would we ever find any of them again?

Dead tired, both Karolina and I fell into bed each night, asking each other: Why? Why are we doing all this? Why have we sold our house? Why have we given up our business? Why abandon our comfortable life with steady income, good friends, nice wines and a school our kids liked so much? And most hard to explain: why are Jessica and Jonathan still so excited about our planned cruise, really looking forward to moving eventually onboard and at last being able to cast off? Have we all become crazy?

It goes without saying that we didn't feel quite as brave as we once had. The closer we got to going, the stronger became our doubts. The confidence I had felt just seemed to melt away under the tiredness that now seemed almost to overwhelm me. Tired of working in the office, tired of preparing the move from our house, tired of endless stowing, of fixing insurance, schoolwork, spare parts, tools; tired of scanning pages from instruction books, recipes, photos and important documents into our computer; tired of choosing which clothes, books, CDs and teddy bears to take onboard.

And still: what we were leaving behind ashore felt less and less important. Countless so-called 'indispensable items', which had not been given away or sold, had disappeared in yet other boxes and been put in the attic of Karolina's parents. Why do we keep all these things? For our grand-children?

And the rest of our 'old world' felt less important, too. New tax laws, political squabbles, stock market going up and down... The News sounded as if it was being transmitted from inside one of those boxes we carried up into the attic, vaguely received and blurred on its muffled way to our minds. Maybe we were too occupied to bother, too focused on a deadline we weren't altogether sure we believed in?

Suddenly, doubt manifested itself again. What did our business clients and suppliers really think when we told them that if they wanted to reach us in the future, they had to dial a satellite phone number, never knowing if we were fighting gale-force winds on the Atlantic or snorkelling in the tropics? Would they ask themselves why? Did they consider us irresponsible and crazy?

Regina was as beautiful as ever, almost ready to cast off, only lacking the necessary bunker of food. She was smiling, eagerly waiting for us in the close-by harbour. It was not Regina, but our old land-life which still was holding us tight with endless last-minute issues to finalise. Why couldn't we just leave shore? With any luck, we would shortly be moving on board; undertaking some final fine-tuning, while we waited for the kids to end their school term.

The next time Jessica and Jonathan went to school, it would all be very different. For a start, their regular teachers would be ones they'd known from birth — their parents. But there would be special teachers, too — new places, new cultures and new experiences. How would the two of them cope with all that?

How, indeed, would we all change once we'd cast off? What would life teach us, living so closely together on a cramped 40-foot boat, almost constantly underway? We would be so close to Mother Nature with all her impact and beauty, and, at the same time, so far away from normal shore life? Why did we even think we wanted to find out? Why couldn't we just go on like most others, taking the easy track? It would have been a lot less trouble, that is for sure!

When the time finally came for us to watch our home-port disappearing in our wake, I hoped then I would to come to understand why we did all this.

CHOOSING AND PREPARING YOUR BOAT

Boats must be a choice of the heart at least as much as the head. When you've skinned your knuckles for the nth time trying to un-jam the aft-head sea-cocks or just been handed the bill for a new main sail or, worst of all, watched a younger model overhaul you to windward, it helps a lot to have a deep reserve of affection for your cruising partner. So, buy a boat you like the look of. Happily, boats with graceful, balanced lines generally sail and sit in the sea better than less-shapely designs.

You will have some idea of how much you can afford to spend. Look only at boats priced 20% below that figure and, if buying second-hand, aim to knock 15% off the asking price. All that apparently 'spare' money will vanish soon after purchase.

Unless you're feeling bold, buy a 'standard' boat with a common rig and layout. If you're buying an older boat, look for a type still widely manufactured — even if the particular maker has now disappeared. When thinking about size and displacement bear in mind the weight of fresh water and other stores you will need to carry, but also don't forget the benefits of speed.

If your boat has not crossed oceans before, leave plenty of time (preferably years) for upgrading. One good way of assembling a list of jobs to do is to ask a surveyor to examine the boat and list the changes that would be required if you were going to offer the boat for charter off-shore. Another good list is that required for entry to the Atlantic Rally for Cruisers (ARC).

Magazines often produce articles reviewing gear used on rallies. Look out for common problems. Gadgets that have just come on the market are probably best avoided. And always bear in mind the possibility of a complete loss of electrical power. Try to keep things simple.

Days and sometimes weeks spent on a single tack can put particular strains on the rigging. It's best to get the rigging examined by a professional - at which point you can discuss this. Don't forget also that you'll need to protect sails and running rigging from chafe.

And if you expect someone else to sail with you, make sure they get a say in all of these decisions, even if you finish up doing most of the work.

Koshlong - a steel, centre-cockpit, 45-footer - the choice of our Canadian cruising friends

Start of the Tall Ships Race, Stavanger, Norway

Chapter three
In which we finally get underway

THE WAKE

One rainy day in early June it was finally time to leave. On countless occasions I had imagined how this precise moment would feel. In my dreams, it had all been so easy: we would eagerly steer out of our old home-port of Ystad in southern Sweden, heading off into adventure. The sun would shine from a blue sky. Happy faces full of expectation would be seen all around us.

When the big day came, it was all very different. Heavy rain clouds were hanging low with drizzle in the air. It was so cold, hardly any people were out and about. Apart from the weather, we didn't mind the solitude at this emotional moment. It was actually very much according to our wish. We hadn't disclosed our departure day to anyone, not even to ourselves. The reason was very simple: we just didn't know! We wanted to leave when we felt ready, neither to force ourselves, nor to feel any pressure regarding a set date.

Since we never seemed to get ready, and still felt stressed, we left anyhow. And it happened to be on this wet, cold and grey 13th of June. Did I ever mention that a seaman does not leave on a 13th? We were so exhausted, we even forgot about our superstition.

No big farewell party waving from the shore; no local newspaper present; no announcements about "the heroic family conquering the seven seas", which immediately would have been misunderstood as a circumnavigation around the world by most, anyway. The past hectic days with thousands of small things still to be undertaken, combined with hearty and warm farewell visits by family and friends onboard as well as ashore, now lay in our wakes, even before the last mooring line had been taken in.

After the decision to go, the moment of actual departure, leaving behind that family and those friends, is perhaps the hardest part of the whole process.

I told everyone and ourselves that the world, for sure, had become smaller these days and that visiting each other was far easier today. Cheap airfares, satellite telephone, Skype and e-mails would all keep us together. I tried to reassure family in particular that this cruise was nothing but an ordinary, somewhat prolonged, sailing holiday. It did not sound too convincing to me. And not to them, either.

Family, good old friends and newly made friends, all were now left behind. It felt as if we had thrown them all overboard, to disappear out of sight in our wake. Only waves remained, washing over memories. I held back my tears, facing into the wind, and guessed that this would not even be the last time we had to suffer the pain of separation. Leaving sailing-friends yet to be made was something I was afraid would become a component of a cruising lifestyle.

Twelve months later, my presumption was not only proven correct, but was felt all the more sharply. How could we have guessed that each separation from the cruising community was to become just as difficult a goodbye? The people we met during the cruising year, the friends we made, the days we shared, the adventures we experienced together: all this has, for us, become the essential core of our cruising experience.

Parting and meeting again are the waves of human relationship. The pain resulting from separation is the price for good friendship; reunion is the reward. Not until this interaction is in equilibrium, do we understand what real friendship means and can accept a departure as a new beginning.

Fortunately, there was something deep inside me whispering the sweet words of a wanderer, encouraging me to explore the world and make new experiences — and to make new friends. Luckily, I could still hear this soft voice in my heart, although barely.

The summer night had by now slowly fallen over Kattegatt. It was just after midnight on the third day of our adventure. It was chilly. I felt a bit lonely on my night watch with everyone else on board fast asleep. I remember thinking that summers come late in these latitudes, if at all. Was it crazy to begin our cruise northbound? Somehow it felt peculiar that Regina was steadily sailing on a northerly course along the Danish east coast while we were really planning on sailing south into the warmth!

I was looking back again at our wake. What impressions had we left ashore? How would we be remembered back home? Wake fades quite quickly, I am afraid. Just think of the wakes we must have made in our careers! How long would we be remembered? And if so, as what?

I turned my head away from memories and checked our compass course. I made some corrections on the autopilot. Our next port of call: Unknown. "I'll sleep on that decision", Karolina had said an hour earlier when she had turned in, leaving me with the boat, the night and my own thoughts on possible landfalls. Maybe we should sail to Aalborg in northern Denmark to see Karolina's uncle who lives there? Or to Skagen, possibly, on the very tip of Denmark? Some good sailing friends were moored there on their way out on a sabbatical year, just as we were. Or why not head for my mother, who was currently staying in Lysekil on the Swedish west coast? Better yet, possibly, sail directly to Norway from here, taking advantage of the fair winds?

I suddenly realised we also had family and friends further on.

It was finally time to look ahead.

CRUISING SKILLS

If you want to cross an ocean and have never sailed at all, you have got quite a bit to learn. But there are plenty of people who manage it. We met people on their way to the Pacific with no more than three or four years' experience. If you want to learn fast, schools accredited by an organisation like the UK's Royal Yachting Association (RYA) are a good place to start. Going for weeks or weekends with a variety of schools will give you the benefit of the wisdom of multiple instructors and experience of a variety of conditions. Build experience by offering your services as crew via a note on club notice-boards etc. You'll find most demand for crew for delivery trips at the start and finish of a season. Signing up to crew on a season's series of races is a good way to assure regular practice.

If you are a more seasoned sailor, it is reasonable to set off aiming to build experience as you go along. The summer before you go, try to do a few longer trips and overnight sails. It is important to be honest with yourself about any gaps you may have in your skill-set and to practise awkward but important things like man-overboard drill.

Another skill you will definitely need is that of a junior maintenance engineer. However new your equipment, something is bound to break, even if it is only an impellor. You will certainly need to be able to carry out a basic service of your engine. The ability to use a multimeter to trace electrical problems can also be useful. But the list of difficulties you are likely to encounter is limited. Write your own list and think about what you would do if one or two or three of those events occurred at the same time.

Lastly, at least one member of the crew should have first-aid skills. There are plenty of short courses available. And your own family doctor should be willing to talk you through the main risks.

Celestial navigation is not as difficult as it first appears

Encountering a replica Viking ship off Norway

Chapter four

In which a guide helps us find our way

THE PATHFINDER OF LISTA

Suddenly, she was standing there, right next to the boat. We had arrived in Farsund, Norway, after 29 hours at sea, covering 177 miles from Nibe in Denmark. She was smiling and wearing a bright orange T-shirt with the words 'Lista Guide' in large letters. She welcomed us to Farsund and talked about the beauty and exciting surroundings we had come to: the Lista area. All nice and well, but we were dead-tired after our long leg from Denmark.

The day before, we had sailed into the Danish Limfjord from Kattegatt, past Aalborg and had motored through the crooked natural channel cutting through Denmark from east to west. The Limfjord is very shallow. I do confess: no fewer than three times we actually touched ground. The first time, we did not even notice. Looking at the log, we realised we were making no more than a single knot of speed while the engine was still turning normally. Obviously, it was not just a matter of heading on a direct course from one buoy to the next. We had cut the curve a little too tight and were suddenly ploughing a lonely furrow; making our own channel outside the fairway, as was becoming a habit for us in general. Luckily, it was just a matter of a little helm to port and we were out in the safe, main channel again.

The second time we ran aground, I had turned in. I didn't notice anything this time either, which could have something to do with the fact that I was deeply asleep – stretched out in my bunk. In any case, my sweet sleep came to an abrupt end with Jonathan proclaiming: "Daddy, now we have run aground again!"

But this time, we were stuck in harder. We had to figure out how to widen up our just-made furrow, to make it big enough for us to back out again. The bow-thruster came in handy - it's not just for tight harbour manoeuvres! Pushing the bow repeatedly from one side to the other with the thruster, we managed to work the keel free, digging ourselves out. Soon we were afloat again and on our way to Nibe marina, which lies about half-way along the Limfjord.

You might ask yourself why we couldn't learn a bit quicker, but it was really not our fault that the marina, proudly declared as having a depth of 5m on the chart, was, in reality, rather less deep. A well-proven trick did it this time: some more revs on the engine and we could dig our way through to a berth. It was more like a car-park than a marina. Having thus 'parked' the boat, we were firmly standing in the mud. No rocking to sleep this night!

Luckily there was no tide to speak of, so we trusted to the fact that if we got in all right, we would get out the same way the following day. At that time, we considered this as a problem from what would be an uncertain future, anyhow.

Nibe, our resting place for the night, was where Karolina's uncle Björn and his Danish wife Annette lived. They invited us over for a pleasant afternoon in their picturesque garden. It looked so beautifully untouched, as if nature alone had been the creator of this typical Danish atmosphere. I said something about the "wild" and "untreated beauty", referring to the plants which seemed to enjoy a free and unrestricted life with Björn and Annette. Björn politely explained that a lot of effort lay behind achieving this appearance, and that gardening was a serious hobby of Annette. Oh, well, again this showed my limited understanding of the subject. As so often with me, I couldn't resist making the odd comment, nevertheless: I drew some improper parallels to women's beauty, suggesting that make-up was possibly justified to a certain extent after all; I meant, to make men believe it's all natural beauty, so to speak.

Karolina asked me to please explain what I meant more precisely. I realised it was time to change subject. Björn helped me out by starting to tell tales about the Vikings and the fact that they had settlements very close to their home. These had only recently been excavated. They had even built a copy of an old Viking house.

"That's interesting!" said Jessica, having recently studied Vikings at school, "But how could they know where to find the old settlement?"

"Do you see that hill over there?" asked Björn, pointing with his hand towards a mound. "From up there some people saw that the grain grew differently, forming a sort of distinctive shape. It grew better at some places than at others and so they believed that the soil must differ because of underlying human construction. Would you like go and see it?"

We were soon all sitting in his car – driving along small side roads taking us to the old Viking homesteads. It was a magical feeling. For Jessica and Jonathan the Viking age suddenly felt very real.

Björn, who could sense our enthusiasm, continued: "Not far from here, the Vikings had a huge fortification as well, built under the famous Viking Harald Blåtand. There are four of these known here in Denmark and they are all called Trelleborgs."

"Trelleborg?" Jessica asked, "But that is what the city in southern Sweden is called. I have been there many times taking the overnight ferry to Travemünde in Germany! Maybe there has been a Viking fort as well in Trelleborg?"

"I guess so. This Trelleborg here is called Aggersborg. Overlooking the Limfjord, it is the biggest one of them all – with a diameter of no less than 240m. Do you want to see it as well?"

Of course we did! And so Björn drove further west to Aggersborg, explaining that the archaeologists were not sure what this fort was for. Or better: whom it was built to resist. Either it was against invaders, which, at first thought, seemed to be the most obvious reason to build a castle. Or there was also another possible motivation to build this huge circle of walls: namely to protect the authorities against their own people! Why? Well, Vikings did not pay taxes with the same enthusiasm as today's good citizens. Vikings were said to protest wildly when the king's soldier came to collect the duty. A rolling head was certainly not an uncommon answer when asked to pay the dues imposed onto these free men of the North.

Tax squads with military protection were therefore required to ensure the necessary respect for the King's authority when out on tax-collecting tours. Off duty, these tax collectors needed to find a refuge somewhere, giving shelter against the revenge of their own countrymen; hence the Trelleborgs!

I personally liked this idea of the huge Trelleborgs' being the tax authorities of the Viking age. It had obvious similarities with today's official apparatus to administrate tax collection and to invent yet new ways to fill the public treasury.

How about the Vikings who still refused to pay and did not succeed in sending the tax collectors to Valhalla? They fled and sailed away on their long boats, joining new settlements far away from the long arms of Harald Blåtand's men.

Still having my recent observations regarding gardening and women in mind, I avoided further comments on similarities between Trelleborgs and today's tax authorities.

The following morning, after a wonderful complete night's sleep, we continued through the Limfjord westbound. The grey weather with drizzle was the perfect accompaniment to our feeling about leaving the safe but shallow Limfjord for the altogether more threatening North Sea. Thyborøn, at the exit into the North Sea, does not have the best reputation as a safe haven.

The lee shore of Denmark in a westerly gale has become many seamen's last berth. The shallow sandbanks give a steep and dangerous sea; the ports that could have served as refuges are scarce, while getting out to deeper water is often impossible, transforming this coast into a rat-trap. An easy way to find Thyborøn from the sea, so they say, is to just follow all the wrecks, and then to keep in the middle.

At 2130, while other sailors headed for a harbour, we continued out into the black North Sea initially on a north-westerly course, leaving Denmark in our wake. Fisher, as this area is called, was known to us purely as a weather forecast area reserved for tough fishermen; men content to have gales as their companion. We had actually never really cared about where exactly Fisher was. It had been, until now, beyond our horizons.

Building permanent boundaries in your mind is especially destructive. Experience is built up in small steps by constantly pushing the boundaries a bit, slightly exceeding your previous achievements. Not by much, and never all at the same time, but step by step. Would our latest step – to leave the shelter of the Baltic – prove one too far for us?

To our surprise, Fisher did not feel much different from any other waters we had sailed on. The wind was light; although a distinct swell could be felt. It was exciting, but not frightening. We had picked our weather window with care, something we would continue to do. I believe that bad weather can easily provoke fear and stressful discomfort, not to mention seasickness, the illness most sailors suffer from, including us. For the best chance of safety and harmony on board, patience is the key: time to wait for a good weather window and then to have the courage actually to leave before the weather-shutters close once more.

Stretching ourselves into the North Sea was not so bad, and we even enjoyed our passage northbound. In retrospect, this crossing to Farsund in Norway was one of many small steps that led us to the big stride of an Atlantic circuit, comprising two ocean crossings. At this stage, crossing the Atlantic was still difficult to think of and we talked very little about that option. None of us dared to imagine ourselves thrown out into the middle of the Atlantic. Visualise just the two of us adults, with two children, in a small sailing boat with masses of water around. Imagine that the closest shore was several weeks away and that no other vessels had been seen for days and days! Could you? For us, crossing Fisher on the outside of Denmark to Norway was adventurous enough. For now, at least.

With pride and near disbelief, we jumped ashore with the mooring lines in Farsund, Norway, on 17 June after a 29-hour non-stop sail from Nibe inside Limfjorden. We sat back down in the cockpit tired and happy, enjoying the beautiful scenery around Farsund.

And suddenly there she stood, this nice lady in the orange T-shirt, welcoming us to Farsund and asking if we were possibly interested in a guided tour around Lista.

Her name was Marita, and she ran a small touring operation called Lista Guide. Flexibility was the most attractive feature of Marita's business, so we agreed to take a tour with her as our private guide the following day.

Next morning, we were still eating breakfast when Marita arrived, as agreed. We discussed the options and then decided to go for historical spots. These would be of particular interest to Jessica and Jonathan, who were collecting material for their school work on board.

Half an hour later, we all sat in Marita's red Renault Mégane. Constantly laughing, she drove us to fantastic places, so picturesque, so exciting for the children and so beautiful for us adults! A private guide, taking her time, letting us explore nature and historic places at our own pace, is a luxury you seldom find. The fact that she had previously been a pre-school teacher gave her an immediate bond with Jessica and Jonathan, who really liked her.

We drove past six Viking graves, visited the renowned lighthouse of Lista and saw amazing rock carvings from the Bronze Age, as well as going hiking in deep, dark forests and high hills. The kids learnt how to look out for poisonous snakes and I learnt that after you've turned 40, it gets harder to cross a swamp by balancing on a narrow log.

High up on a Norwegian peak, we had a tremendous view over the hills to the north and the flat landscape of Lista to south. We were also told about the historical significance of the hilltop on which we stood: ever since the Viking age, right up to the Napoleonic wars of the early 19th century, this place had been used for communications. This was one of the many locations where fires were lit, in order to pass on important messages up and down the Norwegian coast.

Jessica thought this was fantastic. Had she not learnt about these in the Viking museum of Roskilde? These bonfires were used to warn about approaching enemies. Jonathan had listened carefully about the communication system of the Vikings and finally asked: "But Dad, why didn't they just use their cell-phones….?!"

The Pathfinder of Lista helped us to understand that we had found our own path: our adventure had finally commenced, with thrilling sailing to fascinating places, meeting wonderful people.

Wasn't this what cruising was all about?

HANDLING UNDER POWER

Marinas may look like car-parks, but getting your boat in and out of them is not at all like driving a car. Crucially, the water through which you are travelling will usually itself be moving. Any wind will push or turn the boat. At low speeds, the boat's propeller will turn the boat as well as move it forwards or backwards. The underwater shape of the boat affects how it handles. And it's the back of the boat that turns the boat around its keel, not the front.

As with sailing, there's not much alternative but to have a go — and schools are acutely aware of the need to build confidence in this area. Try, if you can, to start by practicing in open water. Get a feel for how sharply the boat can turn both to port and to starboard. See how long it takes to bring her to a halt by going into reverse and have a go at maneuvering in reverse. When in reverse, stick to small rudder movements.

Once you've worked out which way the propeller kicks the stern in reverse, try turning the boat by putting the wheel hard over to turn the bow in the opposite direction and keeping it there while shifting from forward to reverse gear for a multi-point turn through 180 degrees.

If you're approaching a marina or dock, practise the necessary manoeuvre in nearby open water to check the current tide and wind effects. Have plenty of dock-lines and fenders rigged and ready well before you get to your destination. Talk all of this through with the rest of the crew and make sure they also get a chance to have a go.

Navigating through the Norwegian oil fields

North Sea and sky

Chapter five
In which we leave the land behind

VIKING AND BEYOND

The decision was anything but easy. It was a major decision from our new, modest perspectives and down-to-earth way of living. Or should I say 'down-to-sea'? No, not the decision to give up work and house and move onto the boat; we were past that. Living on board felt already very natural.

This was our first big sailing decision; how would we cross the North Sea? The simplest option was to leave the sheltered waters of Norway and to sail beyond the area known in the Shipping Forecast as South Utsira into a new area of sea known only to us from the radio. Even for Scandinavians, there is something both exciting and daunting about the name Viking. These patches of sea look small on a chart but can take more than a couple of days to cross. And now we faced three of them. After Viking there would be Forties. Only after that would the shores of Scotland offer us refuge and welcome. It sounded like half an ocean!

As ever when planning a passage, the question was two-fold; which route to take and what weather to wait for? Our first thought was to go via the Shetland islands, since, despite lying even further north, they are actually some 80 nautical miles closer to Norway than Scotland itself.

Friends with similar plans had tried a couple of weeks earlier. They had met gale-force headwinds and had a long story to tell about the harsh, cold and unfriendly North Sea. Despite being very experienced, after many hours fighting against waves and wind, they had finally given up. Dejected, they had turned back south and taken the route via the Kiel Canal, Germany, Holland, Belgium and France to head eventually over the Bay of Biscay to Spain. We wondered whether we were being too bold to consider crossing the North Sea at all?

We had enjoyed the pleasant sailing in Norway and had no particular desire to leave. At the same time, we knew we had to do something or our trip would end here.

Norway is such a fantastic cruising ground, hardly recognized by the mass of sailors. Only the 'connoisseurs', who are willing to sacrifice a warmer climate and accept the many rainy and cloudy days that go with cold water, come here. Their reward is an untouched and beautiful sailing area with extremely friendly people. There is no need for Europeans to go to Canada, Alaska or even Antarctica for adventure and untouched beauty when we have Norway in our back garden.

Karolina, who had sailed the entire Norwegian west coast, kept telling me with great passion how the beauty and wilderness gets better and better the further north you go. For us, Lysefjorden, close to Stavanger, was as far north as we would get on this occasion.

The waters in and around Lysefjorden are amazing. The Fjord is more than 300m deep and the steep Fjelds rise up more than 600m on both sides, giving a total above and below water of almost one kilometre of vertical wall.

It was a magic moment for us entering the Fjord. Shortly before reaching the breathtaking Preikestolen or Pulpit Rock, we found the perfect hiding place, famous from the legend about the hiding thief. The name of this tiny creek is Fantahålå. Fanta means thief and Hålå is hole. The legend tells how a fugitive sailed into the creek and hid behind a rock. The police could not see him hiding and continued into the Lysefjorden. The hiding place was perfect and boat and thief were given up as lost. Of course, we, too, had to find this narrow hole with its steep walls to see if we could find sanctuary, and hide from the rest of the world.

The Norwegian Fjords are so sheltered, we had almost forgotten about the open sea to the west. Even the lower temperature felt agreeable in here and it was only when family and friends back home called that we envied their hot, summer days. We were really lucky if the temperature got up to 18°C (64F) with the sun shining for at least part of the day. On the other hand, the days are long that far north in June so the sun had many chances to show up, sometimes at the most unexpected times of day (or night!)

Cruising around the area of Stavanger, we started to monitor the weather forecasts closely. We were all too conscious of the importance of our next decision. This would be our first passage of several days and nights at sea. Choosing the wrong time to leave could upset the entire project. If this did not turn out well for all four of us, one of us might even decide to play their 'veto-card' and the trip would be over.

We needed to be prepared to leave the sheltered Fjords for the North Sea, crossing as soon as the forecasts suggested a good weather window. It is an enormous advantage in these situations to have only the weather to worry about. If you have work to get back to or guests or crew to collect or drop at fixed dates, it all becomes a much tougher compromise.

It would take two to three days to cross over to Scotland. We would pass the Greenwich Meridian and start to chart our progress in positive, westerly angles rather than the easterlies we were used to. Psychologically, this would feel like a big advance.

Of the two of us, Karolina is the better equipped to make this sort of difficult decision. She combines facts, forecasts, navigational considerations and a touch of female intuition to reach her conclusions. She worked out when we should leave, which was the most appropriate route and which was the target destination that best fitted our plans and the tidal almanac. By discussing the passage together, including the children, everyone onboard felt involved. Our team began to build. There can only be one skipper onboard – that's essential in an emergency – but we always tried to find time to discuss all our plans.

We finally took the decision to leave on 24 June. The forecast wasn't perfect. It rarely is. We had to make good speed on the first day so as to reach the Viking sea area as quickly as possibly. Otherwise, we might get caught by gale-force winds, which were predicted to blow down the Norwegian coast not long after we left. If our calculations were correct, we would succeed in leaving the coastal area with a good but not too strong wind and would be safely into Viking before the gales struck Norway. We reckoned we would find no more than a pleasant 15-20 knots of northerly winds all the way, if we could maintain a reasonable speed. So, not only would our judgement be tested by the decision to go but our ability to sail would be tested by the requirement for speed. It would not be the last time we were grateful for Regina's slippery hull and powerful sails.

We set off with a little bit of a lump in our throats, apprehensive as the Norwegian shore-line slowly dropped behind. But gradually, as mile after mile disappeared into our wake, the fear dropped away. And then, in the middle of that short night – our first night in the North Sea – something happened that made us all feel luck was with us and our decision had been right. It was 0100 but I just had to wake the others. All around the boat there were dolphins. There must have been about a dozen. That far north there is still plenty of light on a summer's night and we could clearly see our visitors jumping and playing and shooting back and forth under Regina.

The dolphins came back the following morning and again in the afternoon. Jessica was especially excited. She had always dreamed of watching free-living dolphins playing at the bow! And these ones were really showing off, jumping wildly, even turning in the air and landing on their backs, then quickly returning, looking up at us as if to check that we had seen and appreciated their tricks.

We couldn't have asked for a better start. We felt as though we had been welcomed. Our confidence grew.

PLANNING A SHORT PASSAGE

Passage planning is a whole art to itself with several specialist books and dedicated software systems available. But there are some key things to think about. The important advantage of a passage lasting no more than three days is that a modern weather forecast should predict developments for that period with near total reliability. It is still necessary to use the forecasts appropriately. Allow for a margin of error. This is particularly important with wind direction. Finding yourself tacking, when you'd thought you'd be on a beam reach could seriously upset your plans.

The time span of just under three days will most probably not allow for a complete adjustment to the sea. To minimise risk of seasickness, check the sea state just as closely as you do the weather. Waves lag behind winds and can travel for a long distances, so don't sail immediately after a gale. Waves from abeam and winds from astern is the worst combination.

Avoid everyone onboard getting tired at the same time when night approaches after a long day at sea. Begin a watch-keeping scheme immediately, allowing for part of the crew to rest and stay fresh ready for their turn in the cockpit.

Think about shipping lanes, fishing areas and other hazards, and try to time those for daylight hours. Tides may become relevant when you near shore. Choose a destination that is easy to get into whenever you arrive and plan to reach an unfamiliar destination during daylight. Remember it is easier to slow down than to speed up. Have a number of alternative plans and charts to match.

Provision for twice your scheduled time at sea and tell someone you're going and when you plan to arrive.

Nosing into Fantahålå, Lyseforden, Norway

Entering the Caledonian Canal

Chapter six

In which we hunt a Scottish monster but settle for
Scottish marmalade

THE FRIENDLY CANAL

The calm, quiet Caledonian Canal was exactly what we needed after the excitement of crossing the North Sea. The mountains embraced us as if to say "Welcome back to the land." The crossing had actually not been anything like as bad as we'd feared. And it had been quick. The 280 miles from Stavanger in Norway to MacDuff in Scotland had taken us no more than 43 hours – less than two days! The speed of our grand little floating home was amazing. Hallberg-Rassy, originally known for their sturdy cruising yachts, have magically worked a new element into their latest designs: speed.

It was hard to believe: we were in Scotland already! We had crossed a big sea and it had given no pain other than a bit of lost sleep and a bit of sea sickness. Suddenly, once in the canal, there was no stress, no worry about checking weather windows, no tides to think of and no anchorages to judge. It was just about keeping in the middle and passing through the odd lock. In total, there are 29 locks. The most dramatic flight consists of no less than eight consecutive locks, making up the famous Neptune's Staircase at the western end near Corpach and Fort William.

Of course, every piece of information we could pick up along the way was used for Jessica and Jonathan's education. I read the brochure and explained: the canal took 17 years to complete, but when the first locks opened in 1822 it was only 14 feet deep instead of the planned 20 and, therefore, too shallow for many of the increasingly large ships of that time.

From a political perspective, however, the huge building scheme had been successful, providing work and helping ease the flow of emigration from the Highlands. A second phase of construction ran from 1844 to 1847, completing the long hoped-for direct route for full-draught vessels, connecting the east and west side of Scotland. By using the Caledonian Canal, vessels could finally avoid the hazardous route around the north coast and through the notorious Pentland Firth.

The most important lesson for the children, I thought, was not the size and dates of the canal, but the fact that it was constantly behind the evolution of ship-building. Even the second phase was overtaken. By the time it was complete, sailing vessels were in decline and steam ships were large enough to make a safe passage around Scotland.

Jessica and Jonathan marvelled at the scale of the construction. Had it all been a waste of time and effort? Not quite, but I wonder what Thomas Telford, the engineer, would have thought, had he known what sort of craft would be using his once so prestigious construction in our times. Carefully maintained to top standard, it allows thousands of pleasure craft to take advantage of the beautiful and significantly shorter route through Scotland. Or sailors go just to enjoy its tranquillity, be they on a rented barge, a canal cruiser or a private yacht. And as one of them, we could well understand why.

Scotland is famous for its friendly people, but the Canal outdid even our expectations. Every person we met seemed more helpful than the last. As we approached Inverness at the start of the canal we were hailed by VHF: "Swedish yacht, this is Wild Eve. Over." What could they want? Only to ask us whether we planned to enter the canal that day and, if so, did we want them to ask the lock-keeper to hold the gate until we could get in? How kind! We met a bus-driver, who got out of his bus to point us in the right direction. The lady in the post office made several telephone calls on our behalf. And nobody in the queue seemed at all upset. Helping the poor, lost foreigner was a task for them all.

After the first few locks, we got more confident in handling the boat. It was good practice to manoeuvre alongside pontoons and lock walls. We got better at using the propeller and bow-thruster. We were learning as we went along and that, too, was good.

All the lock-keepers were kind, patient, friendly and helpful and were easily recognised as the only ones along the canal wearing life jackets, which was one of the many decrees stipulated by a new powerful institution called 'Health and Safety', or so we were told. One lock-keeper complained she was not even allowed to change a light bulb any longer. 'Health and Safety' made it necessary to call an electrician for this simple task. We couldn't believe it, until we had some direct experience. In one marina where we stopped for a night, we asked for a connection to shore-power. Normally you pay an extra fee and then just plug your electrical cord into the plug closest to your boat and that's it. But this socket was secured shut with a padlock. No, not to prevent theft of the electricity, but in the name of 'Heath and Safety'.

Before we were allowed to plug anything in, we had to read a densely-packed A4 page of text, which, in essence, explained that electricity might become hazardous under certain conditions. After I had signed to say that I had read all this, the friendly harbour master followed us back to the boat, which was berthed at the other end of the marina. I was asked to plug our shore cable into the boat and then to pass the other end to him. He alone was allowed to connect it to the mains, using his key to unlock the socket. "This way", he explained a little embarrassedly, "the handling of electricity is restricted to those with the appropriate training."

"What about the electricity on board?" I asked, amazed by these detailed precautions. "Oh, that's not our problem", the harbour master explained. "On board, it's your responsibility as skipper. It's all explained on that sheet of paper you signed, remember? You connect the cable to your boat and I plug it into the shore socket. That's the rule. I'm sorry. I don't understand it either…"

As the days passed and we progressed along the Canal, we began to breathe more slowly. The pace of life had at last wound down after the hectic weeks before departure and the exciting crossings, first over the Kattegatt, then from Denmark to Norway and finally the big one, across the North Sea to Scotland. Like a balloon losing its air, we just sat there in the cockpit doing nothing but enjoying the scenery, the Scottish people and our new lives. It's amazing how long it takes before you fully realise that you've left — and your journey is underway.

The Caledonian Canal links the North and Irish Seas via a series of deep and impressive lakes or lochs. Loch Ness is probably the most famous and definitely the biggest and deepest. I was keeping a sharp look-out for Nessie, the monster, while standing on deck rinsing off North Sea salt. I used fresh-water taken from the lake via our deck-wash pump, feeling very clever. It turned out to be a totally pointless exercise, as it rained cats and dogs the moment I had finished. We had a good laugh. At least the children were pleased we'd used Nessie-water to rinse Regina.

Around half-way through Loch Ness, there's the impressive Urquhart Castle. Surrounded on three sides by water, its shape and placement is every bit as romantic as you could wish for a medieval castle. It dates back to 1230, with settlements on the peninsula going back to 597.

Urquhart Castle's history is hard to match. At first, the Scots and English fought over the castle, and it changed ownership a couple of times. Then, from 1390 for about 150 years, it was the Scottish kings trying to defend themselves against the MacDonalds. (No, they didn't have the golden arches, that came later!) The MacDonald clan, with their incursions coming from the west, styled themselves the 'Lords of the Isles'. Both parties took turns to besiege, occupy and own Urquhart Castle with it swapping back and forth many times. This complex interplay of Scottish history led to further conflicts in 1513 after which it was finally besieged and plundered by the western clans in 1545. It was repaired, but fell into decline until one last action, when a small protestant garrison holding the castle in 1689 held off a much larger Jacobite force. When the garrison later left, they blew up much of the site. It served then as a convenient local quarry. Much of the stone and building material has gone, I presume to help build or repair local houses.

Of course, with that sort of history behind it, we had to investigate this mystical place ourselves. Just next to the castle, we found a private jetty, where tourist boats dropped off their hordes of eager visitors. There was a sign, which we did not quite understand, explaining when it was and was not permissible for other craft to use the jetty. We moored anyway and dropped off our own horde of Jessica and Jonathan with Karolina following close behind. I settled down with a good book and a most beautiful view of Urquhart Castle.

Suddenly it turned up: the tourist boat! The captain popped his head out of the window on his cabin. I greeted him politely and tried to excuse my limited knowledge of local mooring etiquette by pointing at my Swedish ensign. The friendly captain replied he would use the opposite side of the jetty. I could stay just so long as I made room for a second tourist boat coming in about 2 hours. At the same time, he encouraged me to go and see the castle. That was much more important, he said, than worrying about where we were moored.

I must confess our further sin in that we, by using this private jetty, had already got into the castle compound. When Karolina asked another Scotsman where the entrance was, to buy a visitor's ticket, he just responded: "You are already inside, why bother?"

After the imposing castle, we continued towards the end of Loch Ness and to Fort Augustus. No, sadly, we didn't see Nessie, apart from on the many postcards and souvenirs available in all the shops around the loch.

We tried to avoid buying too many souvenirs but, in a local garage, I could not resist a jar of marmalade made with 10-year old The Macallan Single Malt Whisky. It may have been something to do with the air and the scenery but it seemed to me that this was the best marmalade I had ever tasted. With fresh boat-baked scones, that marmalade and a cup of tea, Scotland was as delightful a place to be as I could imagine.

In less than a week, our inland waterway holiday was over. One more lock and we would be out of the sheltered canal and sailing on the breathtaking west coast of Scotland. Once more we would have tides, fog, currents and weather to cope with – but also beautiful anchorages and more friendly Scottish people.

Tea time in Fort Augustus

TENDERS

The tender is your car, your workhorse, your truck. It will take you ashore, to other boats or to that turquoise snorkel or dive-site you just read about. It will transport groceries, cooking gas, fuel, spare parts and guests. Your tender will do all this for you in a variety of weather conditions.

The faster and sturdier your tender is, the more freedom you have when it comes to choosing where to anchor. A tender and outboard capable of planing will mean you can drop your hook in a quiet, safe corner of the anchorage but still get quickly and drily to the landing dock.

But don't get carried away. We met couples who were not strong enough alone to lift their tender and outboard up the beach. The tender has to be hauled onboard regularly and you must be able to stow both it and the outboard safely while on passage. If you have room, the ideal place for the dinghy on passage is on deck. It's a good idea to fit some lifting points so that it can be hauled up with a halyard. If the engine is heavy, it may need a separate lifting arrangement of its own.

Try not to leave the tender floating behind your boat overnight. It is a very easy thing to steal and if the wind gets up and flips it over, the engine will be damaged. Lifting it to deck level with a halyard is a popular option. Ours settled most easily with the outboard pointing into the wind. When you go ashore, have some means of locking the engine to the tender and the tender to the dock. You can do the latter with a piece of light-gauge chain which can also be used for anchoring the dinghy when you want to snorkel or decide to wade ashore rather than risk the breakers.

Buy an engine that everyone onboard is going to be able to start, including any children. It will, of course, be easier to get spares for better-known brands.

Exploring Lysefjorden, Norway by dinghy

The early fisherman catches the fish

Chapter seven

In which we swap a chipped mug for some clean washing

THE FOG LIFTS

I was about to push the door open, but did not have much hope; the hairdresser looked closed. The windows were dark and only a small sign on the outside revealed that this was a 'Hair and Beauty Salon'. The description, I thought, sat a bit uneasily both with the shop itself and with the surrounding town of Mallaig in general. Mallaig is a genuine fishing village just south east of Skye on the west coast of the Highlands of Scotland. I liked the essence of Mallaig, which is anything but fancy. This small town is surely as it always has been: a real fishing village.

To my surprise, the door to the 'Hair and Beauty salon' was open and through the dark I could make out a lady cleaning the floor further back. No other person was visible, and definitely no clients. I asked if they had time to cut my hair that day. The response was polite, friendly, but clear: "No, no — we are very busy. But there is another hair-dresser in Fort William, if you want to try that one instead. You just drive down the main road." She pointed in a direction out of Mallaig.

Fort William? Did she really mean the Fort William at the end of the Caledonian Canal? That was where we had come from a few days before. I paused. It had become difficult to believe that, for some, Fort William was just the next town, easily reached by car. If you had one, that was.

It struck me how fast these noisy, energy-hungry, carbon dioxide-emitting things could move you from place to place. Having mainly sailed in rural areas of late (like the Caledonian Canal) we hadn't encountered many cars for weeks. For us, cars and traffic now felt rather alien and dangerous and not just because in Scotland they drive on the 'wrong' side of the road. It was their speed that felt so out of keeping with the world around us. Are people really in such a hurry? Why? Are they running away from something? Where are they going?

I could still remember how important it had once been for us not to slack for a moment. All those things we had to do by some ever so important deadline. If time was not exactly money, it had still seemed very scarce. Always busy, busy, busy!

I wasn't yet sure whether it was true but I felt I was actually getting more done now than I had when every day was a rush. I used to own a fast car. I used to leave my cell phone on. I used to insist on the fastest possible internet connections.

It was strange, but I even slept better and more deeply now. I was no longer mentally exhausted when I turned in. When my body asked for rest, it felt perfectly reasonable and rational to simply lie down and sleep. Before, I'd thought of sleep as a necessary evil. Sleep, so I had believed, was a waste of time and prevented me from performing and working. The less I slept, the more I would achieve. It seemed so obvious. What an absurd attitude. I worked until late at night and my constant fatigue made me irritable and not very pleasant to be around.

Living ashore, my brain had been full of problems to solve, all at the same time. My thoughts had been turning round in circles and it had not always been easy to find tranquillity. And then came that terrible spiral I used to get into when I got stressed about not getting to sleep, and that, itself stopped me sleeping. I would lie awake, acutely aware that my alarm clock would be ringing a few, short hours later. I would tell myself I had to fall asleep, and fast! Everything was planned and scheduled. Now I thought back to those times and smiled. Now I went to sleep when I was tired.

Waking was the same. I had hated that old alarm clock. It always seemed to go off when I was in the middle of a dream. If it could just wait a few minutes, I would think, the dream would be resolved, my rest would be complete, I would be refreshed and ready to face the day. But no, never those few more minutes. It is a totally different feeling to be woken by the cry of seagulls. Sleeping onboard is one of the great pleasures of cruising.

There were many ways in which we already felt more in tune with nature. I felt it in my breath. Now I breathed in and out at a natural pace. No more gasping and panting. I had started to accept the tides as a sort of the breath of the sea: in, and out, in and out – every 6 hours. We lived with these tides, sailed with their currents, moving in harmony with the wind and waves. I had come to recognise that trying to force the pace was pointless. Going with the flow would give us a knot or two. Pressing on against the current just meant going slowly.

As I'm sure you can imagine, I was deep in thought as I slowly pushed shut the door to Mallaig's busy hairdresser. There was no reason to be disappointed. My hair was in good enough shape to last to Dublin or even beyond. Who could tell? And who cared, anyway?

Outside, I joined the rest of the family and we continued along the main street of Mallaig. As we walked, there were busy fishing vessels on one side and model fishing boats in the window of a toyshop on our other side. Those replicas were there to encourage the next generation of fishermen, I guessed. At the end of the street, between the railway station and the fishing harbour, we made out a sign saying Fishermen's Mission. Outside, on the doorstep, a weather-beaten man sat with his recently emptied cup of coffee in his hands. "Are yo' goin' in?" he asked. I nodded hesitantly. Well, why not, I thought. "Could ye' take my cup inside, please?"

This was how we got to know the Fishermen's Mission of Mallaig: with an empty blue cup in our hands, which had just warmed a tired Atlantic fisherman.

A spacious canteen opened up further in, with numerous tables spreading out. There they sat, the heroes of the sea, I thought. The lines in their faces told tales of icy storms on unforgiving winter seas, days of good catch and days of disappointment. Some had a cup of tea, others a warm soup, and others were there just for a chat.

I passed the empty blue cup to a lady along with a 'thanks' from the man outside. At the same time, I asked if it was true that men coming from the sea could get their laundry done here. "Of course!" was the immediate reply. "If you stay away from home, you certainly need laundry done, don't you? You see, we have many foreign seamen staying here, some, for instance, from the Baltic countries. They all work on fishing vessels." The lady looked outside the window as a fishing vessel made its way to sea. After a short pause, she continued thoughtfully: "It would be too far for many of them to go home between trips. But we have also Brits staying here, of course. All are welcome at the Mission!"

The lady looked at our bag and asked: "How much laundry do you have? We close at noon on Saturdays, you see…but if Angus could wait…" She looked over to a bunch of men at a table close to a window. One of them looked up from his playing cards and nodded in a friendly way. The lady looked pleased and continued: "Well then, I could do your laundry first. Come again at noon and I will have your clothes washed, dried and folded."

When we left the Mission, we felt we had something in common with the sea and its people. We all shared the same cold, misty drizzle that awaited us outside but we were in high spirits.

Through the rain, we went for a walk while waiting for our laundry. We passed the fishing harbour once more, saw a seal swimming around the boats, looking for leftovers. When we eventually returned to the Fishermen's Mission, we found all our clothes in the same bag but now, for a reasonable fee, clean, dry and folded. We will always remember the Mallaig Fishermen's Mission.

It was still drizzling and quite misty when we motored out of Mallaig. Was this typical for a Scottish summer? As always, I was following the weather carefully.

The barograph read 1033.5 indicating a beefy High Pressure. But even though the electronic instrument showed a friendly sun symbol on its display, there was no sun visible to us through the mist. If this was Scottish summer high pressure, what did Scottish winter low pressure look like?

At Sanna Bay, north of Tobermory, we met a Scottish family and asked what they thought about the weather. Bruce and Christa with their three children were experienced cruisers sailing a 52-foot Moody called Palandra. Strangely, as we thought, they had no complaints about the weather. It was a fine day, they said, why didn't we all go to the beach together?

That sounded good. Our only problem was the cold. How were we going to play when we could barely stop our teeth chattering? Bruce and Christa just laughed at us soft Scandinavians, gathered their beach toys from Palandra and dressed for a summer's afternoon on a Scottish beach. Their solution was as simple as it was efficient: wetsuits for the entire family. Luckily, we had packed ours as well, somewhere deep down in a locker. Now suitably attired, our day on the beach turned into a great success, despite the low temperatures.

Bruce and Christa wanted to invite us to what they said was Britain's most remote pub. They explained it was just a day's sail from Sanna Bay and showed it to us on the chart. There, a few miles east of Mallaig, into Loch Nevis, was a place called Inverie and a pub called The Old Forge. According to Bruce, it was so remote the nearest road was 60 miles away. The place was only accessible by boat or a lengthy hike.

There was not much to discuss. Of course, we wanted to discover this remote place, especially when guided by such a nice Scottish family. We both arrived in the afternoon of the following day and picked up one of the buoys provided by The Old Forge. It felt right to be arriving by boat. There were a couple of 4X4s visible ashore. They'd been brought in by boat and did not even carry licence plates. The only road for them was the dirt road connecting the pub, the church, the old school, the post-office, a couple of houses and the huts further up the mountain.

I was impressed by the number of buildings at such an isolated site. Bruce explained: "Remember: what we call 'remote' wasn't necessarily any more remote than many other places before cars!"

He was right. The church, the pub, the houses and the school all suggested a once very active community, which, to me still looked quite vital. Here, travel by boat was, and maybe still is, every bit as natural as by car.

Over a pint of ale and some hand-dived local scallops from the loch, we discussed our new cruising lifestyle with Bruce and Christa. For reasons I didn't yet fully understand, they wanted to know if we had already changed life-style. We'd been away now for more than a month and they wanted to know if we felt we'd moved on a stage yet. I paused. It wasn't easy to explain how I felt. I tried a metaphor: "I don't know if you recognize the situation: it feels like a curtain has lifted and our range of vision has increased. We seem to understand things more clearly, as if a smoke screen had faded away. It's a bit like that, I think."

And as if nature were listening, the Scottish fog began to clear. All of a sudden, we could see beyond the few metres of green at the water's edge and right up the hillside. What had earlier been no more than an inkling of an island covered in fog, was now a beautiful vista. Just as I felt clarity inside, so there came clarity outside.

It had taken a month for our inner fog to lift. Up until this point, we had been aiming for a fixed target, namely to go cruising. We had put a lot of effort into getting our project started without really seeing how it all would develop. Not until now.

We began to lie back, open our eyes and appreciate what this new life-style really meant. What we saw was the beauty of simplicity. We didn't miss the expensive trappings of our old, shore-bound lives. We were actually happier with less!

I couldn't help thinking of St Francis of Assisi. In the early 13th century, St Francis gave up his life as the son of a wealthy merchant, exchanging it for harmony with nature and God. He taught that it was vital we should all listen to our inner voice, the voice of God. St Francis believed that by giving up possessions, he could own everything, as nature belongs to everybody. He believed in travelling to meet people and to make peace. St Francis had a point, I thought. Doesn't monetary wealth always come with a sort of spiritual impoverishment?

Christa and Bruce began to talk about their own experiences. They had taken a three month sabbatical the previous winter. They had moved to Switzerland and put their children into a Swiss International School, while Christa and Bruce had focussed on finding time for themselves, being with their children, going skiing and enjoying Switzerland. This sabbatical had been of great importance to them, they explained, as they could now see things more clearly, both at work and in their personal lives. It was clear to me that their mental fog was gone. If you could have seen them playing with their children on the beach or making music with violins together in the cockpit, you would have agreed with me: this family was firmly welded together and genuinely happy. We wanted to become like this as well!

Christa and Bruce were the first people we met who were already tuned into the 'cruising frequency'. We were still on the verge. What we didn't know at that time was that we would meet many more such people as we sailed. Making new friends is perhaps the most pleasurable part of voyaging.

It was time to make progress — leaving the fog behind!

SAILING IN FOG

There are two types of fog — sea or advection fog and land or radiation fog. Sea fog is formed when warm, moist air moves over cold water. It's most common around northern Europe in spring and early summer. There will be wind and the conditions may last for some days especially with southerly winds. Sea fog typically stays until the weather system changes, for instance, with the arrival of a cold front.

Land fog is more common in late summer, autumn and winter and is formed when the ground cools during a calm, clear night under high pressure. The fog may drift down rivers and estuaries and even over coastal waters but it should disappear quickly once the sun rises or the wind picks up.

It is good practice to keep track of the dewpoint, which can be found on some internet weather sites. This is the temperature at which the air becomes saturated and fog of whichever sort forms. If your outside temperature drops close to the dew point, watch out.

Getting caught in fog at sea can be quite frightening. There are various sound signals that you must make and listen for but it is often hard to tell from where a noise is coming. Visibility will be worse on the windward side of any land mass.

Even with GPS and radar, it is important to plot your position carefully when there's any danger of fog and, if you're worried about ships, finding shallow water and waiting is often the best tactic. Always assume another vessel has not seen you and, above all, be patient. If you have a radar but are not familiar with it, practise before you find yourself in fog.

Ligthhouse in Sweden

Fingal's Cave, Staffa

Chapter eight
In which we go back to Viking times

NORTHERN REMOTENESS

It was July 20 when we met the lady on Islay. She owned a Bed & Breakfast place and was in the process of launching a website about her little hotel business. The home-page was almost complete; just a good photo of her house was still lacking. She was hoping for a sunny day to take the desired picture. "I've been waiting for quite some time," she said, "I'm sure there will come a fine day sooner or later, certainly during autumn."

During our Hebridean cruise, we had heard this before: namely that October was a good time to visit Scotland. The water gets warmer, resulting in less fog; and swimming, apparently, is more pleasant in October than it is in July.

"But winter – oh, that's dreadful!" the Bed & Breakfast lady continued. It turned out she'd been living on the island since childhood and knew what she was talking about. "What do you do during winter?" I asked.

"My business doesn't require as much attention as in summer, obviously, when I work until one in the morning and then have breakfast ready at seven, every day of the week. What do I do during winter? Well, last winter – I think it was in March – I went to Paris for a couple of days. That was great...!" The lady halted for a few seconds – going back in her memories – and then laughed again loudly: "They thought I was crazy, these French people!" she recalled, with a big smile on her face. "They were all complaining about this extraordinarily freezing 'spring', while I was running around in a T-shirt! But when I mentioned I was Scottish, that seemed to explain it all. They all looked at me with compassion, saying no more...." Another hearty laugh before I asked if she liked her life out here. "Yes, yes! This is much better than a 9-to-5 job on the mainland! You meet so many nice people. Did you know, by the way, that 90 percent of my guests are Swedish?" "No!" I said, "How come?" She gave me another of her broad smiles: "Whisky!" Well, that said it all, I thought.

Islay is pleasant, but not quite as intriguing as the mysterious Barra. We were halfway there and still could not make out the island, despite a rare sun, and blue sky. Gradually, we began to realise why. Barra was hiding inside a huge fog bank enclosing the entire Outer Hebrides.

It was strange, knowing there were islands nearby while all that was visible at sea level was a cloud. All day had been bright and sunny and we had enjoyed a most beautiful Scottish morning at our anchorage on Canna before starting our sail to Barra. It had been so gorgeous, I had even felt like an early swim; or better still its Swedish equivalent, the so-called 'dip'. It must be something that affects only Scandinavians. You suddenly get this exaggerated eagerness, all confused with a sort of national pride. You believe you have to prove your Nordic heritage and get in the water no matter what the temperature. A 'Swedish dip' is done by immersing your entire body into the freezing sea for a fraction of a second. The goal is to keep the experience as short as possible. The reward is breakfast in a sunny cockpit with a freshly brewed coffee in your hands, a towel around your body and confirmation that you are still able to withstand a certain degree of torture.

I was getting ready to strip off when I took a look at the thermometer. The water was 11°C (52F). Maybe I didn't have quite as much Viking blood as I'd liked to think. Could we just skip straight to the coffee? No. I wanted to see how the propeller looked; whether it had grown any barnacles or weed. Propellers are so important, there should be a little window in the hull under the engine room or in the aft cabin, so you can get a glance of what is going on underneath.

In the end, I compromised and put on my wet suit. As soon as I was in the water, I could feel the icy water trickling in. I started to breathe more quickly and my heart began to beat faster. This was cold, no doubt about that. I understood even better now that this was definitely not a sea to fall into. There must be no falling overboard from Regina!

How did the propeller look? I almost forgot to check, but, yes, it looked fine and wouldn't need any scrubbing until we reached warmer waters. I would have said the same, even if it had been fully fouled.

Back in the cockpit, I enjoyed my coffee and what was a magnificent morning. The west coast of Scotland is another great and under-rated cruising ground. There are many protected bays, thrilling and beautiful scenery and, yet, it is almost deserted. On a morning like this, it was hard to understand why.

The sunshine kept up with us for quite a lot of the trip to Barra, until a few miles from our destination it vanished as we sailed into a great, grey, damp mass. It engulfed us completely. Plunging deeper and deeper into the cloud, it was as if we could hear a voice whispering: "So long! See you later, on your way out of the Hebrides."

The radar and plotter guided us safely into Barra's sheltered Castlebay. We grabbed one of the guest buoys and sat down to admire the scenery through the mist. What a remote place! Suddenly I got an immense feeling of satisfaction. We had made it all the way to the Outer Hebrides!

Sailing-wise, this had been no big deal; but emotionally, it was definitely an achievement. As so often before, I thought of the fact that a big goal, which had once seemed so difficult, had now been achieved. Looking back, it was nothing but slowly taking one step after the other. Every journey begins with a single step and every little step that follows takes you closer to your destination.

Surveying the castle in the middle of the bay, seeing all the brownish-grey houses ashore, I recalled an experience from my youth: I remembered one of my first days back at school after a long summer holiday. We got new maths books. Flipping through my new educational challenge, I turned to the pages towards the end of the book. "Oh no!" I had thought. "This is impossible! I don't understand any of this." I remembered how I had stared at the Greek letters and weird equations and formulae that filled the book's final pages. I did not even recognise this as maths. To my big surprise, at the end of the same semester, I got to those pages and they were no more difficult than had been the very first ones. It was all a question of going step by step, completing each chapter before beginning the next.

Barra, or in Gaelic, Eilean Bharraigh, is said to be the most romantic of the Hebridean islands; and the reason for that is not hard to find. Its unique physical setting – with the Kisimul Castle on an island in the middle of Castlebay harbour – was stunning, even on a misty day like this. I could feel its ancient past, its social history, its Gaelic culture and its Celtic Catholicism. Inhabited by over a thousand species of wild flower and about two thousand people, Barra is anything but dull. The close-knit community with the wild Atlantic to the west as its only neighbour really knows how to have fun: the 'ceilidh' dances and social gatherings are legendary, and everyone is welcome.

There had been two churches in tiny Castlebay, but it seemed one had turned out to be sufficient. The smaller had now been left to the winter gales. It was a sad sight and I wondered what was worse: this soon-to-be ruin or the church in Tobermory which was now a souvenir shop? What should be done with churches when souls have drifted away?

We, too, soon had to drift away with the tide. We'd like to have stayed longer, but a low-pressure system with a cold front and gales was approaching and we wanted a better hiding place, further inshore. Castlebay harbour, though lovely, was too remote to get stuck in for long. We were just beginning to think ahead to our crossing of the Bay of Biscay – a task we had to complete before the summer grew too old.

The rain rattled on the coach roof as we anchored in the southern end of Tobermory bay. Here we stayed as the cold-front went over. Then we pushed on south towards the island of Iona.

On our way down the west coast of Mull, we passed close to Staffa, where there are several caves at sea level, of which Fingal's Cave is the best known. Mendelssohn wrote his 'Hebrides Overture', also known as 'Fingal's Cave', in 1830 after a journey to Scotland. During one stormy night, he came to the island of Staffa and was overwhelmed by the manner in which the waves break on the Scottish coast. He immediately wrote down what he saw and sent it to his sister, Fanny Mendelssohn: "In order to make you understand how extraordinarily The Hebrides affected me, I send you the following, which came into my head there", he wrote. The sketch he included consisted of musical notes, which later became the opening theme of the overture. Oh, how I wish I could paint in notes like Mendelssohn!

It was 1700 by the time we reached Iona, just south of Staffa, and all the day-trippers had gone. We seemed to have the entire island to ourselves. We anchored across the sound of Iona in a bay called Bull's Hole. With Regina safely hooked up, we launched our dinghy and motored across the sound, past several medieval buildings. There were ruins of an ancient nunnery, but also a very active monastery.

Coming round one headland, we fell upon a thousand year-old but well-kept rectangular building. "Look at this!" I said, pointing at a fully intact chapel we later learned dated back to the 11th century. "Jessica, you're reading a book about two children who travelled in time and landed in the Viking age. I think we've done the same! Look at this church: It's pure Viking!" Jessica looked at me, wondering if what I'd said might even be true. "Do you think we dare enter?"

The door to the chapel opened with a squeaking sound and we edged in slowly. It was dark inside, despite the white walls. An old oil-lamp was hanging from the roof and a plain iron cross stood in a corner. The altar consisted of a simple stone table; and two small pews made up the primitive furnishing. Jonathan, Jessica, Karolina and I stood silently in the centre of the chapel. We truly felt we had travelled back a thousand years.

I closed my eyes and imagined the last Vikings being christened here, of their own volition or not.

And then, as I stood, imagining those Vikings, another ancient sound crept into my head. It was bagpipes. Not loud, but distinct. When I opened my eyes, the monks and Vikings had gone, but the bagpipes remained. "What's that?" Jonathan asked, "It sounds like an old broken oil pump!" Jessica had already pushed the heavy door open to let in the glaring light, the smell of the wild flowers and the sound of the bagpipes. We couldn't see the source. The sound was coming from somewhere behind the hills and was getting louder.

We headed for the music. Soon we were back by the old nunnery and nearby we found the pipers, appropriately attired in tartan kilts. I had to rub my eyes to prove I wasn't dreaming.

Scotland and its people, its history and culture, its scenery and weather — all made for some unforgettable weeks. Our time in Scotland alone amounted to a fantastic holiday. But we were going on; and more adventures awaited us just a few day-sails to the south, in Guinness-Land.

ANCHORING

Anchoring is another subject to which entire volumes have been devoted. It's crucial to recognise its importance. In extreme weather, your ability to fix the boat to the sea floor may be the only thing between you and disaster. Blue-water cruisers generally upgrade their anchors and chain from the standard boat-length issue.

Choose an all-purpose design for your main anchor, such as the CQR, Bruce or Delta, and something lighter for a kedge.

The more chain the better, but for a trip like a North Atlantic Circuit, 60m is about the minimum. Consider using a 'chum' or 'angel'. This is a weight attached to the chain and dropped to just above the sea floor. It improves the angle of the chain from the anchor and acts as a damper, preventing snatching. It's less likely to get twisted up than double anchors and can be recovered before you start pulling the anchor up.

If you don't take the strain off the windlass by means of a break or cleat, you'll need a 'snubber'. This is a piece of mooring line attached at the chain just above the water surface by means of a chain hook. The other end is attached to the mooring cleat at the bow. Avoid chafing by having a piece of water hose around the rope where it goes over the anchor roller. A snubber relieves the pressure on the windlass and saves you from the rattling sound when the chain moves over the anchor roller as the boat swings in the wind.

In stronger winds and non-tidal waters, consider using an anchor sail. This is a small sail hoisted on the back-stay to keep the bow dead in the wind. This significantly reduces the forces on the anchor and prevents the boat sailing to and fro.

And, lastly, if you've not done a lot of anchoring, practise. It is not as easy as it might seem.

Anchored in Aros Bay in Tobermory

Stripped for work in the engine room

Chapter nine

In which we discover the delights of the 'black stuff'

THE 5-STAR GUINNESS

The engine, on which I was lying, was warm. I was more or less naked, having just finished showering. I was cramped. My head hung over one side of the engine and my feet stuck out into the cabin on the opposite side. I was wearing a head-torch and trying to locate the screw that would allow me to remove the shower-drain pump. The hose-clamp was not as hard to loosen as I had thought. That turned out to be unfortunate. I released the hose and got a second shower, directly into my face and right up my nose. It was the water I'd just showered in and was still warm. Recycling valuable 'fresh' water is all very well, but this was too much.

But it couldn't be helped, the pump needed fixing. The motor was running fine, but the valves did not shut completely, preventing the used shower water leaving the boat.

I unscrewed and took down the pump from the wall of the engine compartment and looked at it with suspicion. Another item added to the 'to do' list.

As well as the pump, there was the electrical relay that controlled the regulator for the High-Output Alternator that needed a little tap every time it was supposed to get on duty. Frankly, I could well understand this poor fellow. I had to wake up and get out of my bunk every time the engine signalled that it was ready to let the current pass on to the regulator. If I were the relay, I would also have thought that a somewhat flatter organization would be more in keeping with modern practice. "Go and tell the regulator directly, instead of telling me, the relay, first!" Too many bosses is never good in an organization and the intermediate ones often get jammed, just like my little relay here.

With a gentle smack on its head, the relay eventually did do what it was meant to, but it was not how I really wanted things to happen onboard. In other words, I had to look for a new Mr. Relay. Another item on the 'to-do' list.

At home, I would have phoned the supplier or a chandlery nearby. A couple of calls, and the new parts would be in the mail to arrive at our house a day or two later. With cell-phones and sat-phones, we had taken the phone with us but our mail box had stayed behind. Generally, given all the bills and brochures with which it was usually clogged, this was a good thing. But at this particular moment, I was rather missing our dear old post box. How else was I going to get some new valves for the shower pump and a new relay for the alternator?

As ever, something – or, more accurately, somebody – turned up. We saw Rob and his wife Karen for the first time in Glenarm, when they had jumped off their motor boat to take our mooring lines and welcome us to Northern Ireland. Rob is the kind of person you can't help liking immediately.

Rob and Karen knew good things to see not only in Glenarm but also in their home town Bangor, as well as in most of the other harbours we were to visit in Ireland. Talking through the possible stops along the way, Rob never failed to mention the best pubs for each and every port. "You see", he said seriously, "we always judge the places we go to by the food we can eat and the Guinness we are served. We have a scale ranging from 1 to 5, classifying the stout we drink. A 5-star Guinness is one you never forget, a 4 is one you finish with joy, an average 3-star is a Guinness you drink without a special comment, the 2-star Guinness is one you don't finish and a 1-star Guinness you reject immediately. Of course, we're always looking for 5s and you should do the same."

How could Rob know so much about all the Guinness in every pub? And it wasn't just the pub, he even specified the tap. "When in Bangor", he said, "don't miss the pub called The First Port, but make sure you get your Guinness from the tap furthest away from the door. Don't forget that! That's the 5-star Guinness, but only from that tap."

When we arrived in Bangor, just outside Belfast, Rob and Karen had already arrived, and stood ready on the pier once more to take our mooring lines. It didn't take long for them to tell us where the 5s were, which were the best fishmongers and cafés and, for Jonathan and me, where to obtain the haircuts we had failed to get in Mallaig.

All these pubs were tempting, for sure, but they had to wait right now. I had other, more practical, places to visit. Next to the marina was a chandlery. That was a good start for me in my hunt for a shower-pump valve and relay for the alternator. As it turned out, they had neither.

Next stop was Nautical World in the High Street. Behind the counter was Neil – and I felt immediately that he would go a long way to help his customers. When I told him about by broken pump (which was made by Whale), he looked at me and said: "Didn't you know that you've come to 'Whale City'? Whale pumps are actually manufactured in Bangor, and their head office is just up the road." He continued to explain that he did not have a service kit for our specific pump in stock and that he nowadays had to order every Whale product from England, which took several days and involved transportation costs. "Three months ago", he continued with some sorrow in his voice, "I could just have driven up the road to get the valves for you, but now it all has to go through this distributor in England. New ordering routines, they say …."

Back in the marina, with neither a relay nor a valve but at least with shorter hair and some fresh fish, we found Rob standing by his boat, filling up with fresh water. As always, he greeted us with a big smile, asking if we had found any 5s yet, and what we had been doing in Bangor so far. I confessed I was chasing spare parts, not Guinness, and mentioned the delay with the pump spares.

"Oh I know these guys at Whale! They are customers of mine. Really nice people! Call them and tell them about your problem. I'm sure they'll help. And this relay thing…. Wait, I'll call my electrician, he might know where you can get one." Rob got his mobile phone out of his pocket and dialled a number he seemed to know by heart. While talking to his electrician, he passed the questions to me: "Is it a 12 volt relay?" I nodded. "Does it say 30 amps on it?" I nodded again. "OK. Is it a four-pin, you want?" I nodded once more, now with a thankful expression in my face. "Yes. OK. Bangor Autoparts? Fine. Thanks. Bye." Rob turned to me: "I'll drive you up there, it's just next to the butcher, where they make the best sausages in Northern Ireland. Did you not smell them in Glenarm where we met first?"

"You mean you can smell them all the way from Bangor to Glenarm?" I asked laughing.

"No", said Rob. "I had them on our barbeque, remember? Didn't they smell fantastic? If you want, we can stop by the butcher as well, so you can order some meat and sausages there. If you ask the butcher, he'll vacuum-pack them for you. That's what he does for us. I'll come with you to make sure you get the right sausages."

Not long after, we were all sitting in Rob's car: me eagerly hoping for a new relay and Karolina not missing the chance to stock up our freezer with some good-quality meat and sausages. During the ride, I found out why Rob knew so much about beer taps — not only in Bangor, or in Ireland for that matter, but in many countries worldwide. His company manufactured two million metres of tubing for draught beer every month. The tubes are designed so that beer that's cold in the pub cellar reaches the pub taps in fresh and well-chilled condition. No wonder he knew about pubs and beer.

With a bag full of meat, Karolina was as happy as I was with my beautiful new relay! Now, if the people at Whale were equally helpful, we would definitely have a reason to go out for a Guinness tonight.

I called Whale and talked to a man in the sales department, who confirmed that it was unfortunately impossible to sell any products or spare parts to me, or even to a chandlery in town; it all had to go through the distributor in England. However, he saw one possibility: if I were to make a claim on the warranty, he could put me through to someone who might be able to help.

Half an hour later, I arrived at Whale reception. They were already waiting for me and within a couple of minutes one of my new-found friends had taken the pump apart, showed me that some hair had got stuck in the valves and had fixed it.

If this wasn't worth a Guinness, then I don't know what is. The entire Regina-crew went out to a pub, where Karolina and I enjoyed a Guinness which I would class as a very strong 4. I had never had better.

Maybe you have some prejudices against stout? Maybe you have only experienced a 1 or 2-star Guinness? Or – even worse – only had stout out of a bottle or a can? Maybe you have not yet visited Ireland, and especially not Dublin, nor have you tasted a Guinness out of a tap made by Rob and his 70 employees? In that case, you have my sympathy. You have not yet tasted a real pint of Guinness! At the same time, be happy, since you have still something great to look forward to.

Smooth, black and with a most wonderful foam topping. That foamy head stays beautiful throughout the entire enjoyment of the pint, right to the last drop. Guinness is like ice cream. Guinness is like chocolate, the best dark chocolate you can imagine. It makes me feel good. Whatever the advertising regulator may say, I believe Guinness is good for you. Guinness also means friendship, since the ideal pint is drunk with a friend. And if you're not with a friend, in a pub that serves good Guinness you soon will be. After a pint of Guinness, you take a more relaxed approach to everything – even a bit of recycled shower water in the face.

Since Jessica and Jonathan could not share a Guinness with us, we found them some delicious dark chocolate. Karolina liked that too, almost as much as the Guinness. She is our family's biggest chocolate fan, closely followed by Jonathan.

It wasn't long until we got to Dublin. Dublin is the home of Guinness and is definitely a city with a bit of life to it. In fact, it was a bit overwhelming after the tranquil Hebrides.

Founded by the Vikings as a major trading post, Dublin later became the centre of boat building for the Norsemen. It has always been a magnet for the itinerant. If it was once a bit of a 'forgotten' city, it has now definitely awoken and is a popular and cool place to visit and live. We saw building and construction sites everywhere. It felt like a booming city.

To reach Dublin, we berthed Regina in Malahide, just a 20-minute train ride north of the city. If Rob had not recommended it so strongly, we would never have dared enter, as the chart showed sandbanks covered by no more than 0.3m of water at low tide. Regina draws 2m so we had to get our tide calculations right.

Malahide was a haven of calm compared to the busy city of Dublin. Flowers were hanging from each and every window, most of which seemed to belong to pubs. We took another tip from Rob and stopped off at James Gibney's & Sons, where we enjoyed a very, very strong 4. The atmosphere was fantastic. Everyone was watching horse-racing on a big flat-screen TV. As far as I could see, the Guinness was going down quicker than the horses were running.

Our last day in Dublin took us to the Guinness Store House, the original brewery. We learnt how Arthur Guinness bought a run-down brewery in 1759 and started at first to brew ale. At that time, there were more than two hundred breweries in Dublin, of which twenty were nearby. Competition must have been stiff, but demand was strong. Beer, remember, was then thought to be safer to drink than water, which could be contaminated.

Arthur Guinness was smart enough to distinguish himself from the other brewers by following a trend then fashionable in London. A new type of beer called porter had become very popular. So, in 1799, he decided to brew his last ale and concentrate instead on porter. This became a very successful recipe. Arthur Guinness was a good entrepreneur with a feel for trends and an appreciation of the value of scale. At the same time, he was known to be very generous, granting paid-for holidays for his employees, offered 10-15% higher wages than others, launching Dublin's first Sunday school, and providing workers' widows with pensions. Because of the pension, mothers were said to tell their daughters to marry themselves a Guinness Man, as he was valuable alive or dead.

At the Guinness Store House, we were shown how the four ingredients, barley, hops, water and yeast finally become Guinness. The only thing I possibly could criticise was the claim that wine-making consisted of nothing more than crossing grapes and letting them ferment, while brewing beer, and especially Guinness, was a much more complicated process. Well, I guess, everyone believes in their own products.

The tour ended on the 7th floor, at the very top of the brewery. With its panoramic view of the city, this is said to be Dublin's highest bar and is named 'Gravity'. And that was where we finally found it. This Guinness, pumped straight from the brewery below: this was a 5-star Guinness.

SPARES AND TOOLS

The spares you carry will be determined by the gear you have on the boat and the route you plan to take.

Before you go, write down telephone numbers and e-mail addresses for the brands you carry. Ask the manufacturers if they sell a suggested spare part kit. A complete list of parts is invaluable, especially for complicated items such as your engine or your rig. Knowing the part number makes it all much easier.

If you've bought a new boat, the manufacturer should be able to supply you with a list of key spares, along with other useful information. Owners' associations are also a good source of advice.

Your tools should be sufficient to do the basic maintenance and to fit all those spares. Some people choose to buy good, stainless steel tools and to keep them oiled and rust free. Others prefer to buy cheaper and expect to replace. Give yourself time to build up a set of tools. Experience over a season or two doing your own basic maintenance will give you the best idea of what you need.

It helps to not have to get out a big, heavy tool-kit every time you need a pair of pliers or a screwdriver. An extra set of the most frequently needed tools within easy reach will make life easier.

Plan to have enough filters and oil for at least a couple of oil changes and carry enough fuel filters to cope should you take on contaminated diesel.

One spare that every boat should carry is a complete pump for the heads. It's not much fun trying to clear or repair one of these while at sea.

Finally, don't hesitate to ask a cruising friend if you need to borrow a part or a tool. Helping fellow sailors is one of the great pleasures of a trip like this.

Temple Bar, Dublin

Our gennaker worked well and was not hard to handle

Chapter ten

In which we take the blue-water baton

TRANSFORMATION AT SEA

I climbed the companionway, breathing deeply as I took in the huge Atlantic swell that was rolling towards us from astern. I turned around. The log said 9.94 knots. The stern rose, the water rushed below us. It felt like Regina was flying.

I had not been able to get much sleep. This wasn't simply because the boat was rolling fairly wildly. There had been a constant stream of giggles and laughter coming from the cockpit and I had wondered what was going on. From time to time, I heard a "Woooooooohhhh! Look at that one..."

Karolina, Jessica and Jonathan seemed to be having a great time. I was too anxious to be able to rest properly. It's not every day you set off on your first crossing of the notorious Bay of Biscay.

I had heard them preparing dinner earlier, laughing about the tomatoes rolling around in the galley. Jonathan had been standing on his toes trying to stir the pan. One minute he could see the entire contents of the saucepan from above. A moment later, as Regina rolled, he was looking up at the saucepan's bottom.

By the time I joined them in the cockpit, most of the supper had been eaten. They must have had good appetites.

It's interesting how the body adjusts to a new environment. We had by now got our 'sea legs'. None of us felt badly seasick any more. That was a big relief, albeit one that lasted only until the start of our next passage. As much as time spent at sea gets one used to its movement, growing confidence also helps significantly, we found. Being a bit frightened often triggers a feeling of sickness. How often have I heard wives, married to macho seaman, say they don't enjoy sailing much because they get seasick? Their salty husbands should ponder whether it might be the other way around: could it be that their wives don't enjoy the way their husbands sail and that's the reason they get sick? Those men would find it much cheaper to help their current wife enjoy sailing than to trade her in for a new model. It doesn't take much. A woman who hasn't done a lot of sailing will enjoy learning with a sympathetic teacher, just as much as will any man. And if that means slightly fewer miles are covered, so what? Half a day's fine-weather sailing across the local bay might be just what the novice sailing wife needs to build experience and confidence. And if, at the end of such a day, the husband produces an enjoyable meal, he'll be another step towards having an enthusiastic and seasickness-free spouse. Oh, and he shouldn't forget the washing up. At this stage, that's the skipper's job, too.

I was still standing in the companionway, collecting my thoughts and wondering at my wife and children eating and laughing while the biggest waves I'd ever sailed in rolled relentlessly under the boat. The swell had built while I had been lying in my bunk. I asked Karolina if it had been like this for long. She told me I'd get used to it. We discussed reefing. There was an argument for taking in some of the mainsail, especially as it was now getting dark. On the other hand, we needed speed to get to La Coruña ahead of a gale predicted for later in the week.

Using the Iridium satellite phone, I sent off a request for a GRIB weather file to see the latest forecast for the Bay. The GRIB file came back and I downloaded it into the MaxSea navigation software we used. It said there was currently a steady wind from the north-west of about 20 to 25 knots. That was pretty close to what we'd got and that was why we were making such fantastic speed. Overnight, it was predicted to drop to some 15 knots. We decided to keep the main and genoa as they were and to continue our joy-ride over the Atlantic waves.

Crossing the Bay of Biscay had been something we'd thought of as both a threat and thrill. Or maybe a thrilling threat? Neither Karolina nor I, however, liked threats and neither of us are big thrill-seekers. Always in the back of our minds were the numerous stories we had read of Biscay's storms and dangers. Although we knew that the most perilous times were autumn and winter, and we were crossing at the end of July, the Bay still had a reputation that made us both feel a little bit frightened.

Twice before we'd had this feeling of butterflies in our stomachs when leaving port. The first time had been when we were casting off from our home-town after saying 'good-bye' to family and friends. The second came when we were about to set off across the North Sea. This third time seemed even worse than both of the previous occasions. Biscay would be our longest leg to date. We had few friends who'd crossed it happily or otherwise. And we knew the weather could not be relied on, even in summer.

Karolina and I carefully studied forecasts for all the areas we would cross on our way from Kinsale, Ireland, to La Coruña, Spain. The first area was called Fastnet. That, of course, reminded us of the 1979 Fastnet Race in which 15 competitors lost their lives in a storm very close to where we would begin our trip and at not that different a time of year. The next forecast area is called Sole and it was only after that that we would enter the area actually called Biscay, finally making landfall in an area called Fitzroy, close to the notorious Cape Finisterre of north-western Spain. All these huge patches of sea had to be crossed by us – and in one go. It was more than 500 nautical miles and would probably take Regina some four days and nights to cover. The thought was both grand and scary.

Jessica and Karolina went to sleep shortly after dinner. At least Jessica did. Like me, I don't think Karolina found it easy to get to sleep.

Jonathan and I were now alone on watch. It had become totally dark. This made it feel even more strange. We were rushing along at eight and a half and sometimes nine knots – able to make out neither the waves under us nor those around us. We could feel them lift the boat and hear them hissing beneath us, but not see them. It was like driving on a motorway with the accelerator right down, running full speed ahead into nothing but darkness. Suddenly, there was a big bang and a huge wave from the side broke against the hull, the spray pouring over deck and crashing onto the windscreen. What power water can have! "Did you get wet?" I heard Karolina's voice from below, still not asleep. "No, no, I'm dry as a lizard in Arizona. But that must have been a big wave." There was a swirling noise from the deck as the water found its way to the scuppers and back to the dark ocean below.

I fetched some nuts, which we had purchased and saved specifically for difficult nights on Biscay. This was one of those, I'd decided. Though anxious, I couldn't help finding it cozy sitting under the spray-hood listening to all the water rushing by, feeling the steady movements of the boat, even if I didn't see much. With no moon, it was easier to see the stars. There were not many vessels around, and the few that we did spot on the radar were fishing boats. These may not be big or fast but they can be frustratingly unpredictable as they turn this way and that, guided only by the shoals of fish they are following on their undersea sonar devices.

"Jonathan, are you awake? Don't you want to go to sleep?"

(He jerks awake) "Me? – No. I'm looking at the stars. Daddy, all these stars, are they also turning around other stars, just as we travel around the sun and the sun in its galaxy?"

We talked about the stars we saw and the ships we could see only on the radar. We discussed radar range and frequencies, why VHF can't be heard behind high islands and how the Iridium satellite phone works in the Gigahertz range. We talked about the difference between geostationary satellites and others. Jonathan spotted a satellite in the night sky and we wondered what type it was. A spy satellite, maybe?

More to talk about! Why are such spy satellites needed? What can they see and how are they being used? And so the questions went on. It was a conversation I will never forget.

At midnight, Jonathan finally turned in, with his life-jacket still on, sleeping in the saloon, ready, as he explained, for his next watch. Jessica, on the other hand, had earlier put on her pyjamas and was sleeping in her aft cabin berth as soundly as if we we'd been anchored in a sheltered harbour.

The black night now belonged to me alone. These first hours after midnight were still quite chilly. Maybe that would change further south? Regina was pushing on quickly. I could hear and feel the waves still passing swiftly under her hull. I was a happy man. I felt a deep gratitude for the good fortune that had brought me to this time and place. Yet again I was thinking about how we'd turned our lives through 180 degrees. Funny, I thought, 180 degrees is exactly what I could read on our current compass course heading south. This was the most thrilling and exciting thing I had ever done in my life. And the best thing was that I was sharing it with my wife and our children. Could happiness like this ever last? Knowing was not important. The moment we were in was what counted. And right now, Regina was happily charging though the seas. Jessica, Jonathan and Karolina seemed happy. Biscay was being friendly, despite the power of those waves. And I was in the middle of it all, in the centre of my personal joyride.

During the morning of the second day at sea the winds had eased, just as predicted. Once more, I was climbing the companionway, but this time I had been able to catch some short hours of sleep. The waves had decreased in power and size and we were only making some six or seven knots. I looked around at the grey sea, still half asleep. Suddenly I heard water breaking close by. I turned my head and I could see them approaching from all angles: dolphins! This was a smaller species, even more playful than the ones we had seen on the North Sea. Jessica and Jonathan were, of course, excited and we all went up to the foredeck, to watch them play, jump and swim back and forth under Regina's bow. As Jonathan leaned over the side, one dolphin came to the surface and blew spray up into his face. "I got a kiss!" he shouted. We felt that we could almost touch them. Watching dolphins is a more than adequate trade for little sleep in a rolling home.

On our third day at sea, sleeping became much easier, a fact which could not be explained by exhaustion alone. I suddenly felt less tired and more relaxed, with more energy and ability to concentrate on enjoying the sailing.

We had all gathered in the cockpit for dinner, when I noticed a sailing vessel approaching from the south-west. We had not seen much traffic at all and no sailing boat for a long time, so we all got excited. I commented on its strange heading as no port or land laid in that direction, at least not anywhere close. No sooner had I mentioned this to the others than the VHF called for attention. "Sailing vessel, this is Stella Maris – OVER." I grabbed the microphone and pressed the transmit-button: "Stella Maris, this is Swedish sailing yacht Regina. Are you the red boat heading north-east?"

Of course it was!

Never would we call up another boat just to say 'hello' when sailing in our home waters. There, there were so many boats and, anyway, why would you call somebody you didn't know? What would you say to them?

But here, in the middle of Biscay, it felt different. We eagerly wanted to know who they were, where they came from, their destination and if they had encountered any problems.

It was with a completely new feeling that I now spoke with Stella Maris over the VHF. It was with a sense of fellowship. The skipper of Stella Maris talked to me as if I were a true blue-water sailor and no longer the dreamer I had been before, walking the dock-sides of our home port with a wistful smile. I suddenly felt I might have something in common with my idols from those countless hours I had spent reading sailing memoirs.

We learned the secret of Stella Maris's heading. Their last port of call had been the Azores and before that Cape Town, South Africa. They were heading home for Kiel in Germany after a five-year circumnavigation. They took it for granted that we, too, were out on a grand tour, and asked about our plans. They talked about Tahiti, Bora Bora and Rarotonga in the sort of way we would talk about islands in the Baltic.

Thinking about our exchange, after Stella Maris had disappeared over the horizon, we felt the baton had been handed over to us, here in the middle of Biscay. Stella Maris was coming to the end of 5 years at sea and we were just setting off – heading into who knew what sort of adventures.

Deep inside me, I felt that I was now one of them. Not as experienced, still standing at the doorstep, but clearly beyond week-end and holiday-sailing.

It was in the Bay of Biscay that we became blue-water sailors.

BISCAY TACTICS

For northern Europeans, crossing Biscay is the first 'big one'. The Bay's ancient reputation is the result of two geographical facts. Its western edge coincides with the start of the continental shelf and a steep upward slope to the seabed. When big waves rolling eastward across the Atlantic hit the shelf, their energy is compressed and the waves become shorter, steeper and much more dangerous.

It is also a bay that faces the prevailing winds. Escape from its rocky eastern edge is almost always something that has to be done against the wind. There is nowhere to run to.

Modern weather forecasts take away most of the threat, but not all. For many yachtsmen, Biscay is the first time they set out on a passage that will last longer than the 3 days of a reliable weather forecast. Falmouth and, to an even greater extent, Kinsale offer a good chance of beam winds, but Normandy is a day closer. If that still looks like a bit of leap, you can work your way down the French coast until you feel like cutting the corner to Spain, though you will then, probably, have to tack to La Coruña.

So many books to read

Marina games in La Coruña

Chapter eleven

In which we make landfall at the end of our most challenging passage yet

SPANISH WARMTH

The third morning on Biscay felt different. Not only had we got accustomed to the rhythm of the sea; but also the early light appeared brighter than the previous dawns. The sun rose from behind a cloud-free horizon and seemed to light up our whole lives. The wind blowing into my face was different as well. It lacked its customary chill. And then there were the colours. The Atlantic sea had changed from steely grey to a deep blue. It was so beautiful.

The sun had only just risen when I began to feel uncomfortable. Something was disturbing me. Something on my body felt superfluous. Oh, it was my fleece sweater. I took it off and the warm winds raced around my limbs. It felt like a warm shower of air.

There was no mistaking it: we were heading south. I dug out the shorts I had not worn for at least a year. Good-bye warm, practical layers. And from that day on, our dress stayed as simple as that. Not until the Azores some eleven months later, would it be necessary to put on anything other than shorts and a T-shirt. We became big lovers of the lower latitudes.

With balmy winds embracing us and with the sun some 20 degrees above the horizon, we spotted land. This was where Biscay ended. We'd done it. Zigzagging between a dozen or more Spanish trawlers, we finally moored in La Coruña on the afternoon of the 2nd of August. We'd covered 536 miles in three days and six hours. It was an impressive passage-time and a credit to the boat.

I jumped ashore. In my hands I held the mooring line and under my bare feet I felt the sun-warmed Spanish soil. I was proud and happy.

We rang home and were told that in Sweden, it was 13°C (55° F) and rainy. Our friends talked about the fact that autumn had arrived with the rowanberry trees now standing in their full splendour. In Scandinavia, it is the arrival of their red berries that traditionally marks the end of summer. Our friends grumbled that summer had never come. School would start again shortly and life outdoors would come to an end. The long winter of hiding from the weather and each other was already beginning.

With so many people complaining about the climate at home, I couldn't see why more didn't chose to live in another corner of Europe, most logically somewhere southern. But what did I hear myself saying? Wasn't it me who had agonised so long over our decision to get away? Hadn't we thought of hundreds of reasons why we should stay where we were? We thought we knew what we had; school for the children, jobs for us, the house we lived in, gadgets we owned, the local grocery store we knew, the friends we enjoyed. Didn't I remember how difficult the decision had been? And now? I was sitting in the cockpit enjoying the shade of our bimini as I took in the view. The locals were busy but still looked relaxed. It had to have something to do with the climate.

In contrast to the Mediterranean coast of Spain, the tourists here were mainly from inland Spain itself, many from Madrid coming to enjoy the relative cool of Galicia. La Coruña may have felt hot to us but it was an escape for many inland Spaniards. For us, it was a new experience to find a coastal town in Spain, which had remained so 'Spanish'. We liked La Coruña a lot.

In the morning, I left the boat silently, with the rest of the crew still in bed, walked into the still quiet and sleepy town, found the bakery and bought fresh bread. I did my best to trouble shopkeepers and people in the street alike with my limited knowledge of Spanish, trying to improve my vocabulary. The chance to learn or improve a foreign language is yet another benefit of this sort of life.

With the warming sun, I returned to Regina to enjoy breakfast with an awakening family in the cockpit. To one side of us, we had the city of La Coruña and to the other side we overlooked the growing number of yachts gathering after successfully navigating Biscay. Many would continue southbound. How many of these were planning an Atlantic passage and how many would prefer the Mediterranean? After our triumphant crossing of first the North Sea and then the Bay of Biscay, we began carefully to consider our options. La Coruña, we reckoned, would be a good place to find others with whom we could discuss next steps.

As we sat enjoying breakfast under the bimini, we looked at the boats around us. They appeared so professional and well equipped. Wind generators, solar panels, foot-steps on the masts, wind-vanes, EPIRBs, man-overboard equipment, canvas to provide shade…, you name it. There was no doubt that this was a port filled with blue-water sailors. Regina might not have been as elaborately equipped as some but she fitted in pretty well. I was pleased.

One of the yachts carried a familiar name. It was shiny yellow with a huge sun awning covering the entire deck. A wind-vane at the stern stood alongside a red and white British ensign. On the hull, in big letters, it said 'Sarah Grace'. Hadn't we been in e-mail contact with this British boat, having found each other through the family pages of noonsite.com?

Two girls were playing on foredeck: the younger one climbing up the cutter stay like a monkey, with her small hands and feet clinging onto the thin wire. Within a couple of seconds she was half way up the mast. The girls looked to be similar ages to our children. They looked natural and uninhibited. They certainly seemed to be having great fun together.

I pointed at the girls on Sarah Grace and said to Jessica and Jonathan: "Look! I think I know this boat. If I recall correctly these two girls are called Otti and Mimi. Don't you want to go and say hello to them?" Jessica and Jonathan gave me a couple of shy looks. "Us? But we don't know any English. What should we say?" "OK", I replied. "We will go there together after breakfast."

Not long after, we knocked on Sarah Grace's hull. We introduced ourselves, which turned out to be unnecessary. They had already seen us coming into La Coruña and had cheered us in, already knowing Regina and her crew from our web-page. It didn't take many minutes until we felt as if we had known each other for ages, both families sharing the same sort of home and a recently transformed lifestyle. The kids went off playing with water on the pontoon, while Chris and Sophie invited us onboard. Soon, we were deep in discussion about our experiences of the Biscay and thoughts on an Atlantic crossing.

Chris is a medical doctor and Sophie a dentist, which gave us a great sense of security. What good news to have a doctor and dentist close by! Chris and Sophie, on the other hand, couldn't wait until we, as engineers, had a chance to look at their laptop, which was not working properly, or talk to them about their engine, electrical systems and water-maker. It was clear we had a lot to share.

The discussion carried on through SSB-HAM-nets, home schooling, whether to take extra crew for the Atlantic, whether the Cape Verdes were worth visiting and if it was true that Madeira had a new marina.

Discussing issues and problems, asking questions and helping each other would soon become an important and valuable part of cruising. It was true that many other cruisers were just as new to ocean sailing as we were, but we all held individual pieces of information. Adding them all up, the sum of knowledge became considerable. And not just know-how was happily shared among the yachties, but also charts, books, spare parts and tools. A colourful alliance binds the yachting community into a great symbiotic network.

After a cup of coffee we talked about our sailing background. Chris had already sailed from South Africa non-stop to Europe in his youth. This made him a very experienced sailor in my eyes. He, on the other hand, thought we were the big sailors, since we had crossed Biscay all the way from Ireland, instead of taking smaller hops along the coast as they had done. The fact that he had been out for weeks on a wide ocean was waved away by Chris as something done long ago. At that time, he was just part of a crew with no responsibilities or any real insight to what was going on.

A humble attitude to life, nature and the sea is typical for cruisers. Very few consider themselves to be very experienced or to take anything for granted. Blue-water sailors respect the power of nature and their fellow cruisers. Ask a real yachty – with tens of thousands of miles under the keel – if he or she has experienced any real bad weather. It's likely that they will claim that they have not, adding something like 'not any real bad weather, at least'.

This sort of modest understatement was new to us, and very different from the empty dockside boasts we'd often heard in local sailing clubs. Really experienced blue-water sailors acknowledge their worries and fears. They know their limits and rarely show off.

We immediately liked Chris and Sophie, and Jessica and Jonathan seemed to enjoy their new companions every bit as much. Watching them throwing water at each other, it was clear the communication was mainly body-language.

Despite that, for Jessica and Jonathan it was great finally to meet children of their own age. We hoped also that they would soon start to pick up some English, which for them was almost non-existent at this stage. As it turned out, English would soon become their natural every-day language as they met more and more boat-kids along the way. If someone had told me in La Coruña how good their English would be in a year's time, I would not have believed it. It wasn't long before (like many of the other kids) they were devouring Harry Potter in the original.

Sitting laughing in the cockpit of Sarah Grace, we agreed we were all glad to leave the cold north. Sophie had grown up in the tropics and loved the climate and warm water. She couldn't wait to sail further south. Obviously, for them, returning to the tropics included an Atlantic crossing. How about us?

We had seen how boats crewed by retired couples with little time pressure often chose to cruise the Mediterranean before heading further afield. Cruising families, on the other hand, often opted for the Atlantic circuit as they wanted to be able to swim and sail during the northern winter.

The question was: would we do the same? Clearly, the kids seemed to have great fun playing together with Otti, Mimi and other new boat friends such as Anna and Eddie from the British yacht Tamarisk which arrived shortly after us. Jessica and Jonathan were soon asking if we could stick with Sarah Grace and Tamarisk for longer. I swallowed. Sarah Grace and Tamarisk both had decided to sail to the Caribbean for winter. The crew of Tamarisk had even bought places on the Atlantic Rally for Cruisers (or ARC) and were – to an extent – committed to leaving on the 22nd of November for the big crossing. I explained to Jessica and Jonathan that sticking together would mean that we also would have to cross the Atlantic. Their reply was instant: "So…?"

The longer we spent in La Coruña the more an Atlantic crossing looked like a logical option for us. The fact that so many boats in La Coruña were actually planning an Atlantic circuit was impressive, as was the diversity of yachties in the marina. Couples, singles and families formed a colourful mix, all with one shared aspiration: cruising.

I thought of Jonathan Livingstone Seagull. I knew how he felt. In the story by Richard Bach, one gull becomes an outcast because he is different. He does not want to live for food alone but wants to master flying. He practises his flying and ignores the rules of seagull society. At the very end of the book, he finally finds like-minded friends and together they form a new, independent society supporting and encouraging each other. We sailors were all Jonathan Livingstone Seagulls.

During one walk up to La Coruña's ancient Roman light-house (which is said to be the oldest working lighthouse in the world) we found a mosaic compass rose. Each cardinal point held a symbol of what could be found in that direction. With a little shock, I noticed that the West, to which we were headed next, was marked with a skull and crossbones. This was the dauntingly-named Costa de la Muerte, or Coast of Death. Here was a trip we were going to take carefully!

VISITORS

Welcoming family or friends onboard for a few days' stay can be fun for all involved. It can also turn out to be rather awkward. A couple of small but delicate suggestions should make it more likely your experience is a positive one.

A useful rule is to allow visitors to choose dates or place but not both. They will want to book flights early but the chance of you being able to predict a place you want to be or are able to get to on a particular date months ahead is small. Several cruisers we met regretted commitments that forced them to break away from 'the gang' and sail back to places they had already been in less-than-ideal weather. In the Caribbean, one thing that will help your potential visitors is the fact that flights between the islands are frequent and well-priced.

An invitation to spend time on a 'yacht' may give some people the wrong impression. Make sure they realize just how small the living space on even quite a large boat is. It's probably a good move, too, to make clear the relative simplicity of life onboard. If they come expecting flash restaurants and an endless round of activities, they may be disappointed. Packing a lot into a short time is not what cruising is all about.

Stress that the luggage allowance on board is significantly less than that offered by most airlines. Guests should bring only the most essential items and pack these in collapsible bags. Essentials may, of course, include spare parts for the boat and anything else you particularly need from home.

To avoid problems later, start by going through the boat 'rules'. These may include use of freshwater, use of the head, avoiding cockroach infestation, fresh-water rinsing after a swim, washing off salt and sand from feet in a bucket and all the other little things that make life easier for all on board.

Don't aim to sail too far with your guests. Cruise short distances on fine days, leaving plenty of time for exploring, swimming, snorkeling and relaxing. Make clear that it is perfectly alright to ask for some time on your own, like a walk ashore or time alone on the foredeck.

Having friends or family visit is not just a pleasure in itself but helps you understand how your life has changed and gives you both a link that will help your relationship after you return.

Mosaic compass rose above La Coruña

Heading for the Costa de la Muerte

Chapter twelve

In which the children start school with 'James Bones'

HEADING SOUTH DAY BY DAY

The summer break from school had been appreciated both by the children and by their parents. It had been good to be able to concentrate on the voyage and the boat without having to worry about another new challenge in the form of home-schooling.

But we knew that if our cruising year was to end happily, school would have to be a major part of our daily lives. We'd prepared for this and had plenty of books and other learning materials on board, but we were still a long way short of recognising how big a thing schooling is for cruising families.

Galicia was the perfect place to open our onboard school. We could now make progress in day-sails along the Rías. These Spanish alternatives to the Norwegian Fjords cut deep into the mountainous shore-line. Many are thickly forested, with dense pines sweeping down to deep, blue, cold water. The short sails between stops allowed us to do school in the mornings, while still moving on during the afternoons.

We rounded a fog-enshrouded Cape Finisterre and Costa de la Muerte with our eyes glued firmly to the radar, and settled to a pleasant pattern of day sails from Camariñas via Muros and Portosin to Combarro and then to Bayona.

At Portosin, we left the boat and took a bus to Santiago de Compostela, the end point of the legendary pilgrimage from Southern France. The whole route is 780 km (485 miles), which is a long way to walk. We guessed, however, that quite a few of the pilgrims we saw had done at least part of the trip by plane or car.

Why go all that way to Santiago de Compostela? It's to see 'James Bones', as Jessica and Jonathan called him. We had to go into quite a detailed explanation of what it was all about. We told Jessica and Jonathan about the belief in the power of holy relics and how James had been one of Jesus's apostles. The Faithful believed that his bones now lay within the Cathedral.

The story tells that Saint James once wandered this route himself, preaching and converting people to Christianity. At that time, the Romans called Galicia 'Finis Terrae', or the 'end of the world', hence Cape Finisterre.

James returned from France and Spain to Palestine and, in about 44 AD, was arrested and tortured to death. His body was stolen, according to the legend, brought back to Spain and buried. Much later, in 813 AD, the story goes, a hermit called Pelayo heard music in the wood, saw a light and found the grave. He called the place 'Campus Stellae', meaning 'field of stars'. Not long after, Saint James became the Patron Saint of Galicia.

For Jessica and Jonathan, it was fascinating to think that thousands of people still walked this ancient route to see the jewel-encrusted casket behind the thick bars. It was the ideal project with which to start school.

Exactly two months after we cast off from our home town in Sweden, at 10am on August 13th, the school books were taken out of the locker. With great eagerness, we went through what we had been discussing with the teachers before we left. Then, we began to plan the goals for the week, as we would do on all (or almost all) the Monday mornings to come. We jointly decided how far Jessica and Jonathan respectively wanted to get in their books by Friday and what should be written by then. Jessica decided to write about 'St James Bones'. After that, she wanted to create a story set on the Irish Coast. Jonathan also decided to write about Santiago de Compostela. He would also complete the first of the bi-weekly travel logs he had promised his old classmates at home.

Karolina and I were pleased with the enthusiasm with which Jessica and Jonathan turned to their school books. We planned three hours of school per day, five days a week. If sailing meant having to miss a day or two we would catch up at the weekend. I enjoyed those early lessons and looked forward to more. Jessica and Jonathan did really well... but I can't pretend it was all easy.

When we met other cruising families, talk would often go as follows: The husbands would quickly get involved in deep discussions about batteries or gearboxes while the mothers would carefully ask each other about school. "How is school on your boat?" one would ask. "Not easy" was a typical answer. Of course it is hard to be a parent and a teacher. We had to encourage our children to do the required work, even if it felt dull to us. Once we'd decided that some of the chapters in the exercise books could be left out, the children realised that a certain amount of negotiation was possible. It wasn't unheard of for us to spend more time discussing why something had to be done than doing it. The planning sessions on Monday mornings, for instance, soon developed into complex rounds of bargaining. "Do I really have to do this?" was a frequent question, often followed up with "but I have done so much work already!"

As none of us were trained teachers, judging our students was an issue. How much work – and what results could be considered a 'pass'?

Maths was the easiest subject to mark. We knew exactly how far we had to get within a certain length of time so all we had to do was stick to the timetable and mark the answers. English as a foreign language was, in a way even easier, as it was basically learnt by doing. Among the many boats with children we met, we stuck mainly with the English-speaking crews. French boats tended to stick with other French boats and we didn't meet many Scandinavian or German boats with children. We weren't too disappointed about that. It meant Jessica and Jonathan had no choice but to speak English. Written English, however, was still a subject for school. But with the children both seeing first-hand how important it is to speak English, little persuasion was necessary. In fact, both though English was 'cool'.

The hardest subject on which to judge progress turned out to be our mother-tongue, Swedish. Some comparison could be made with other children, especially those doing correspondence courses, but, with so much being done in English, it was very hard to decide how much progress it was reasonable to expect in Swedish.

Reading was not an issue for most boat-kids, who eagerly devour book after book during long passages. For geography and history it was not difficult to find enough material to study. In our case, without a plan from a correspondence school, we could make a free choice based on where we were. We made up projects, interweaving various subjects. Our first projects were about the Vikings, following in their wake until we got to Spain. Then we switched to Columbus. From Madeira on, volcanoes became a favourite, with fascinating examples to study not only on Madeira, but also in the Canaries, the Caribbean and, later, in the Azores.

Technical subjects came up naturally as we discussed the various systems on board, did routine maintenance and the occasional repair. Plus, Jessica and Jonathan both took a great pride in preparing meals on board.

At first, I thought aerodynamics, electricity, thermodynamics and meteorology would be too difficult for a 10 year-old child to understand. Apparently not! The children were interested because they saw how relevant it all was to us. We were, to an extent, relying on our own technical skills.

So, were there things we would have done differently in our school? There were a few. I think our expectations were too high. School took more time and involved more hassle than we anticipated. We had been mistaken to believe that school could simply happen between 0900 and noon – with eager kids who wanted nothing else but to work efficiently so they could go swimming or playing afterwards. If I had been them, I would have worked hard during long sailing passages to get more time off while at anchor. Further, I had hoped that they would work more on their own, while I could be writing or doing some repair jobs onboard. But kids are not adults and any frustrations were completely outweighed by the simple joy of spending so much time together.

Supporting each other within the yachting community worked wonderfully. There were always fellow cruisers who held special knowledge. For instance, it was a quite different experience for the children to have art classes with Liz, an artist from Australia we met in the Canaries, than if Karolina or I had tried to explain the fundaments of painting. Or when Chris, the doctor, guided the children through the La Coruña museum of the human body.

How did the children cope when they came back? Fine. None of the cruising kids we met have had any problems resuming school. Jessica and Jonathan were well ahead of their school-mates when they came back after a year and don't remember (or, at least, say they don't remember) what a hard time it sometimes was to get them working.

The cruising ground of northern Spain gave us a delicious foretaste of the world to which we were headed. The climate was warm, the waters inside the Rías were sheltered, the small fishing villages were friendly and the cruising community was beginning to grow. Each day, we got to know new cruisers, many of whom we would meet again and again during our voyage. In particular, we noticed three categories of boaters: British and French boats on their annual summer cruise to Spain, returning regularly from year to year; a second category, like us, on their first voyage south, planning to turn either left or right at the bottom of Portugal; and a very small third group of boats on their second escape from shore-life. Our initial encounter with this group was in the form of Bernardo.

We first met Bernardo in one of the many beautiful anchorages of Galicia. We had just anchored for the night when a dinghy with a 15hp engine and carrying a sunburned guy with long, wild hair and beard approached at high speed. Like his dinghy, his shorts and T-shirt looked well worn and showed evidence of many hours in the sun. He waved at us as he neatly swung alongside Regina. He stopped the craft, stood up and held onto the toe-rail of our boat. "Heh", he greeted, "I saw you coming in and noticed your Swedish ensign. You're Swedish? So am I! My name is Berndt. But that's only for the people ashore. When I'm out cruising, I'm Bernardo! So you may call me Bernardo!"

I don't remember asking him aboard. But within a flash he was sitting in our cockpit with a cold beer in his hand. He must have looked thirsty in the hot sun. Installed under our bimini with his beer, he glowed like the Spanish sun. Here was a man who knew how to enjoy life.

It didn't take long before Bernardo began to tell the story of his three year cruise to the Caribbean. I can't remember why he came back but it was certainly something he regretted. "Oh, it was dreadful coming home! The people were so short-sighted. They wanted nothing more than the lives they had always lived. I felt so boxed in! Nothing whatsoever had changed during the years I had been away. Even the climate was still the same old unbearable freezing cold!" He looked at his cold, damp can of beer as if it reminded him of Scandinavian winters, and shivered at the thought. He looked up and continued: "Three long years I stayed at home and tried my best to readjust, but it simply didn't work! I worked hard, saved every penny and now I am off again! Finally! I hope I don't have to return for a long time! How about you?"

I was a bit overwhelmed by his appearance, his candour and his blunt views about our home country. Compared to him, my recently cut hair and fresh T-shirt must have looked very conservative. I could just about make out that his T-shirt had once been green; I could still read the name of some remote Caribbean island and something about 'living slow'.

I told our story and said that we had just arrived at this anchorage, would stay overnight, have some school in the morning and then leave the following afternoon to continue along the Galician coast southbound.

Bernardo looked like Baloo, when Mowgli tries to bellow like a bear. He shook his head and stared at us with big eyes and pity. "You're new to cruising. Don't make the mistake I did the first time. I rushed through this area far too quickly. Where are you going, anyway? The Caribbean will still be there when you get there. No, my friend, pick a place you like and stay there for a while. I have been at this anchorage for a week now. I like it here. I'm beginning to get to know the place and will probably stay for another week. It's inexpensive and the people are friendly. When I've seen it all, made some new friends and enjoyed the place, then will be the time to move on. And when I leave, I will remember the town forever. Come on. Stay a while. Let loose!"

I admit I had some difficulty in finding his level. On the other hand, he made such a laid-back impression, taking the days as they came, which was attractive. How little did I understand at that time! It would take another full month until we entered into this later stage of relaxation. Another couple of cruising months later and I would consider his outer and inner appearance as totally natural. No longer would I judge people by their hair-style or clothing. With clothes slowly fading in the tropical sun and shaving on an occasional basis, I would soon look a bit like Bernardo and not be bothered by it.

And, as Bernardo so rightly said, next time, we will explore the Rías of Galicia in more depth, taking it easy right from the start.

CHILDREN'S SCHOOLING

Generally, cruising itself offers a lot of opportunities to learn, and boat-kids pick up much from each other and their ever-changing environment. Plus, they benefit from so much time in adult company.

If you plan to take your children away for a year or more, you will have to check the regulations in your particular country. You then have the option of buying a programme from a commercial supplier or sorting it out yourself. A commercial supplier, often a Correspondence School, has the advantage of giving you a set curriculum, which is not negotiable. You can be confident the lessons are right and adequate and that the work is being properly assessed. Work can be sent to and fro via the Internet. Parents finish up more like coaches than teachers. Some cruisers think this sort of arrangement is too formal. Often, the children have to study subjects which have no relation to their current surroundings. Who wants to learn about moose when you have turtles and dolphins swimming around?

The alternative is to set up your own curriculum. A bit more work is required on the part of the parents; but it will often be easier to motivate the children. Try to agree on a topical project. It doesn't take a lot of imagination to work in some maths, reading, writing, painting or model-building. Have the children make a 'country book', with a chapter for each country visited. Depending on their age, suggest they draw a map, buy a typical postcard, find a local stamp and write about the language, the environment, the currency, the industry, the climate and some history. Together with a couple of photos, these essays can then be scanned in and posted on the children's own web-sites or e-mailed to grandparents or friends back home. Ask the readers to give positive, inspiring feed-back to the children.

Getting in contact with other cruising families is fun and rewarding. From time to time, exchange kids during school and do specific subjects jointly. Put together a small kit before you go for experiments. Plan to do things with electricity, light and mirrors. Aerodynamics can be discussed while setting the sails and meteorology is best learnt by following the weather forecasts and watching the sky.

When in an anchorage with other children, try to agree with parents on a shared time for school. You can invent signal flag signs meaning school is happening or not.

You will know your children better than anyone and you will know best how to keep them learning. Just don't underestimate how big a job it is!

At school

Using the tide to do a bit of maintenance in Povoa de Varzim, Portugal

Chapter thirteen

In which we try our absolute hardest to put you off cruising

THE BAD BITS

"Come on, Leon! Tell us the truth!"

The appeal came from my sister Jenny, who called us on our cell-phone while we peacefully strolled along the beautiful sea front. It was late at night, but the entire town still seemed to be out eating, drinking or just enjoying the warm night air. The buildings were beautifully lit, as so often in southern Europe. It was a delightful Portuguese night. I hadn't worn socks since La Coruña and I loved being able to wear just shorts and T-shirts, even late into the evening.

What could she mean, my dear sister?

"I've been following you on your web-site. OK, it's fun to read, but, Leon, tell me, it can't always be as beautiful and romantic as you describe. Leon, you must be more truthful when you write. You can't just paint a glamorous picture of cruising. You must put in all the bad bits as well."

It's good to have a truthful sister, who says what she thinks. A critical reader is essential. But 'the truth'? I really loved our new life-style and didn't want to swap it at any price, especially not if it meant being buckled up in an office chair again.

Having said that, cruising is not always a bed of roses. It has its ups and downs. I wanted to do as my sister asked, and so wrote my next web entry about nothing but the tough times we'd had so far. I hope no one thought I was complaining.

So, what is it really like sailing with two children on a 40-foot boat?

First of all, I need to mention that I am fortunate enough to be very happily married. If I were not, sailing would definitely be less pleasant. Not a few cruises have ended in divorce. A bad partnership is unlikely to get better at sea. Every little domestic crisis is exaggerated on a boat. If you don't like cooking, you will like it even less on board, without a dishwasher, with restricted worktop space and limited water.

If, at home, your neighbours or the tax inspector give you raised blood pressure, you will find ample scope afloat for similar moans about fellow boaters not handling their vessels correctly or immigration officials taking bureaucracy to new extremes.

Living on a boat is, of course, very different from living at home. For example, take the normally fairly easy task of doing your laundry. Some larger cruising boats have a washing machine installed. There are laundrettes in many marinas, but not all. And if there is one, it's often busy. Experienced cruisers always do a bit of washing whenever the opportunity arises. Another option is to give your laundry to someone to do it for you, but that often means planning, waiting and surprisingly high bills. To avoid digging in your laundry bag and giving one of the less grubby items a second or third outing, washing by hand is the answer, be it on deck, on the pontoon or in some quite out-of-the-way places.

I remember one occasion when doing the washing became a great social event. The local open-air beach showers offered plenty of cold water, a nice sandy floor, a beautiful view and, most importantly, company. We filled the big buckets many cruisers carry just for this purpose and started washing by hand and, sometimes, feet. Commenting on the various techniques and inspecting the finished articles kept us laughing all afternoon. An onboard washing machine would definitely not have been so much fun.

The laundry was then carried back through the village and hung up between the stays, shrouds and mast – providing some pleasant decoration. The hot sun did the rest and a couple of hours later everything was dry and it was just a matter of stowing it all back in the lockers.

Space to put things is another problematic issue. It comes up everyday, and the smaller your boat the more of a problem it is. We try to stow gear logically, but as we often changed the places where things were put, in a constant search for the ideal solution, the game of finding things never ended. Turning the boat upside down in search of that printer cartridge I knew I had somewhere took time and was frustrating. I promised myself to be more organised and to stow things in dedicated plastic containers.

In a shop recently, I found a new type of Rubbermaid plastic box in a size we did not have before. I was as happy as a boy on his birthday when I discovered that it fitted precisely onto a previously unused part of the shelf under the galley sink. To the left and behind the waste pipe, to be precise. What a success. What we would put into the new Rubbermaid box? Not a clue. Air was in it, right now. But I was sure, we would eventually find something suitable. The important thing was that we had a box that fitted a space.

The specific corner of the shelf under the sink I am referring to was slightly difficult to reach, unfortunately; you needed to bend over the rubbish bin with your head down and your arms up to get to the new Rubbermaid box. Sniffing garbage while trying to reach the box upside down in a rolling sea would not be good for nausea. Aha, I thought. I know what to put into the box: seasickness pills!

Talking about seasickness: yes, we all get that. It's not pleasant, but doesn't prevent us from cruising. The saying is that seasickness comes in two stages: Stage 1 is when you are afraid you will die and stage 2 is when you are afraid you will not die. A cure, fortunately, is easily found: as soon as you reach land, you get better. The trick is to survive in the meantime.

There are things you can do to minimise seasickness. Picking some good weather for the start of a long leg is one sensible step. To have two or three fine days in which to get used to the motion gets the whole voyage off to a good start. That's one reason I am personally no great enthusiast for organised rallies, where the entire fleet is encouraged to leave on a specific day, irrespective of the conditions. If the weather is bad, seasickness will follow.

Of course, seasickness is not the only medical problem you may face. You or other members of the crew are no less likely to get ill or be injured than you are at home. We were lucky and only needed a doctor a couple of times. Karolina got an ear infection and the children suffered tropical ulcers when some bites and cuts got infected. The worst part, thankfully, was tracking down the medicine we needed.

Good-quality medical assistance was available in almost all the places we visited. That's not so true when crossing the Pacific. We did worry a bit about injuries when far offshore, and made more effort to look after ourselves. A serious injury would, of course, be a 'bad bit' of cruising. But there are risks at home, too. On balance, we thought, cruising did not present significant additional risk.

Grocery shopping is another issue. It usually takes a while to find the supermarket (which, in places, will not be that 'super'.) Getting lost in new towns is a common occurrence. Of course, that can turn a shopping trip into a more pleasant afternoon. There always seem to be cafés. The sight of locals sitting in the shade, drinking beer and eating grilled sardines, is pretty tempting. And why shouldn't we join them?

Without a car, we always have to work out how much we're going to be able to bring back. Could just Karolina and I go? Or did we need Jessica and Jonathan to help with the carrying? Leaving the supermarket, we would look like back-packers, too heavily loaded for the local heat.

Of course, brands, labels and products vary from country to country, and sometimes it was a bit of a struggle to work out what was inside. One day I found a whole litre of 40% spirit for just a couple of Euros. What a bargain. I think it was vodka with aniseed flavour, but that was not what concerned me. It was strong, and that was the main point. This wasn't for me but for the fish. When you catch a fish from a yacht you have to kill it. And you want to do that without getting too much blood on the deck of your boat. So, many blue-water sailors pour alcohol into the fish's gills. This kills them without too much mess. So far, alcohol had been quite expensive' and industrial spirit with all its additives did not sound too inviting as fish marinade. Vodka with aniseed flavour should be perfect for killing the fish we caught. Or rather, the fish we hoped to catch.

One more thing you don't want to bring back to the boat from a shopping trip is a cockroach. These are common in shops in warmer climes and will often hitch a lift in a box of purchases. We once found a huge passenger in the dinghy one night on our way back to Regina. This almost resulted in all four of us jumping into the water with the cockroach left alone to pilot the dinghy.

An even worse thing to get onboard is a bag of cockroach eggs. These are often laid in fresh food or in cardboard packaging. The bag is no bigger than half a fingernail but within it are hundreds of tiny eggs. So, how do you keep them off the boat? Everything has to be inspected carefully before it is allowed on board. Sitting on the dock removing all packaging becomes part of the shopping routine. The plastic bag inside a cornflakes carton has to be taken out. Toothpaste has to lose its little box and a six-pack of beer can only be allowed on after it has shed its cardboard wrapping. All this also helps save space and the amount of rubbish onboard.

If you do get cockroaches on board, there are ways to get rid of them. Either you sail a long way north (or south) to freeze them to death. A normal Scandinavian winter might do. Or you can smoke them out by fumigating the entire boat – twice. The cockroaches may decide to leave. But you may have already decided to depart yourselves. Luckily, we never had to try either of these solutions, having been spared an invasion, possibly thanks to our cockroach phobia.

Another difficult issue is money. We became quite sensitive to prices while cruising. Without money coming in, we had to look at our costs all the time. We'd been surprised by how much we'd had to spend on harbour fees. The occasional luxury of eating out was part of our budget, but we found the cost varied significantly from country to country. Having said that, a good bottle of wine quite regularly found its way under the floor-boards, which we called the 'wine cellar'. But why is it always the best bottle that breaks in a heavy roll?

Though we were careful what we spent on ourselves, the same was not true for the boat. Regina had her own budget. A thousand Euros for new batteries in Portugal was not to be discussed. Period. They were simply needed and had to be paid for.

Did we miss the car? No. We didn't even think of it. It had become so natural to walk everywhere. At the checkout in one supermarket, I noticed a woman behind us who had bought loads and loads of bottles of wine and water. How could she possible carry all these home? Then I remembered she probably had a car waiting outside.

If you think shopping took up a lot of time, it was nothing compared to boat maintenance. Preventative work and repairs constantly needed doing. A clogged-up toilet or a water-maker making anything but water were frequent issues among yachties, as were non-functioning generators or communication devices. They all give you grey hairs. I don't know if you ever get used to the fact that so much gear needs to be looked after and that you are the only repairman likely to do it. But you learn new things all the time and get a better and better understanding of how your boat works.

Of course, it helps to have a good and well-equipped boat in the first place, but you can't predict every surprise. For some reason, our inflatable man-over-board life-buoy suddenly inflated inside the locker where it was stowed. The force of the compressed CO_2 was amazing. Getting the thing out of the locker was almost impossible: the more we tried, the bigger it got. It finished up as a full evening's task.

Then there was the time we dropped anchor outside the marina of Cascais in Portugal late one evening. When Karolina put the propeller into reverse to dig in the anchor, an awful sound of banging against the underneath of the hull could be heard. Our rope-cutter had done its job, cutting an abandoned floating line into pieces, so the engine was still running, but some rope was now stuck in the rudder, slamming loudly against the hull. So, the following morning was time for a swim again, in distinctly cool water. I got the rope free from the rudder and pulled at the line at the end of which turned out to be an anchor. It was home-made — from four iron rods with welded triangles at their tips. Not worth keeping.

The day before my sister Jenny called, we had got our new batteries. It should have been a straightforward 'old out — new in' operation. But when I took the old batteries out of the battery-box, I noticed that the box itself had broken and needed some reinforcement. So a full day had to be given over to repairing the box.

The computer was always a struggle. Getting things like 'com-ports' set up right for communications or navigation often took hours. Finally, gas can be less than a 'gas'. Getting your bottles filled for cooking can take hours and involve many long walks.

So, the daily tasks on a boat take time. Some people said I'd given up work. I said my new occupation involved being an electrician, carpenter, plumber, rigger, mechanic and, of course, teacher. Was it any wonder I'd not had time to play my guitar?

Is all this difficult stuff enough to outweigh the good stuff? Well, that is a question for you. And you can't tell until you try, right?

We tried. And the moments when we felt we might like to give up and go back to our old lives were truly very, very few.

INSURANCE

Of course, one thing you can do about the 'bad bits' is to buy insurance. Not all cruisers insure their boats, although many countries and almost all marinas require third-party liability insurance.

When you compare quotes, consider more than just price. Service can vary quite widely. Look for a well-established, specialist insurer able to understand the complexity of an extended blue-water cruise. Ideally, the company should have a worldwide network of agents and partners.

There are surprisingly few insurance companies that cover blue-water sailing. That's not because such sailing is particularly risky. It is that managing claims far from home is so expensive.

Compare insurance companies by looking at the premiums they charge for the entire planned itinerary, how they depreciate the value of equipment and what stipulations they have, such as being outside specific areas during certain seasons. If you don't understand the small print, ask.

Of special importance is the third-party liability insurance, which most countries require you to have. Make sure the sum is big enough to meet those requirements.

Health insurance is also an issue, which needs to be dealt with in advance. Check how long you can travel with your current arrangements and make additions as necessary. Some boat insurers offer health insurance as an add-on.

Interestingly, health insurance for cruisers often works out less expensive than the equivalent ashore. That must say something about living on a boat!

Cascais, Portugal

Leaving our mark in Porto Santo

Chapter fourteen
In which we take a decisive right turn

AN IMPULSIVE DECISION

It started with Karolina thinking aloud. "What would happen if we steered a bit more to the west?" She pointed vaguely at the horizon beyond the starboard guardrails. "That's the way to Madeira, isn't it?"

We were on a 25-mile leg from Cascais heading south along the Portuguese coast. It was the 13th of September and a fine, clear day with just the right amount of wind from just the right direction. Our plan had been to find a change of scene, having been in Cascais for a fortnight.

After such a long time in a marina, Regina's movements at sea felt unusual. It is a shame how quickly you lose your 'sea legs'. But there was that fantastic feeling of freedom as, once again, we hoisted the sails and felt the water rushing by Regina's hull. Cascais, which is close to Lisbon and amply supplied with restaurants and things to do and see, is a perfectly pleasant place to spend time. But we had still begun to feel a slight sensation of 'harbour rot'.

Harbour rot is not uncommon among cruisers who have tied up for a length of time. One gets used to harbour life, forgets about the wonderful movements of voyaging, gets lazy and slow to the extent that leaving port becomes less important and is constantly postponed. Fear is a little bit of it, too. We have met sailors who have stayed in the same port for years. The infection is particularly common in the Canaries. The Atlantic lies next. Sailors badly afflicted by harbour rot say they will leave later; but some never do.

Harbour rot is not the same as feeling settled, unhurried and without the need to move on for its own sake. Sailors who stay because they have found their dream destination are happy people. Sailors who have caught harbour rot do actually want to continue, but don't dare to let the mooring lines go. Stuck in planning and preparation, some even get the disease in their own home port and never go anywhere.

Luckily, our touch of harbour rot in Cascais was very minor. But to avoid its growing inside us, we planned to sail just a few hours to a nice anchorage a little way south. It was wonderful to be out in the fresh air under a blue sky accompanied by the northerly winds that are typical of this part of Portugal in summer. Sailing conditions could not have been better and we were really enjoying the trip.

"Why don't we do it?" Karolina asked again.

"Do what?" I replied, still daydreaming a bit.

"Alter course."

"Karolina, please, we planned to sail for four hours, and now you're talking about sailing for four days and nights instead."

"Why not?" said Karolina. "The conditions are great, the weather forecast for the next five days is ideal. We've topped up with food and water. Why don't we sail to Madeira?"

I saw she had a point. If you know that a leg of four or five days lies ahead, nerves begin to build. At least, they do for me. By altering course right now and heading straight for Madeira, we could avoid that pre casting-off anxiety.

And after all, Madeira is part of Portugal. It's really just another island off the coast, isn't it? We had told our insurance company we might be heading offshore and, though I tried, I could think of no reason why we couldn't go to Madeira. I got the sat phone working and sent off an e-mail to my mom and Karolina's dad, telling them of our plans. Then, as Karolina had suggested, we changed course to 225 degrees – a course that would take us to Madeira.

What a feeling!

I had been dreaming for years about leaving continental Europe, but never really believed I would do it. I had read the pilot books; imagined how it would feel to set course out into the big ocean. And now, we'd done it simply by adjusting the autopilot. It was so easy. In life, a small alteration in course can sometimes lead to big changes. We didn't even fully understand how we had got into this situation. We hadn't thought about it for very long. And now we were doing it and it was going to make a big difference.

It is a lesson I now try to apply to the whole of my life. Chances have to be grabbed. But they often don't require big changes. Be it the offer of a new job, a new friendship, a new experience, a voyage, or the chance to take a sabbatical sailing year, think hard before you let such chances go by.

Darkness fell, but it was warm, and we continued to make good progress towards Madeira. I had read about such nights hundreds of times, sitting at home in an armchair. And now here I was with the stars above, wearing just a T-shirt and shorts, reaching in a northerly Force 5 wind, sailing at 7 knots, heading for a tiny island out in the Atlantic. I had never had a 13th of September like this before. Should I pinch myself? Had I somehow fallen into one of those books? No. The truth is that sometimes dreams and reality are closer than you think.

As I sat in the cockpit watching the horizon and checking the instruments, I thought about my old self, sitting in my office, in front of a computer screen, talking on the telephone. I remembered thinking how important all those tasks were. But also thinking that the more I did, the more I felt my efforts were insufficient. I remembered thinking more about the things I thought I should have done rather than the jobs I was doing or had finished. All the while, outside the office window, rain fell and cold winds blew. I thought about all the people still stuck in their offices when they would rather be cruising in the warm Portuguese Trades. Maybe you are among them?

Another thought struck me. Had I been disloyal by fleeing from that cage while my colleagues remained, still locked in? It was a depressing thought. But I don't think it is a charge that sticks. Karolina and I had worked hard for years and paid plenty of tax. We were paying for the trip ourselves and had a tight budget to stick to. Still, it felt like wealth. There had been enough members of our family and close friends who had been struck by cancer, some even leaving this earth much too early. When you've lived through such experiences, you realise the importance of living for the day. I was content I could permit myself to enjoy the cruise. In fact, the only right thing to do was to value and appreciate our good fortune. These big questions were ones we found many cruisers asked themselves.

Bang! My thoughts were rudely interrupted. Something had hit the boat. What was it? The night was dark and I couldn't see much. The sound did not come from the hull; it was more like something had hit the coach-roof. I went below to fetch a flashlight. I was quickly up again and leant outside the cockpit, shining the torch up the deck. What I saw made me smile: our first flying-fish on deck. A true blue-water sign. The poor thing was fighting for its life. The first flying-fish is for the captain, I have heard, to be fried in butter for breakfast. This one was different. The fish was still alive and so was I. We were staring at each other. Life and death are so close, sometimes, and I had the life of this first flying-fish in my hands. I gave him a second chance, and threw him back into the Atlantic.

I leaned back in Regina's cosy cockpit. I was sleepy, notwithstanding all my philosophising, or perhaps that was what had made me drowsy. The radar confirmed my look-out: no traffic within 12 miles. We sailed towards the half moon, leaving the Portuguese mainland far behind. Portugal is a fantastic country, friendly, impressively modern and actually still inexpensive (except, perhaps, for the marina fees). The history, scenery and people all make it worth a visit.

The following morning greeted us with a beautiful bright sun, blue sky and blue sea. I had never seen such a blue. It was a deep, saturated blue, a blue that I had previously only come across in the virtual world of Photoshop. Now I knew why they called it 'blue-water' sailing.

During the second night we passed south of the latitude of Gibraltar, another thought that gave me a thrill. But still, our passage felt more like a sail out to a relatively nearby island rather than a long sea passage. Were we becoming blasé? Where was the anxiety we had felt in the North Sea, let alone while crossing Biscay? This leg would be as long as Biscay at around 500 miles, but it felt so different, so much less dramatic.

The reasons, I think, were various. The temperature and weather made a huge difference. The sea, the swell, the wind, the movement of the boat all felt so much more comfortable when the bright sun was shining and the wind was blowing gently from astern. Our old worries about running into weather fronts and low pressure systems, hoping they would speed up or slow down, was something we definitely didn't miss. Following the weather forecast had become a pleasure.

As well as better weather, we now had less traffic to worry about. Gone were all the twisting, turning, unpredictable fishing vessels. When a cargo vessel showed up, we almost welcomed the break from endless sea. Tracking the echo on the radar and making an alteration to our course was a straightforward business. With steady winds, sail changes were needed less often. In fact, we often went hours without having much to do. We could just enjoy the sea and the sky and the speed with which Regina was flying over the waves.

Despite being cruisers, we all appreciate Regina's ability to sail at reasonable speed. We don't want the racing type of speed, where trimming is obsessive and everything is sacrificed for another fraction of a knot, but we do like the feeling that we are making good progress, minimising the time spent at sea and have the ability to outrun bad weather if needed. Plus the movement of the boat is more comfortable once a reasonable speed is reached.

Though we say we're not racers, we don't like to be at the back of the fleet. We were all pleased that a boat that left Cascais just before us reached Madeira a full day after our own landfall.

Taking turns sleeping, at night and during the day, the time passed quickly. Jessica and Karolina felt sick on the first and second days, but were better on the third. Jessica wrote e-mails to friends while Jonathan read about planets and stars, fascinated by the fantastic night sky you get at sea.

On the third day, the wind dropped to the point where we either had to start the engine or dig out the light-wind gennaker in its long, tubular bag. The children had named the sail 'Nessie' after the similarly shaped monster in Loch Ness. I wasn't convinced we should bother. We'd only about six hours to go. It felt more like time for the fenders.

We had to remind ourselves that six hours was more than a usual day's sailing back home. If we had been lucky enough to sail with the gennaker for such a long period of time back there, we would have thought it a great day. So, out she came, Nessie in her long bag, and we enjoyed a wonderful afternoon ghosting along at six to seven knots despite there being almost no wind. The sea was flat. Was this the mighty Atlantic? What a way to arrive in Madeira!

Jonathan saw it first. "Land ahoy!" he shouted, excitedly pointing towards the horizon. It is hard to describe how I felt. Out of the sea, in the middle of nowhere, somewhere in the Atlantic, the tips of several high volcanic mountains peeked out of the sea. Even with the GPS it still felt like a miracle to find such a small island on such a huge sea.

It was great to arrive but sad also that the passage had ended. There would be longer stages ahead, I hoped. We had been tired for the first two days of the passage, but the third had been pure pleasure. What would Madeira and its little neighbour Porto Santo be like? Now was our chance to find out.

SEASICKNESS

Seasickness is not much fun and needs to be taken seriously. The dehydration it causes can be a serious health risk, and its impact on the capacity of the crew to keep the boat safe is important. Luckily, there are things you can do about it.

Not everyone is affected in the same way. Learn how seasickness affects you. Reading, particular sea conditions, tiredness, smells, eating and heavy weather are typical triggers.

It helps to get a good night's sleep before starting a passage. Try to avoid too much alcohol, coffee and heavy food. Drink plenty of water and make sure you feel confident, warm and happy.

Before you head off, prepare as many below-decks jobs such as cooking and navigation as you can. If you have wet weather gear to take off, do it in the cockpit. Once down below, lying down with your eyes closed is often most comfortable.

Stress is another trigger, so stay busy, keeping your mind on things like steering or trimming the sails. Feeling that you have control over your situation is helpful. Try to make the boat's movements as comfortable as possible. You may be able to do this by reducing sail or altering course slightly.

Many people find they get less sick as the sailing season goes on, so avoid making your first sail for a while a long and difficult one. Try to cast off on a fine, calm day. That way you can get used to the movement gradually. Most sailors will have their sea legs within a day or two.

Some sailors say vitamin C helps a lot. Others swear by crystallized ginger. Others use medicines. Ask a physician or pharmacist for a recommendation.

And if all that fails, have a two to three-litre container with a lid standing by. Don't lean over the guardrail. It's dangerous. And take comfort in the fact that you should feel better after you've fed the fish. And when you've been sick, drink water and try to eat something sweet and full of calories.

Madeira's storm-buffeted north coast

A three-boat school outing

Chapter fifteen

In which the children lead us to the top of the clouds

NEW BOAT KIDS

The news spread like wildfire. New boat-kids had been spotted arriving. And a whole bunch of them! A boat with three girls on board was said to have tied up on Porto Santo. The resident children rushed from boat to boat spreading the news. The new boat was berthed on the reception pontoon.   Like an official welcoming committee, the children marched down to meet the newcomers.

The new boat's name intrigued and excited. What could 'Koshlong' mean? And the flag at the stern was quite unfamiliar. It was red and white with a leaf in the middle. One of the children remembered seeing it in a schoolbook and declared it to be the Canadian ensign. Canada. Where was that? In North America. Wow! Had they really sailed all the way from Canada? Excited and happy, the children cheered the Koshlong girls ashore.

Sondre, aged ten, from the Norwegian boat Galadriel, stood a bit in the background with his smaller sister Synne, who was seven, close by. Otti, from Sarah Grace, who was just a couple of days short of her 11th birthday, made the first move. "Hi!" she said. "Where do you come from?"

The oldest of the Koshlong girls spoke for her sisters: "We've just arrived from the Azores. I'm Emma, this is Rachael and this is Chloe."

"Cool!" said Otti.

The number of boat-kids is limited, so every boat with children is welcomed with great eagerness by the others. We had heard rumours of more children on their way via continental Portugal, but Canadian Koshlong was a total surprise. We parents followed along to say "hello" and soon discovered that Dan, Sue and their girls were planning a crossing from the Canaries to the Caribbean.

The Koshlong girls were no less thrilled than our children to be making so many new friends. And Otti, who had been thinking a lot about her upcoming birthday, rated the arrival of new play-mates above any of the other presents she'd been expecting. Though Karolina and I were pleased to meet the Koshlong crew, we couldn't know then how strong our bond would become. We would stick together during good times and bad, staying side by side, supporting each other and becoming best friends for life.

On board Sarah Grace, preparations were fully underway for Otti's 11th birthday. In fact there was not much for the parents to organise. All they had to do was keep watch while the children played on the beach and swam in the sea.

Otti had written invitation cards for all her friends. These were beautifully decorated and carefully put into home-made envelopes and sent over by dinghy-post. Ours was addressed as follows:

Jessica and Jonathan

S/Y Regina

Stern Cabin

Porto Santo Marina

At Anchor

The big day finally arrived and all the kids dressed up for the party: swimming clothes, a towel as well as new shorts and a T-shirt for afterwards. Porto Santo was the first place we had reached where it was comfortably warm enough to swim in the sea. The thermometer on the boat gave 22°C (72F). Only Sophie, with her tropical childhood, thought it was still a bit too cool. The kids played on the beach, while the parents watched from the nearby marina bar. Surely, these were the happiest children in the world?

When they weren't swimming or playing, the children worked hard on the 'boat logos' that are traditionally painted by passing crews on the walls of a harbour. These involved several days' work on design, preparation and painting. The children helped each other, sharing paint and making suggestions. If you pass through Porto Santo one day, don't forget to look out for our paintings. Each was made with love and hard work.

We all found Porto Santo the perfect oasis. The fact that this tiny island in the Atlantic was nothing but a pretty barren volcanic tip made it no less charming. Few tourist visitors to Madeira make it to its little neighbour. And there is not, in truth, a lot to see. But the people are friendly, the beaches beautiful – and, at the right times of year, there are lots of blue-water sailors.

Porto Santo's position well off the normal tourist track helps make it a charming and tranquil place to be. We would look for similar places in the Canaries, the Caribbean and the Azores; and we would find them. Our own little paradises – shared with only a few other cruising boats and locals. It was a revelation to me how concentrated mass tourism remains. There are still plenty of unspoilt spots not far from many vacation centres and there is no better way of finding them than by yacht.

Many of our sailing friends chose to stay on Porto Santo for a week or more. We stayed for two. Had we by now finally got our second wind? After all, we had been out cruising for three months by now and finally got rid of our rush to move on. We'd reached our destination: namely the state of voyaging itself. We had found Porto Santo. We liked it, so we stayed. Leaving? Maybe tomorrow. Or the day after. Or next week.

Was this the stage Bernardo had been talking about? I often thought about our conversation back in Galicia.

For the purposes of onboard school, Porto Santo had a big place to play in our ongoing Christopher Columbus project. The books told us that he had been refused support by the Portuguese, who did not believe in his crazy ideas to sail westwards to India. We wondered whether the Portuguese had already understood enough about navigation to realise that the world must be much bigger than Columbus thought? Or did he guess he would find something else first?

Anyway, Christopher Columbus turned his back on the indifferent Portuguese and tried his luck with the Spanish King Ferdinand and Queen Isabella, instead. Excited by his promises of gold, they chose to believe his wild theories. Hence he sailed under the Spanish flag. Had King John of Portugal been just a little more gullible, it might have been that country that colonised Latin America. And if that had meant more trade and less pillaging by the Europeans, how would that have changed history?

The fact that Portugal denied Columbus' request for ships in 1484 is rather overlooked by the Portuguese living on Porto Santo. On this island, he is still celebrated as one of them and raised to the sky as a Portuguese Hero. The reason for this is that Columbus is closely related to Porto Santo – thanks to a clever marriage to a Porto Santo girl.

Bartoloméo Perestrello, a former student at Henry the Navigator's school on mainland Portugal, had been one of the men who discovered Madeira. As an acknowledgement, he was given its smaller neighbour, Porto Santo, to rule over as governor. Whether Columbus married Perestrello's daughter for love or money is disputed. The fact remains that Columbus' liaison with this noble family on Porto Santo gave him both a short-cut to the aristocracy and a knowledge of the Atlantic Ocean. Could he possibly have heard tales about land far, far out in the west, long before his own adventurous sail to 'India'?

For us parent/teachers, it came in very handy when the entire island of Porto

Santo held a Columbus Festival to celebrate their hero. It lasted three days and involved sand sculptures, music, theatrical productions and a water-borne tour by a replica of the great explorer's ship, the Santa Maria. What more natural environment could there be for a history lesson? The children were eager to learn as much as possible about Columbus.

All the boat-kids we met, we liked. They live in close quarters with their families and treat their siblings as partners, their parents as collaborators and other children as valuable friends. I have seldom seen such caring children, always keen to look after each other and make sure no one is left behind. Bullying never happened. They just can't afford to jeopardise friendship. Possibly it was also owing to the fact that they part and meet again regularly. Their joy at each reunion touched me deeply.

Different ages, genders or cultural backgrounds proved no problem when it came to playing together. They lived in a world beyond prejudices and fashion, not knowing what was 'in' and what was 'out'. Boys were allowed to play 'girls' games' and older children felt no awkwardness playing with the younger ones. One could see their imaginations' being fired by their adventures. Their intellectual development, I thought, was fantastic. Their different cultural backgrounds were never a big deal. We were all different, just as the boats on which we lived were all different.

In some ways, they lived in a totally sheltered world. In others, they were close to nature and always aware of dangers. How many normal children see a risk of ciguatera when eating fish or think of impetigo when they get a cut? What children worry that their home might drift away if the anchor doesn't hold? And how many keep a regular eye on the barometer?

The limited space on board prevented any of us from carrying bulky toys or big games. As a result, the children had to play more creatively than they did at home. For hours, they would make bead jewellery, for instance. Passing jewellers' displays ashore would inspire them to make similar bracelets or necklaces. Sometimes they would criticise the commercial jewellery, arguing that they could do better. I wonder what the store-keepers thought, hearing these ten-year olds discussing their merchandise?

With plenty of paper and pens, watercolours or acrylics, these children could do wonderful paintings and drawings. One of the boats had modelling clay on board. What a treat! The kids gathered on that boat and for days made miniature sculptures, furniture and food; putting it all together in one little doll's house.

Collecting items was very common among the children, though not quite so popular with the parents who had to stow the treasure on board. But small shells, stamps and postcards from each country we visited was fine. The boats were all quite heavy with souvenirs by the end of the cruise.

None of us had TVs on board, and nobody regretted their absence. For the occasional movie-night, all the kids would gather in one boat. The dads would get some corn popping in the frying pan, while the laptop played a DVD — with its sound blasting out of the boat's stereo speakers.

When the children were on one boat, the adults could get together for a drink under the starry sky on another yacht. That way, the parents were always nearby — but sufficiently far away for both generations to feel they were by themselves.

Even the youngest children quickly learned how to drive the dinghy, how to start the outboard and come alongside a bigger boat or dock pontoon. I've never heard of any 'reckless driving' by live-aboard kids.

Boat kids get used to taking responsibility. Often they had the safety of their families as well as the boat in their young hands. On watch, on longer passages, they knew that if they didn't keep a sharp look-out, the consequences could be fatal. But none of them went too far. They recognised the point at which it was necessary to call for an adult.

A boat is a home with many more hazards and breakable bits of gear than a house. Just take the fact that using the toilet is not straightforward. Valves have to be opened and shut in the right order, the pump is manually operated and you need to be careful with the paper quantity. So it was a joy to watch Jessica and Jonathan's new friends treat Regina with every bit as much care as we did. They would bring their dinghies alongside with care and climb onboard knowing what to hold on to and what hazards to avoid. They would go round the deck and down below, interestedly comparing their friends' boats with their own, commenting on various items and asking intelligent questions about the technical systems.

Sometimes our small guests stayed longer than for the afternoon after school. Sleep-overs were popular, often with the younger child going one way and the older one the other. They loved sharing their cabin with a friend, showing them where everything went and enjoying their company.

Between the boats, we used the VHF as a free telephone and the children's on-air discipline was every bit a match for the adults'. Even two-year-old Nancy on Wild Alliance knew that every sentence finished with an "over". She once knocked on the door to the crew cabin and shouted from the outside: "Can I come in? Over!"

Despite their discipline, the children's use of the VHF sometimes caused embarrassment. One day all the parents except Dan from Koshlong were in town grocery shopping. Dan was left behind to look after all the children on the various boats. Some kids were on Koshlong working on a crossword puzzle and others were on Sarah Grace playing a game. Everything was going smoothly so Dan decided it would be alright for him to walk around the marina to say 'hello' to another yacht he knew.

"Kids, I'm just going over to the other side," he said to the children on Koshlong, "I'm taking the handheld VHF, in case you need me. I'll be back soon."

"Sure" said Emma without lifting her head from a difficult clue in the crossword puzzle. Jessica was trying to help, but her English was not quite up to it yet.

Dan had got about half way round the marina basin, when his handheld VHF went off: "Sarah Grace, Sarah Grace, Sarah Grace, this is Koshlong, Koshlong Koshlong. Over." Dan turned up the volume to hear what was going on. He could hear Otti answering. "Koshlong, this is Sarah Grace. Go ahead. Over." "Otti. Hi, this is Emma. How do you spell 'atmosphere' please? Over." "Emma, I don't know really. Over." "OK, I'll have to call my Dad, then. Never mind. Over." "Standing by on channel 72." – "Standing by. Out."

Dan had stopped, not really knowing what he should do or say. Had this taken place in a deserted anchorage somewhere only the boats directly involved would have heard. But this was a busy marina and the channel we were using – 72 – was also being used by yachts on the famous Blue-water Rally. Two fine English gentlemen, known as 'Rally One' and 'Rally Two' could often be heard on channel 72 making announcements for participants.

Dan could see people sitting in their cockpits nearby smiling. Had they heard? It didn't take long until a new call came. "Koshlong Shoreparty, Koshlong Shoreparty, Koshlong Shoreparty, this is Koshlong, Koshlong Koshlong. Over."

'Koshlong Shoreparty' was Dan. The kids had heard the expression being used by crew on a super-yacht and thought it was cool.

Poor Dan took up his VHF and whispered urgently: "Emma, what do you want?"

"Koshlong Shoreparty. This is Koshlong. Hi Dad, how do you spell atmosphere, please? Over."

"Emma, please!! Not over the VHF!"

And then, like an ostrich, Dan turned off his handheld VHF. He looked around to check if anyone had seen or heard and quickly continued his walk as if nothing had happened.

Soon, Dan thought better of it. Having turned off his own VHF, he couldn't follow what was going on any longer. He'd better keep an ear on the children, he reckoned. He turned his VHF on again and tuned to channel 72. There, he could hear a clear, friendly, masculine voice spelling out "...– P – H – E – R – E". His own daughter replied: "Unknown-vessel-calling-Koshlong, this is Koshlong. That was very kind of you! Thank you! Over."

"No problem. You're welcome. Thought I'd help out since no one else seems to be willing!" came the friendly voice again. The exchange had entertained the whole marina. We never did discover the identity of the friendly speller.

The VHF and the Single Side Band radio (or SSB) were our main source of voice communication between the boats. The Iridium satellite telephone was mainly used for e-mails or the occasional call home, but was too expensive and too private for our daily inter-ship communication. We all wanted everyone to be involved, to help each other if needed just as if we belonged to one big family: the yachting community.

The few boats without SSB felt a bit left out. These yachts did not always know where their cruising friends would gather next. We didn't always stick together and it was nice to go our own way for a bit and then to get back together. Deciding where to sail and what to see were always the top items on the SSB, as they were for family discussions. The children's words were given substantial weight. We always tried to make unanimous decisions. The only time their wishes were vetoed by us parents was when we decided to sail back home after one season in the Caribbean. Jessica and Jonathan wanted to prolong our sabbatical with at least another year. Karolina and I thought that it was right time to sail back to Europe, and for the children to go to a regular school with professional teachers. Today, Karolina and I both question our decision, but that is another story for another day.

After two weeks in Porto Santo, we were ready to hop over to the main island of Madeira. We had heard of great hikes on Madeira and wanted to walk the famous Levada trails as well as try our luck on the very tops of the island's high volcanic mountains.

The pleasant day-sail between the two islands was just made for racing. We all started at the same time with the boat-kids busy trimming sails and doing their best to get an extra tenth of a knot. "Look! Sara Grace is hoisting its gennaker. Quick get 'Nessie' out of her bag." All the boats put up their light-wind sails. It was brilliantly colourful.

For the children, the 30 miles over to Madeira were as exciting as the America's Cup. I can't remember who won. We all made it to the barbeque in Quinta do Lorde. All that mattered was that it was fun.

The next day we went on a hike. Some of the parents went off to organise three rental cars. One was red, another blue, and the third, a shiny silver. The kids thought they looked fantastic, and eagerly looked forward to a trip up into Madeira's mountainous interior. We packed the cars with picnics, kids and walkie-talkies. In the front seats sat a map-reader and, to his left, a driver. Off we shot in a line towards the mountains.

Seeing the world through your children's eyes is one of the great pleasures of a year like this. This is especially true of outings and excursions. They see things we don't notice, small details that define the bigger picture. Jessica and Jonathan each had an inexpensive digital camera and took photos I would never have thought of. Later, it was often the case that I would ask for one of Jessica's photos, having missed a great shot she had noticed.

Back home, hiking had often been accompanied by grumbling about the length of the walk, the hills, the temperature or the time it all took. But after three months of no car, Jessica and Jonathan were used to walking and enjoyed sharing the exercise with each other and their friends.

The Levadas are the irrigation channels built to bring fresh water down to the drier agricultural areas on Madeira. Most have paths running alongside them and the gentle incline makes for ideal mountain walks. We completed one of the lower walks and then drove up, into the low-lying cloud, almost to the very top of the island. We parked the three brightly coloured cars and climbed.

I am glad our family and friends back home did not know about the Madeira-hikes until afterwards. Unsurprisingly, our relatives and friends at home were more worried about storms, pirates and sharks than our shore excursions. Each time they heard we were safely moored in a marina or at anchor, they relaxed and stopped asking nervous questions. They simply believed we were safe ashore.

Partly swathed in cloud, we carefully tried to follow the path along the edge of the extinct volcano. Visibility was minimal in the cloud and it was difficult to follow the trail. The only reason we could go on was that the cloud spared us the view down. On the north side of the ridge, clouds were blown up from the Atlantic. On the south side, they disappeared leaving a fantastic view. From time to time, we walked out of the clouds or they drifted away slightly. It was then that we realised just how dangerous the situation was. We were hiking on narrow shelves, which sometimes turned into some sort of balcony and sometimes formed bridges. On all sides were drops of hundreds of metres.

One trail took us to some stairs consisting of hundreds of steps leading up to another summit. It felt like they were taking us to heaven. Who had built these steps and why? Were they like the builders of Babylon, trying to find a way to God?

The kids did great, as so often, and hiked with joy, and did not show any fear. This was fun, they thought, and rushed ahead. They did their best to follow their parents' pleas not to lean over any edges or to run in fog but it was hard to suppress their natural enthusiasm. Disney could never have built such an exciting environment in plastic. The reality of the Madeiran mountains far exceeded any theme-park.

Hiking high on Madeira

COMMUNICATIONS

The days of Poste Restante and picking up dusty, long-awaited packages at remote post offices have long gone. If you have the budget, you can even surf the Internet in the middle of the ocean.

Short-range radio communication will be via VHF. Newer sets have unique MMSI identification numbers and can transmit that number, a distress call and your GPS position at the touch of a single button. Have a spare aerial so you can transmit even if the mast is lost. A handheld set is a good additional back-up. Newer models are waterproof and may float.

Long-range communications will be via MF/HF radio (usually SSB) or satellite phone. An SSB is expensive, needs proper installation and training to operate. But, thereafter, is free and generates a great sense of community and comradeship with other users. With a modem, you can also use your SSB for sending and receiving emails. A satellite phone is generally easier for emails and good for private or business conversations. The cost of air-time via satellite varies. On both SSB and satellite phone, it pays to compress incoming and outgoing emails.

WiFi internet connections are available in some surprisingly out-of-the-way marinas and anchorages. To get connected, it will help to have a separate, amplifying aerial you can place on the cabin roof or even pull up the mast a bit. Skype is ideal for talking to friends and family at home.

You can save money on your mobile phone by buying SIM cards locally.

Communication is important. Children, in particular, like to know where their cruising friends are and what is going on at home.

———

A taste of Funchal, Madeira

Hurricane Vincent roaring by our marina on Madeira

Chapter sixteen

In which we lose a battle but become more confident of our overall strategy

VINCENT, SALVAGE AND GRACIOSA

One hundred and twenty miles. That is about as close as you ever want to get to a hurricane. Even if this one was dying as it limped weakly towards Europe, it still felt unpleasantly vulnerable to be this near to Hurricane Vincent. The fact that this year's alphabetical naming of tropical storms had come to the letter 'V' so soon merely added to the sense of threat, as did Vincent's unusually southern track. Normally, hurricanes have died out long before they get this far east and they usually choose a route significantly further to the north. Spent hurricanes do strike Scandinavia once in a while and we call them 'autumn storms'. The one now threatening Madeira was a lot more frightening than any of those.

At the time, we did not know this would not be our only encounter with a hurricane. Not only would we meet another but it would be while we were sailing in the open Atlantic.

But our introduction to hurricanes was an interesting one. Vincent passed just a little over a hundred miles north of Madeira. At the time, we were moored in Quinta do Lorde marina on Madeira's southern side and had no desire whatsoever to try our luck at sea. Fortunately, this new marina felt pretty safe, even with such destructive force such a relatively short distance away.

We sat in the cockpit, watching the huge waves breaking over the massive harbour walls as well as over the breakwater further out. The marina entrance would have been impossible to get through without putting the boat and ourselves into serious jeopardy. So we stayed.

Being trapped inside a half-completed building site, as Quinta do Lorde then was, seemed quite bearable. We had friends moored around us. The marina itself had not much more to offer than shelter, shore-power and water. Everything else was either at the planning or building stage. Next time we come here, we will most likely not recognize the place. Deserted rocks and cliffs will have turned into a complete village. We had seen the plans. This eastern tip of Madeira was to become a fancy new holiday resort, complete with bungalows, shops, cafés, restaurants, hotels and a town square. The whole project had started, luckily for us, with the marina, which was just about finished. The marina office was still housed in a bedroom in an old hotel overlooking the boats.

With not much to offer in the way of facilities, the marina staff made up for it by being extra helpful. They would do things like drive us hurricane-bound yachties to the next town some 20 minutes away to shop. They arranged our car hire and let us use their internet connection. Harbour fees, it seemed, had been set to reflect the facilities as they would be not as they were, and had scared quite a few boats away. The published fees of more than 30 EUR per night were just not appropriate at this stage, and occupation was low, so a certain amount of negotiating was going on. The best price we called the 'Koshlong Rate' as they had been the first to get the 'weekly fee', the 'ARC rebate' and the 'under 12m rate', all at the same time.

From our safe, if storm-battered base at Quinta do Lorde, we took the bus into Funchal, the capital of Madeira. We waved the bus down outside the marina and climbed aboard. All the seats were filled and so, soon, was all the space for standing. We held on tight as the driver tore along the narrow, twisting roads of this mountainous island. At the sharpest corners, the driver would sound the horn to warn road-users coming in the opposite direction. It all got particularly interesting when the oncoming vehicle turned out to be another bus. I can't tell you exactly how many millimetres there were between the vehicles as we passed. I simply had to shut my eyes. Madeiran driving may not be that bad. It may have been that I was so unused to travelling in any sort of motorised vehicle.

We all wanted to put the drive behind us and discussed how best to spend our day in Funchal. The nearness of Hurricane Vincent had made it rainy and windy. Where better to shelter first than in Blandy's wine cellar? The word 'cellar' is not really appropriate as most of the wine is in an attic. In contrast to any other sort of wine-making with which I am familiar, the wine barrels are stored high up in the building, far away from the cold cellar.

Normally, wine-makers seek a constant, cool temperature for maturing. Not on Madeira. They look for fluctuating temperatures, including up to 30°C (85F) in summer. The aim is to simulate the traditional production process including, as it did, the crossing of the Equator in a ship's hold. Therefore windows are kept open, to let the warm summer winds blow along the corridors, embracing the barrels and warming their contents. Totally oxidised, these wines can last for over one hundred years!

A pleasant and informative tour through the domains of Blandy ended with a particularly enjoyable wine-tasting. We tried wine made from the four noble grapes: Sercial, Verdelho, Bual and Malmsey. These give the Madeira wines their full-bodied, aromatic flavour. Try to avoid Madeiran wine that doesn't mention any of these grape varieties on the label. It will probably have been made with Tinta Negra Mole, which is not so good. The less expensive wines will be labelled simply Seco (Dry), Meio Seco (Medium Dry), Meio Doce (Medium Rich) or Duce (Rich) without naming the grape itself.

We also tried a new type of lower-priced vintage Madeira called Colheita. Originating in a specific year like a real vintage Madeira and, of course, made from one of the four noble grapes, it has not matured quite as long in oak barrels as its genuine cousin. True vintage Madeira has to mature in casks for a minimum of twenty years.

So, in rather good spirits, we left Blandy's and headed for the Botanic Garden. We were actually not going to see the flowers. For us, the trip was about getting permission to visit the Ilhas Selvagens. These are a small group of islands situated half-way between Madeira and the Canary Islands. Sailing to the Salvage Islands, as they are known in English, would mean a detour in our next passage, but would take us somewhere very few people have been. To protect the island's largely unspoilt wildlife, the Portuguese government insists visitors seek a permit.

Our taxi driver knew where the permissions office was, and the man who signed the permits happened to be in the office at the time we arrived.

I handed over our ship's papers and my passport to a female official and waited patiently until all the details were fed into the computer, printed on paper and copied several times. Finally, the bunch of papers was solemnly carried to the Big Boss in his office next door. It looked as though this was all going to take some time. The taxi driver, conscious, perhaps, of his ticking meter, was not in anything like the same hurry as his bus-driving rival had been this morning. He stood patiently next to me looking out of the window enjoying the beautiful Botanic Garden. I could still taste the lovely Madeira wine. After a while, the lady re-entered the office and I got back one sheet of the copied documents, now embellished with a neat signature together with a couple of fancy stamps. This paper allowed us to stay at the Salvage Islands for a maximum of 48 hours. Success! With that job done, it was time for a coffee before we screwed up enough courage for the bus tour home.

Vincent was still doing its best to make us stay on Madeira, so a couple of us yachties gathered on Regina to discuss weather patterns and our planned voyage to the Canaries via the Ilhas Selvagens. It was a 300-mile leg and some planning was needed. It was crucial we got to the Salvage Islands in daylight. To navigate the difficult and dangerous approach, we also wanted as little sea swell as possible. They are not called the Salvage Islands for nothing! Nevertheless, we were keen to give it a try. Just two people lived on the island: the officials who would check the stamped and signed papers we had collected in Funchal.

A couple of days after Vincent had passed, four boats set off from Quinta do Lorde. The Australian crew of Amaranth decided to head straight for Graciosa in the Canaries. Graciosa, meaning 'charming', 'comfortable', 'fun' or 'sympathetic', sounded more inviting to them than anything to do with 'salvage'. That left three boats planning a mid-passage stopover: Starlight from the USA, Koshlong from Canada and Regina from Sweden, each with children on board.

The only bit of Starlight we saw was her stern. I prefer not to take pictures of boats from behind, other than at anchor, but in this case there was not much else to do. Starlight is a Swan 46 designed by Germán Frers, the same designer as Regina. All Frers designs are fast, but the Swan — with its long waterline — was particularly so.

Early on the 13th of October (exactly four months after leaving Sweden), we approached the mysterious Salvage Islands. Starlight, who arrived first, looked for a place to anchor, but still had not found the bay marked as 'anchorage' on the chart by the time Regina and Koshlong showed up.

Starlight's mast was swinging from side to side like a pendulum. Was this the anchorage? It felt about as sheltered as the open ocean. No, worse, actually, as the swell behind the island was shorter and even less comfortable than offshore.

After a discussion over the VHF, we decided to take the opportunity to snap some photos of each other's boats in front of this (almost) deserted island, rather than trying to anchor. Leaving the boats for an excursion ashore looked very difficult. I could not see anywhere to land the dinghy for a start. A visit to the Salvage Islands no longer felt as urgent as it had.

The biggest disappointment for me was that nobody had inspected all that fine paperwork. We could not even see the two officials with our binoculars.

We called up Amaranth on the SSB later that day and told them they had missed a fantastic photo opportunity. They replied that they were just a couple of hours out of Graciosa and would soon be able to have a hot shower and open a bottle of wine with their meal in the cockpit. In contrast to our upwind beat to the Salvage Islands, they had enjoyed a pleasant reach the whole way to Graciosa.

Graciosa is part of the Canaries but, in many ways, has more in common with the Salvage Islands than with a tourist trap like Gran Canaria's Playa Inglés. It's the most northerly of the Canary Islands and is situated within a nature reserve. The settlement consists of just one village, inhabited by some 600 people. The rest is sand: sand on the beaches, sand as pavement, sand as roads, sand uphill and sand downhill.

To our surprise, the village had no fewer than four supermarkets, and several restaurants. Tourists were mainly yachties, together with a few self-caterers, looking to escape the bustle of the world. There are no paved roads and it does not take long to walk around the entire island. It felt a lot like Porto Santo. Once again, we had found our own private little paradise. It was hard to believe that Lanzarote was just a mile or two away.

We stayed for ten days on Graciosa, spending some time in the friendly marina and some outside in the anchorage. Of the thirty yachts in the anchorage, about a dozen had families with children on board. You can imagine what fun these children had playing together. They raced dinghies, kayaked, hunted for treasure and swam in the warm, clear water. Jessica liked a quiet moment to read, lying in the hammock attached to our spinnaker pole.

October the 21st was a big day. Do you know what happened on October 21st, 1805? It was the battle of Trafalgar and this was the 200th anniversary. The parents decided we would all get together for a mass history lesson. We would re-enact the battle – and Nelson's victory over Napoleon's fleet. The children would be the British and the parents would be the French and Spanish. (The parents' plank-walking fate was, therefore, sealed quite early in the day.)

It was at this point that we noticed that one yacht in the anchorage was flying a French ensign. We did not want a diplomatic incident, so some of the parents dinghied over to say 'hello'. It turned out that the skipper, Chris, had been born in France but now lived in Australia with his wife Linn, and they were both quite relaxed about our recreating that dark day in the history of France. They promised to join us for a post-battle beer.

Starlight was renamed Victory after Nelson's flagship. Jack, the eldest of the Starlight boys, took the role of Nelson and ordered the raising of signal flags spelling out the famous declaration 'England expects that every man will do his duty'. The British crew gathered on one of the biggest yachts of the group, Wild Alliance. They planned their strategy while the parents retreated to Aventura, which was now the French flagship, and opened a bottle of suitably French wine.

With their strategy agreed, the British climbed down the sides of Wild Alliance and into an armada of dinghies and kayaks. These they had equipped with an array of water pistols, sponges, buckets and water-filled balloons. A foghorn was sounded and the attack began. More than a dozen heavily armed and frighteningly dressed children started paddling towards us. On board Aventura we drained our wine-glasses without hurrying, confident in the knowledge that the boat's deck-wash pump would keep the marauders at bay for a few minutes at least.

As they neared the French flagship, the children launched a salvo of balloons and sponges. The parents fought back with their own buckets. But the battle swiftly turned in favour of the historic victors. Admiral Jack's tactical master-stroke was to take control of the deck-wash pump. Soon all the parents were in the water and the French flagship was in British hands. The children celebrated by jumping in on top of the adults. There was a lot of laughing. It was the best history lesson ever, according to the children.

After the battle, we gathered on Wild Alliance for an excellent party. Chris and Linn from the French yacht joined us as promised and the gang was getting bigger. October 21st is a date I will remember.

Two days later, it was Dan's 44th birthday, and Koshlong organised another party: a barbeque on the beach. Dan's present from his wife Sue was a bag of ice. Ice is a rarity out cruising and Dan was very pleased. The ice chilled a bottle of sparkling wine and a collection of local beers. We used the same black rubber bucket that usually served for gutting fish or doing the laundry. We were truly beginning to live and love the simple life.

Dan thought this was his best-ever birthday - better even than his 8th when he had got a new red bike. We all agreed that coming away cruising had been the best thing we had ever done and that we did right in making the most of the moment. "Imagine", I said, "if we'd waited another 20 years and it was Dan's 64th birthday we were celebrating. I'm sure I would really regret not having gone earlier. Let's toast the fact that we are doing it now and still have the chance to do it again!"

Dan agreed, smiling with his chilled wine in his hand and mumbled something about Panama and the Pacific. Sue, his wife, who is always very sensible, pointed out that cruising could not reasonably continue forever, however pleasant it was. She might have been right but I didn't want to think about stopping just at this moment.

Dan and I agreed that we would continue to dream. That was the right thing to do on your best birthday ever. We continued talking about South Pacific routes and paradise islands. Sue and Karolina exchanged meaningful looks. They were every bit as much in agreement as Dan and I.

Doing the laundry the friendly way

THE ATLANTIC RALLY FOR CRUISERS (ARC)

Many sailors considering an Atlantic crossing sign up for the biggest and oldest of all ocean rallies, the ARC. Started in 1985 by Jimmy Cornell, it now leaves from Las Palmas, Gran Canaria, and ends in Rodney Bay, St Lucia. About 250 boats take part, most in a cruising section, where motoring is allowed. If you're willing to keep an eye on the numbers signed up and take a bit of risk, you can leave your decision until quite late.

The organisers provide a lot of useful check-lists and carry out a safety inspection of each boat taking part. Participants get a guaranteed place in Las Palmas marina and the option of talks on weather, navigation, safety, provisioning and communications, plus discounts at most chandleries. There is then an organised SSB net during the crossing.

The start involves a Spanish warship marking the line, and lots of fireworks and cheering from the dockside. It is a big, sociable event and not to the taste of everyone hoping for a bit of peace and quiet on their cruise. There is also pressure to go on the pre-planned date, even if the weather is not ideal. That, of course, can be an advantage if you think you will find it hard to take the final decision to set off. To take part or not is a personal decision and there is still plenty of room on the Atlantic for both types of sailor.

Trafalgar Day, 21 October, Graciosa, the Canary Islands

Provisioning in Tenerife

Chapter seventeen
In which we make our final preparations

"SEE YOU THERE FOR CHRISTMAS!"

The words echoed in my head. It felt like an impossibly long way away in terms both of time and of distance. Our friends on the Norwegian yacht Galadriel called happily across to us as they backed out from their berth in Santa Cruz de Tenerife. Their two children waved from the deck. We shouted back, wishing them fair winds and promising to meet again on the small West Indian island of Bequia for Christmas.

We followed their mast as they made their way around the pontoons and out toward the open ocean. They planned first to sail along the coast of Tenerife, then to turn and head west. Soon, we would be doing the same. A strange feeling grew in my stomach. I felt so small; the Atlantic seemed so big.

The North Sea, Biscay, the legs to Madeira and later to the Canaries were short hops compared to what lay ahead of us. Luckily, we were not alone. There were at least 250 boats in Santa Cruz preparing for the crossing. As soon as one left, another came in to go through the same process of preparing and provisioning. And the same thing was happening in all the big marinas around the Canaries. The busiest of all is Las Palmas, from where the Atlantic Rally for Cruisers (or ARC) sets off. That involves 250 boats leaving at once.

It was hard to believe it was so close to Christmas. In shorts, T-shirt and bare feet, I did not feel like I normally did in November. At home, we would have given up outside activities long ago and would have been indoors, in front of the fire with a good book about sailing, dreaming about the sort of thing we were now doing for real. But, as I was discovering, dreaming about an Atlantic crossing is a totally different matter from being in the Canaries, seeing the boats leaving, waving a last 'good-bye', and knowing that soon it would be our turn. It still did not feel real.

All sorts of boats make up the annual Atlantic fleet. There are tiny cruisers, some with men or women going single-handed. And then there are the super-yachts with professional crews. Most amazing to me were the rowing boats. Rowing across the

Atlantic takes at least 60 days. Some were even doing it solo. (I guess you can't say rowers are single-handed.) I wondered whether the rowers really knew what they were getting themselves into. And then I thought: did we?

Leaving aside the oddities like the rowing boats and the super-yachts, most of the boats heading for the Atlantic were about 45 feet long. Regina, at 40 feet one of the biggest boats in our home marina, had felt like a ship when we first bought her, but now seemed quite small. As we stowed the tons of water, diesel and food we would need for the crossing, I was relieved we had not bought the smaller model we had considered.

The reason there are so many yachts in the Canaries at the same time is that the gap between the end of the hurricane season and Christmas, the date by which most people want to arrive in the Caribbean, is only a little more than three weeks. Many of the marinas in the Canaries are fully booked for November well in advance. When we were there, Las Palmas on Gran Canaria, home to the ARC, had no space in the marina. Santa Cruz de Tenerife was fully booked and La Gomera, one of the most beautiful islands, was almost impossible to get into.

Thinking about Christmas made me realise that we had already been away for a long time. Five months had passed since we dropped our lines in Sweden. We were now totally into the rhythm of our new lifestyle, living without the seasons or the stresses that had shaped our old lives. Hundreds of sailors were doing the same as us. Many had done it for years. Some had gone back to the cruising life after trying and failing to return to 9-to-5. Several times I was told that readjusting to shore life was not easy. Some never succeeded and many simply could not see the point in trying. A lot of the crews we met in the Canaries were cruisers who had come back to the freedom of the seas for a second or even third time. We met one Swiss gentleman in his seventies, who was on his fourth circumnavigation.

Among these experienced cruisers, our only novelty was that we were so new to the lifestyle. In their eyes, we were nervous novices, having not even crossed an ocean, yet. This last fact was soon to change, however.

Although we were anxious about the trip, we took comfort from what we had learned over those five months. Like those experienced cruisers we now realised that with stressful jobs, traffic, crime and the rest, ordinary, shore-bound life presented many dangers; maybe worse than the Atlantic. It was not the sailing so much that scared me but the practicalities. Even with a water-maker onboard, we needed to allow for the water-maker breaking and our main tank getting contaminated. We would still have our second water tank. The question was how much bottled water should we also buy and stow.

It was also hard to know how much food to stock. There were issues around what sort of food lasted best and how it should be stowed. We had been reading about how long various vegetables and fruits kept if you treated them in one or the other way. We had read about buying eggs that had not been chilled and being careful to turn them every day, packing each tomato individually in newspaper, not stowing them with any other fruit and the amazing capacity of cabbages to endure for weeks. We had endless discussions with our boat-friends about how much flour, sugar, milk and pasta to buy. It felt quite surreal to stand in a supermarket with several fully-loaded shopping carts. We had never purchased so much food in such a short time.

Karolina, organized as she always is, made menu-lists for each day. We bought according to those lists, with an allowance for extra days, plus emergency supplies like pasta, rice and tinned food.

Interesting items, such as boric acid and condensed milk to feed potential blind passengers, were stocked up together with Cockroach Motels to trap these unwelcome pets. As usual, we checked each item before taking it onboard, and actually found a bag of cockroach eggs on one package from a small shop. That one duly failed the onboard security check, but had we missed any more? What would we do if we had?

I noticed one thing in our pre-Atlantic hysteria. The more experienced sailors were less worried and knew their shopping lists. Their boats were ocean-ready at all times. They were no longer affected by the cockroach fever, either. Getting them on board is not the end of your sailing career, they claimed, and cockroaches can be defeated. Having said that, these experienced sailors were always very careful, putting in a lot of effort to minimize the risk of getting them on board. Checking every item had simply become part of their shopping tour.

The huge supermarkets Carrefour and El Corte Inglés became our main source of food. We visited both of these almost on a daily basis with long shopping lists corresponding to Karolina's menus, and buying stuff in the right order: pasta, rice, water and tinned food first, fresh fruit at the very end. These supermarkets deliver directly to the boat, if you wish, or you take a taxi home with all your groceries, which does not cost much. From El Corte Inglés we ordered vacuum-packed frozen meat, which went directly into our freezer.

Our detailed shopping plans were only distorted by 'meddling' from other first-time crossers, although we weren't, I'm sure, any better ourselves. We all had good ideas, had read a lot about ocean sailing and were very willing to share our good advice and shopping suggestions with each other. As valuable as they were, they all meant we were never finished: buying more and more groceries (as well as boat stuff) to keep up with the many inputs! We didn't want to be less well prepared than anyone else, right?

Storage, food and good bargains were discussed continually. Listen in to these typical dockside snippets:

"Have you seen this great camping lamp I just bought? For just 30 Euros!"

"I bought a Honda 230V petrol power generator today. Really neat! Do you have one as well?"

"Wine is less expensive here. We bought a shopping cart full."

"How many spare halyards do you have, by the way?"

"How much diesel do you carry? We have five jerry cans of diesel on deck in addition to our tanks. Just in case, you know."

"Do you think 200 bottles of water will be enough? I might go and get some more."

"Look what I found! Olive oil in Tetrapaks! Light, easy to stow and produces almost no garbage. We bought 15 litres! I have heard, you can hardly find olive oil in the Caribbean, and if you do, it's enormously expensive! Better to stock up."

"I have this new navigation software, but it won't load on the PC. Do you know why?

"My e-mail software does not talk to the SCS modem for the SSB. Could you come and help, please?"

It was a never-ending story!

People were hanging in their rigs like monkeys, drilling holes for new poles, checking sails or putting on anti-chafing tapes. Jigsaws and grinding could be heard; painting and varnishing was done. New canvas was sewn and bottoms were cleaned.

Oh, I wished I had the tranquillity and self-confidence of the sailors, who had done an ocean crossing before! They had lived long enough onboard to keep their homes in perfect condition and knew what to do.

What we would eat on our 3-week passage? Definitely not dried food and corned beef, although both were on board as emergency rations. We were lucky enough to have a freezer, and this was filled with 46 possible meals for our expected 22-day crossing. It was packed with chicken breasts, minced meat, stewing steak, fish fillets, pork fillets, hamburgers, and even Swedish meatballs (thanks to IKEA on Tenerife!) plus some pre-cooked meals for the first days. The trick is to fill the freezer, yet not to pack it too tight since some air in between the meals is needed to keep everything frozen. Our recipes were easy, yet tasty, and had been tested before on board.

Living on board has widened our scope of recipes and meals, since most sailors show a great interest in food and are happy to share it with equally interested yachties. Rama from Israel, who had lived on the boat for over ten years, showed us how to bake pita bread over the open gas flame on the stove; Liz from Amaranth shared her favourite bread recipe; Dan from Koshlong explained how to use Thai spice, while Val from Valhalla gave us the tip to peel tomatoes directly over the gas flame. Not all cruisers might be as lucky as we were, getting to know Captain Jon on Wild Alliance, who had been a professional chef in his 'former life', and specialised in fish dishes. We all got a crash course in fish filleting and sushi rolling, to be prepared for all the fish we hoped to catch on our Atlantic crossing.

It felt as if we were to eat ourselves over to the other side, arriving with our bellies stuffed with food. I began to look forward to our Atlantic meals!

After two weeks in Tenerife, we had no more space to fill. Furthermore, Karolina was complaining about the fact that we were eating from her Atlantic stock. If we stayed much longer, she argued, we had to replace it, meaning more provisioning, which, in turns, would make us stay even longer. Time to break this vicious circle!

When finally both the Blue Water Rally and the French Atlantic Crossing Rally had left Tenerife, a calm atmosphere spread over the marina. The ARC-fleet, starting from neighbouring Gran Canaria, was also due to depart in the next couple of days. Left were the cruisers, doing it at their own pace, taking weather and their own preparations more into account than a specific starting date.

The rallies had barely left, when the weather situation on the Atlantic became interesting, to say the least. The Azores High, always responsible for stable trade winds, had suddenly retreated to the British Isles, which now experienced an extraordinary High of 1039hPa. With no familiar High over the Azores, the Atlantic lay wide open for strangers to enter the scene. Lows were forecast to show up just north of the planned route to the Caribbean. They would be offering anything but trade winds.

We decided not to leave for the Atlantic with this weather situation, and chose to make a last stop in La Gomera, instead. We had heard so much about these westernmost islands of the Canaries. It had opened up a possibility to get a berth alongside the harbour mole, despite an otherwise full marina.

The very same day the ARC-fleet left for St Lucia, West Indies, we sailed in direction La Gomera. It was a dreadful day, beating into headwinds. We were glad that this was not our first day on our big crossing and that our next port was not far away. At the same time, we thought of the poor ARC-fleet getting this miserable start and wondered how they must have felt knowing that their sailing would continue for weeks rather than hours. Later, we learnt that no fewer than five boats in the ARC-fleet had, in fact, turned around and sailed back to Gran Canaria; among them our friends on Koshlong and Wild Alliance. Leaving a day later made all the difference!

We were not in a rush, and followed Columbus' example: checking into La Gomera for a couple of days before the crossing. Columbus had loaded blessed holy water in La Gomera in order to Christen any Indians he would encounter. The Regina-crew bunkered tranquillity and harmony, instead, before our own big voyage.

We were not alone in our desire to retreat in La Gomera. No fewer than 200 yachts had gathered in this well-run marina and friendly island before sailing to the Caribbean. Compared to Tenerife or Gran Canaria, the hectic atmosphere was totally lacking here, which had its consequences: the marina was constantly filled to its limit. The problem lay in the fact that yachts arrived for a night or two, fell in love with the island and stayed for weeks!

We had equally become fond of La Gomera, but wanted to keep our promise to meet all our friends 'over there' for Christmas, weather permitting.

The meteorological situation on the Atlantic was still anything but stable. One of the Lows was of specific interest. We had been following its progress for quite some days. Soon, this Low earned a name, meaning it had turned into a tropical depression – developing into a hurricane. Its name was Delta.

Remember hurricane Vincent? The alphabet had since run out of letters and the following hurricanes were named in Greek: Alpha, Beta, Gamma and finally, this one, Delta. Never had I heard of so many hurricanes in one season!

Delta's track caused a lot of headache. At first, it had looked quite all right for us with Delta heading north-east towards the Azores. Then, it suddenly turned south: interfering with the classic Canaries-Caribbean trade-wind route and giving some nervousness for the fleet already heading over the Atlantic. So far, all these boats experienced was the total lack of trade-winds, but the track confused us all and was threatening, to say the least.

It became crucial for the boats already on their way to the Caribbean to turn as far south as possible to avoid the strong headwinds closer to Delta's centre. Being aware of their vulnerable situation, we hoped they all had long-term weather forecasts onboard. We sent off an Inmarsat-C mail to one of our friends participating in the Blue Water Rally, who then very thankfully turned towards Cap Verde and did not leave this group of islands until Delta had passed.

Suddenly, Delta changed course a second time, now heading straight for the Canaries, where we were. We had Hurricane Vincent in fresh memory, throwing up heavy seas and winds far beyond what we considered pleasant. The overcrowded small harbour of La Gomera, open to the south-west, felt anything but safe. In addition to that, we were moored alongside a concrete mole in the entrance of the port, which was not a very good place to weather a heavy storm.

Should we stay? Should we leave? If so, where should we sail? Could Delta change track once more?

The hurricane season was officially not at end, yet. Statistically, Delta had a certain right to exist. The same statistics, however, also told about how seldom they form this late in the season, and if they do, should normally be found in the Caribbean Sea, where the water still is warm enough. But do hurricanes read statistics?

The exceptionally warm water in the Atlantic this year was to explain the situation. No hurricane can form if the water temperature goes below 26.5°C (80F). Furthermore, this temperature must be exceeded not only on the surface but also further down: The layer of warm water must be at least 50m (150feet) deep, otherwise the hurricane stirs up the cooler water from underneath and 'kills itself'. Normally the water temperature has gone down enough by this time of the year, ensuring a hurricane-free season. Apparently, this year, the sea had not cooled down, yet. A further sign of our global warming?

Karolina, Jessica, Jonathan and I were leaning over charts and computer screens, trying to get a picture of the Greek letter moving on that huge area of open sea. The visit of Vincent had apparently not been our last engagement with a tropical storm on this voyage. We studied weather faxes, GRIB-files, Inmarsat-C warnings, NAVTEX messages and weather forecasts from France, the UK and the USA. The more information we had, the more confused we became about our own situation and the more difficult our decision became. If we had interpreted the information correctly, we should sail. The decision to leave port in such a situation is so hard, that we desperately looked for clues telling us to stay.

We had conference calls over the SSB discussing the situation with our friends both already at sea as well as still in port around the Canaries. Some had already decided to stay on Tenerife and would not head off until the hurricanes had passed. Indeed, a tempting option!

The ARC fleet, with its miserable start, was doing quite all right, actually. It was far enough south already, most probably not getting in the way of the hurricane. It was worse for us and the others who were still in the marinas: if we left now, would we be fast enough to get south when Delta struck? Time became critical, with the exit door closing very soon. Within a very short time, leaving harbour would mean sailing into Delta, rather than away from it. Yet staying could mean getting closer to the eye of Delta than we ever did with Vincent.

With our Iridium phone we called Commander's Weather, a respected commercial weather routing company in USA. They charge for their service but is a great investment when you need it! They are never further away than an e-mail or a phone call. They give detailed routing suggestions by e-mail, or you just lift the receiver and talk to a weather guru right where you are for a fixed price. Satellite phones do come in handy at times! Some of our friends were also in contact with the legendary Herb Hilgenberg in Canada, who does free and very precise weather routing via SSB for yachts. Rudy and Lilian on their Swiss Ovni Shiva were in contact with a German equivalent meteorologist. For once, all these weather routers were of one and the same opinion: "Leave! – Now!"

And that's what we did.

A truly tough way to cross the Atlantic

ATLANTIC PROVISIONING

Make a plan based on meals you know can be prepared at sea and are liked by all the crew. Add at least a week to your expected crossing time and use that plan to create a shopping list. Prices vary but are likely to be best in big towns with proper supermarkets. Try to buy fruit, vegetables and eggs that have not been chilled. They will last longer. If you have a freezer, buy meat pre-packed and frozen. You can take a few packs even if you have just a fridge.

Don't try to prepare too many meals in advance. A few are helpful for rough weather but too many can get boring and deny you the time-filling pleasure of cooking. Plan stowage to take account of how often you will need things. Tins of ravioli or whatever is your extreme storm standby can be hidden right away. Tins of tomatoes are likely to be used every other day.

Don't forget snacks and treats. You might want to hide some of these for the final days at sea. Try to minimize the packaging you bring onboard. Dried foods, such as pasta, flour and rice, are best stored in sealed bags or boxes. Fruit and vegetables need careful stowage away from direct sunlight. Nets hung from the cabin roof are the traditional solution.

Water is, of course, very important. A combination of boat tanks kept isolated until required and bottled water distributed around the bilges is probably best. Use the tanks first as it is these that could be lost as the result of a single failure.

Keep notes of what you actually use on passage. This will help you refine your lists and plans for future trips.

A last night alongside in La Gomera

Sunset as we head west

Chapter eighteen
In which we sail across an ocean

THREE WEEKS ON THE ATLANTIC

Leaving what appeared to be a safe marina – with no landfall planned for several weeks and a hurricane approaching – was a tough decision, tougher than any since the original decision to go cruising. But many of our friends were already on their way and, so long as we could get south quickly, the winds looked good.

Day 1

It was a strange start to what is usually a three-week marathon. We were not in a rally but we did have an adversary. Our first priority was to out-run Delta. Would our plan succeed? It had worked before, when we followed a similar strategy in the North Sea, heading out before a gale hit us in harbour in Norway. The North Sea, however, was not the Atlantic – and a gale was not a hurricane.

We started ahead and the chances looked good, but we had to keep up our speed. The first hours at sea were nerve-racking, with no wind whatsoever and no option but to motor. Every mile gained getting away from the likely track of Delta was another mile towards safety. We motored as fuel-efficiently as we could. With our Gori propeller in second or overdrive gear, 1400 rpm gave us about five and a half knots and fuel consumption of around two litres an hour.

I wouldn't say we were scared those first hours at sea, watching the Canaries getting smaller and smaller behind us. We were focused on the task in hand. We had made our decision. We had chosen the risks involved in going over the risks involved in staying, and it would be a few days yet before we would know whether we had been right.

After a couple of hours' motoring, the wind set in nicely with a 15 knot breeze from the east, pushing us forward at an excellent seven and a half to eight knots. When the wind picked up further, we made a steady eight knots. At that speed, our DuoGen tow generator made more electricity than we were using. So far so good!

Day 2

The following morning, on the 26th of November, I was lying in my bunk feeling miserable. I seldom get seasick, but this time it had hit me badly. And it was all my fault. I had drunk coffee while washing the dishes at the end of our first day at sea and had already fed the fishes once.

What woke me was the ringing of our fishing tackle announcing that a fish had taken the hook. There was nothing for it but to clamber out of my berth, put on my lifejacket and lifeline and crawl back onto the aft deck and deal with it. Oh, this was a big one! We were fighting for quite some time with the fish diving down and swimming away, pulling out more and more line. After a while it got tired, so I could pull it in a bit closer, then it started to thrash about again and pulled back away. Jonathan stood ready with the (as yet unused) gaff for getting it on board. Karolina had the spirit to pour into the gills. (remember the bottle of aniseed vodka we found in Spain?) And Jessica was ready with her camera.

Feeling distinctly queasy, I fought with the fish. When, eventually, we got it close to the boat, I could see that it was big and blue. With a bit more of a struggle we got it onto the deck, where its turquoise colour swiftly turned to gold. It was a beautiful Dorado. It's easy to see why they are called 'golden mackerel' in some languages. It weighed six kg (12 lbs) and its fillets were big enough to provide several meals. No more fishing for a while, thank you, I thought.

Jessica and Jonathan immediately asked for sushi, but my current state of health made me fit for nothing but plain Swedish dried bread.

Karolina did a great job running the boat, taking care of food and the kids, as well as talking on the SSB on two different nets, while I retreated once more to my bunk. But by the time I was due on deck for my night watch, I felt better. And it was good to be able to give Karolina the chance of some well-deserved rest. We were still racing away from Delta. We reckoned the critical day would be the 28th of November. Two more days and we would probably be as close as we were going to get. That was, so long as we could keep making progress south and Delta stuck to its predicted track.

I started talking to Regina, whispering quietly: "Run, Regina, run south! Run just as Germán Frers designed you to do! Run towards the tropics. Run towards the Cape Verde islands! And we will be safe!"

Day 3

Our third day on the Atlantic was an anxious one. It was nothing to do with Delta, which was still following its predicted track, but was the result of a noise coming out of the engine room. A strange, new screaming sound was worrying us. It did not seem to be the fan belt, which looked tight and sound. Was it the water pump? They rarely fail. What could it be?

We picked up the satellite phone and rang knowledgeable friends and the engine-makers Volvo Penta. The boat was rolling a bit and I was not long over my seasickness. I did not want a difficult repair to attempt. After talking through the various possibilities, we decided it might just be the normal sound of the coils in the alternator. We hoped it was and carried on.

It turned out that we were wrong. And we were lucky to be able to use the motor all the way to St Lucia. The original alternator mounting had cracked and was held in place by the belt alone. The noise was the result of the two bits of metal either side of the crack rubbing up against each other. The belt drove the engine cooling pump as well as the alternator so if it had broken completely the engine would have been unusable. Even though we could have sailed, the engine was our main source of electrical power for navigation equipment, lights and all the rest of our gear. It was a simple matter to get the bracket welded up in St Lucia. A complete break would not have been a simple matter in mid-Atlantic.

This was not what we usually did on the first Sunday in Advent. At home, this was the day the first of the four Advent candles was lit. We usually went into town and looked at the shops' Christmas decorations. It was usually cold, sometimes rainy. At home, we would bake gingerbread, decorate the house, light the fire and think about Christmas presents.

My biggest wish for this Christmas was an engine without alarming sound-effects; and the only candle we lit was the LED head-torch. We used it to light the cockpit table as we ate our evening meal. Jonathan had the prestigious task of carrying the 'candle' so had to keep his head pointing down at our dinner of Dorado fried in olive oil, garlic and lime.

Though warm, these tropical nights were very dark when there was no moon. I thought about the rowing boats. How did they feel so close to the water in such complete darkness? We found the first hour or so of darkness a bit creepy. We got used to it as the night went on but the mood hit us every evening. To help, we tried to gather as a family for our supper as the sun went down.

In my bunk, while Karolina took the first watch, I tried to work out where the noise in the engine was coming from. Within minutes and without an answer, I was asleep.

Day 4

"I kind of like my night watches", said Karolina as she woke me up three hours later. This did not make a lot of sense to me as I forced myself out of my cosy bunk. I was now sleeping well but still not used to getting up in the middle of the night. "Not that I find it easy to get up", Karolina continued as if she had read my thoughts, "but once up there in the dark, I find time for myself, at last." She took off her lifejacket, the personal EPIRB and her sweater, getting ready for three hours of blissful sleep. "Tonight, I enjoyed listening to music using the iPod and could really concentrate on the words of the songs. I had time to think things through, looking up into the eternity of the stars."

Karolina had a point. It was a delight to be able to lie down in the cockpit and to look up at all the stars above, bright and clear with no clouds or city lights to interfere. The night watches also gave me the necessary quiet to update my journal, which had been neglected during our hectic days preparing in the Canaries. I liked the writing. It was my way to capture what I felt and to pass on to others what life on a boat was like.

At ten in the morning, we had our normal rendezvous on the SSB with our friends crossing the Atlantic. We learned that Koshlong had had trouble with their engine from 0200. Sue had hand steered all night while Dan had worked in the engine room. Another friend, on a boat called Coconut, from Norway, had more experience of engines and helped talk Dan through the steps necessary to isolate the fault. It was great to hear on the next net at 1800 that Dan had found the problem – a leak – and fixed it.

As well as technical problems, other popular subjects for the SSB nets were the weather, recipes, our positions and tips for destinations once we had arrived in the Caribbean. Exchanging positions made us feel safer.

During the morning net on the 28th of November, we also learnt that Delta had passed over the Canaries, causing all sorts of damage. Winds of 60 knots, gusting up to 80, had torn away the pontoons we had all shared in the marina in Santa Cruz de Tenerife. Yachties had had to fight to save their boats and many craft had been seriously damaged. Overhead power cables had been broken, cutting off electricity and completely blacking out Tenerife. Two boats in the marina had actually been sunk.

Our friends who had decided to stay had been lucky and their boats were safe, but they had had to fight all night with ropes and fenders to prevent serious damage. They planned to leave soon. We had been right to go when we did but I wondered at how close we had been to staying.

While Delta was wreaking havoc on the Canaries, we – further south – were fine. The only effect on us was some light wind from the 'wrong' direction, making it harder for us to get west; and some uncomfortable swell. I was surprised how far and fast waves stirred up by a hurricane travel on the open ocean.

On my next watch, the smell of freshly baked bread spread through the saloon and cheered everyone onboard. There is nothing like that smell, with its promise of something tasty and wholesome to eat. Fresh bread with just a bit of butter can lift your spirits like almost nothing else: at least it can in a small boat on a huge ocean. It was so good it was all we needed with our supper of Dorado in tomato sauce.

We had by now got into a pleasant rhythm onboard. Gone were the days of seasickness and wishing for land. In the afternoon, we allowed ourselves the luxury of a shower. That also made us feel better.

On the radio, we heard that some of the other boats were totally becalmed and had stopped for a mid-ocean swim, something our children would have loved to do. But with a good wind, we were not able to follow their example. Even if we had taken down all the sails, the mast, stays and shrouds would have been enough to push us faster than normal swimming speed and we did not want to leave anyone behind. Would the fear of sharks have stopped us? No.

Day 5

Our Caribbean Chicken, cooked in coconut milk, lemon and chilli along with bananas – loads of bananas – was delicious. As usual, we all sat in the cockpit at around 1900 UTC after our SSB chat with friends. The anti-slip mats on our cockpit table did their jobs: the bowls were glued to the surface. More mobile, however, were their contents, and the bananas and chicken swirled around according to the movements of the boat. Chasing a piece of chicken was quite a challenge.

As dessert, Karolina had made banana cake. It was the same dessert as the day before. In between breakfast and lunch we served bananas pure or *nature*, as they say in French. Lunch did not involve any bananas, as we still had left-over Dorado, but for a mid-afternoon snack, we had, you guessed it, bananas.

I like bananas but why do they have to ripen at the same time? We did not buy a whole stem as we had heard from other sailors that different varieties would ripen at different times. Not for us. They all ripened together. It was eat them or chuck them. And we chucked very little. Karolina took pride in looking at each individual fruit and vegetable each day, turning them if necessary and getting them out to eat if they had ripened.

We had only been out for five days, but we could already see a trend in our food consumption. Fruit and vegetables were disappearing at a worrying pace, but everything else seemed hardly to have been touched. Maybe that was to be expected given how much we had spent on groceries in the Canaries, more than we usually spent in a month. One contributory factor was that we did not eat so much as in colder latitudes. We just did not feel so hungry in the heat.

Another interesting fact was how little waste we produced. We had disposed of as much packaging as we could in the Canaries. All food waste went overboard together with paper towels. Any plastic was kept onboard, rinsed and dried, before it was packed and stored in our aft deck locker. During our three-week crossing, that locker came to hold just four bags of garbage. Ashore, we produced at least one bag per day: in other words five times as much as when sailing.

On the 29th of November the real trade winds had finally set in, as Delta moved on from the Canaries. Steady north-easterly winds together with big rolling seas came at us from astern, rolling Regina from side to side. With the trade winds came the heat. Our afternoon fresh-water shower on the aft deck began to feel like a real treat. It made us appreciate having a water-maker. After my shower, I stayed for a while on aft deck, with my lifeline hooked on and a banana in my hand. I was sitting with a comfortable back-rest of fenders. We were having a joyous ride over the waves.

Five days at sea and it just felt great.

Day 6

"Please, Dad, be a little less loud! I can't hear anything!" Jonathan looked at me urgently from where he was sitting at the chart table.

"I'm just doing the breakfast dishes" I explained.

"Yes, but not now. Please! It's SSB-time and I am trying to get in contact with Koshlong, Sarah Grace, Aventura and Starlight!"

"This is Regina standing by on 8122, over." Jonathan had picked up the microphone again announcing his presence on the frequency the children had chosen the day before. Jessica was standing beside him eagerly listening to the crackle and noise from the SSB, waiting for a familiar voice to come through. Suddenly, it was there. "Regina, Regina, this is Koshlong, over!" Jonathan answered immediately: "Koshlong, this is Regina, how are you guys? Have you caught any fish today? Over."

I smiled while I carried on with the dishes, this time more quietly than before. It seemed hardly believable that these two kids who had known hardly any English a few months earlier were now talking with their friends over the short-wave radio on which speech is often distorted or drowned out by interference. They called their routine SSB rendezvous the Kids' Net. As well as talking about position and speed like the adults, they loved to talk about fish that had been caught or wildlife spotted.

Today, Jonathan and Jessica had another catch to report – a 1.5kg (3.3lb) Dorado. The children begged for sushi. I offered them a trade: if they would now start their schoolwork, I would cook some special rice for a sushi supper. The deal was agreed and so, after five days at sea, which we decided would count as autumn half-term, the children resumed their schooling. It was difficult to keep the boat going, try to catch up on sleep and encourage the children to do schoolwork. But the combination of sushi and, maybe a bit of boredom, meant they were soon stuck into their books.

In the meantime, the seas and winds had built up further. Running with the wind, we were now rolling heavily. It was more than I had expected. You couldn't move about without first taking a firm grip. Everything slammed about inside the lockers. We tried to stop that by stuffing some with rolls of toilet paper. Other stuff we tied up with rubber bands. But there were still lockers you had to open and close while the boat rolled one way. Otherwise the contents would come flying out. Trade-wind sailing sounds comfortable. This was anything but.

We had now changed course towards the west, away from the Cape Verde islands and the last dry land. Two weeks of ocean sailing lay ahead of us. That was a bit scary. Karolina, I think, had some bad feelings about the fact that no doctor or other help would be close at hand. From now on, it would be only us.

Jessica and Jonathan were not remotely worried. All they were interested in was rolling sushi. The three of us unpacked the sushi kit and took up our positions in the galley, doing our best to remember what Jon, the chef from Wild Alliance, had taught us. Each of us had his or her own task. From the end of this human conveyor belt would emerge our first sushi.

The water bowl was tipped over twice, the wasabi got lost, the seaweed was too wet, the rice was insufficiently sticky (until it came into contact with any part of the boat's interior) and the Dorado was cut too big. But it was great fun. Everything rolled when the boat rolled. We called it our 'self-rolled sushi'. It was dark by the time we were finished. We gathered in the cockpit. I held the bowl with the sushi, Karolina was responsible for the soy sauce and Jonathan was in charge of the head-torch. Jessica, without a specific task, got to sample the first sushi roll. Some of the sushi (the ones Jonathan had made) held considerably more of the hot wasabi than the others and were very spicy. They made tears come to your eyes. Or maybe it was the non-stop laughter. I know I will never forget our rock and roll sushi supper.

Day 7

Bob Marley's rhythmic steel drums did their best to get me into the Caribbean mood. I was listening to my iPod and studying the map of Bequia in one of Chris Doyle's excellent guides. My finger followed the coastline. From the dinghy dock, I turned right by the market and continued along the beachside road towards the little church. In my imagination, I passed the gas station and the customs office, and turned left by the Bequia Bookshop towards the little island hospital. A restaurant called 'Gingerbread' had an advertisement in the book. It looked very welcoming, even offering a WiFi internet connection. Maybe we could Skype home from there? We could certainly celebrate our crossing. Further up the road, I noticed a business called 'Caribbean Diesel'. Maybe they could help us with our 'singing' engine. By turning right behind the church, I could get back to the water. Here, it said 'Frangipani'. It was a bar and café. I imagined myself sitting down for a cool beer in the shade, or why not one of those notorious rum punches for which the Caribbean is famous?

So far, this had happened only in my head, sitting in the rolling cockpit, keeping watch. I wondered how it would all feel for real; actually to stroll around on Caribbean streets after several weeks at sea.

Already one Atlantic week had passed by now. At least, that's what the logbook told us. Without the log, it was hard to know what day it was. The sun rose and then set. We did not adjust our watches to take account of going west, so our 1800 SSB net came earlier and earlier in the solar day. The children were fantastic. They adapted perfectly to a world consisting of no more than a tiny shell floating on an enormous ocean.

With the boat being our world and the ocean resembling an infinite universe, it sometimes felt as if we were travelling through space. Looking up into the night sky, we could identify planets, like Venus, and stars, in their now easily recognisable constellations. They felt closer to us than the islands of the Caribbean. In our small universe, we couldn't see any other souls on the ocean. But thanks to the radio, we at least knew our friends were also travelling alone like small, isolated planets in the same giant universe. We may have been alone but we were not lonely.

The following day, we would complete a thousand miles since leaving the Canaries. A thousand miles is more than many yachties sail in an entire season. For us, it was just about a third of our Atlantic crossing. And there was definitely no turning back. The winds were now steady from the east. We had no choice but to go on.

We actually saw another boat on Day 7. It was a catamaran that overtook us. We hadn't seen a boat for many days, so it was an exciting moment and we called them up over the VHF. I asked when they had left the Canaries. It was silent for while. Then the voice (with New Zealand accent) replied: "Saturday, mate – I think..." I wondered: "Saturday of what week?"

Time is such a subjective thing. What is a day, a week, a month, when you live continuously in the present? Is this how animals and pre-historic humans understood time? We had lost our feel for it. If you, for instance, asked me if a week of ocean sailing was a long time, I could only say: "I don't know." Sometimes, it felt as if we had been out on the Atlantic forever.

I went back to my guide books, moving on from Doyle to the Lonely Planet Guide to the Eastern Caribbean. Were the people really as friendly as it claimed? Would the mood be as cool as the climate was hot? Would it still be beautiful? I realised it would not be an unspoilt wilderness. For that, we would have to go on to the Venezuelan islands, San Blas and beyond. But even if the Caribbean had become a modern tourist-driven society, I was still very much looking forward to experiencing it. Our hope was to find a few of the pearls of the Caribbean, the flora and fauna and the people. We wished to find some comfortable spots that would welcome us just as we were.

Day 8

I was sitting at the chart table. Karolina had just called me for my night watch and I was still not really awake. It was midnight.

Karolina went to sleep quickly, held in her bunk by the lee cloth, rather than my arms around her. For that, we would have to wait another two weeks.

Still sleepy, I was looking at the radar screen in front of me. No ships or boats in sight, just echoes from the waves close to our own vessel. We had met nothing since the catamaran. The only thing we had seen before that had been a German cargo vessel on its way to Houston, Texas. Two ships in one week. There is not much traffic out here.

The meeting with the German cargo ship had been pleasant, with a nice chat on the VHF, exchanging information about cargo, destinations and Christmas plans. I talked about Christmas in Bequia and explaining we were looking forward to a calm anchorage in the Caribbean, meeting all our friends again. The German watch-keeper said he was envious. They would have left the US by Christmas time, heading for South America. Christmas, he said, would be spent somewhere on the high seas. He reassured me that the rolling was bad on his ship, too. I checked he could see us on his radar and he told us we were making a good echo. We wished each other a good watch and signed off.

I looked at the radar again. Still no ships. No squalls either. Squalls, which form during the night in trade-wind areas and can bring gale-force gusts and heavy rain, are another thing you have to look out for. Most show up quite clearly on the radar.

I yawned and looked at the computer instead. I went through all the emails we had received during our Atlantic crossing so far. Many were funny, a few questioning, some were worried: all were wonderful. I read them through slowly again. Out here, these emails meant a lot to us.

I went up into the cockpit and looked around. A warm tropical breeze welcomed me. Everything was dark, no ship was in sight and Regina seemed pleased. So was I.

I sat next to the second radar screen by the companionway. I leaned back, looked at the stars above, and thought about the friendly emails. One e-mail told of the arrival of winter back home. Snow had fallen. How exotic! It was so difficult to imagine an icy, snowy landscape from Regina's cockpit. I closed my eyes and tried my hardest. In my head, the snowy scene looked charming. Would I want to swap? No. I had spent enough long, dark winters watching the occasional snow get washed away by miserable rain.

I got up from under the spray-hood and stood in my favourite position between the wheel and the hood. There was complete darkness below, a great night sky above, and no navigation lights on the horizon in between.

As so often on night-watch, I felt a bit peckish. I went below to find one of the snacks Karolina thoughtfully prepared for each night. She kept telling me not to eat it all and to leave some for her watch later. I did not always find this easy to manage. I grabbed the flashlight with the red bulb and found some chocolate. What a treat!

I went back to the chart table and checked for new emails. There were two: great! They were both from sailing friends. I read them out loud to myself:

"Enjoy your sail! You might never come closer to Nirvana."

"Caribbean is the closest you can get to Paradise – and you can still return home again."

We were actually enjoying the crossing now. The rolling had eased. We were building experience and learning. It bound us together as a family, spiritually as well as literally. If only every day could be like this, with Regina dancing over the waves, we were happy for her and the sea to be our home.

I smiled and looked at the clock. My watch was nearly over. It was amazing how quickly the hours passed just watching and dreaming.

Time for Karolina to read the two latest emails.

Day 9

On the 3rd of December, 9 days out into the Atlantic, not much happened. And that was the significant thing.

We didn't touch the sails all day. The seas had flattened. The trade winds were pushing us gently westwards. Both Karolina and I had got enough sleep to feel rested. And the friends we talked to via SSB were all doing well.

Still, there were jobs to do. I took apart the toilet pump. The job was overdue as water had been running back into the toilet for the last couple of days. It was an easy task, though not one of my favourites, to swap the outlet valve and clean out the salt deposits. It was all done in less than forty five minutes, and with some new grease the pump felt like new again.

We kept checking the sails and ropes for chafing. Lines can be worn through if you don't take preventative action. We put a piece of garden hose around the sheets where they went through the end of the spinnaker pole. I found some unexpected chafing where a cabbage had been lying on some old charts. The miniature movements of the cabbage had rubbed off big areas of shallow waters and rock warnings. The chart was one from home waters. Luckily we would not be needing that for a while.

There are all sorts of things you have to check for chafing. I had heard of sailors who had found their jackets full of holes after a crossing owing to the constant movements in a locker. I had been urged by family members back home to bring my blazer on the cruise, just in case we got invited somewhere fancy one day. I hadn't looked at it since we had left. I decided to check it tomorrow. Not on this perfect, Atlantic day.

Another uneventful event involved a fish — a large one that made off with our biggest lure and hooks. I remembered Karolina quoting a book that warned against using too big a tackle, as big lures attracted big fish, possibly bigger than you would want. In the tackle shop, however, Dan from Koshlong and I had decided we wanted to catch the biggest fish possible. Maybe, Karolina had been right. If it had been a Dorado, I doubt we would have been strong enough to haul it onboard. And even if we had I think I might just have got bored with eating it for the next fortnight.

We found another plastic-squid lure and a new, smaller hook in our fishing box. We had soon caught another, smaller Dorado for tomorrow's lunch.

If only all days on the Atlantic could be like this.

Day 12

Days ten and eleven were also eventless and enjoyable. Each day was now merging into the ones before and the ones after.

Day 12 was a bit special, however. It was the day we reached half-way. We had sailed 1450 miles since the Canaries and we had 1450 miles to go. We were mid-ocean. Land could not be any further away. We prepared a special mid-Atlantic meal and shared our one and only Atlantic can of beer.

From now on, we started our countdown to our destination, or, as our Swiss friend Rudy proclaimed over the SSB: "We're sailing downhill now!" Reaching the top of a mountain is, indeed, something to celebrate and enjoy. But the descent can be just as challenging. So, our feelings were intense, but mixed. We had completed half our task but still had half to do.

This mid-Atlantic position felt grand, no doubt about that. One fact made this situation especially extraordinary for me, personally. I had never really dreamt about being here before. I had long imagined myself steering in and out of ports, sailing in a warm climate, experiencing atolls, lying on deck, even sailing in gales. But never before had I pictured myself in the middle of the Atlantic. Daydreaming is something I have done a lot of – during boring business meetings, in the car, while jogging or swimming, before getting to sleep or on countless walks home from the office at night. Somehow, I had forgotten, or possibly stopped myself imagining us to be more than a thousand miles from land. But now I was here.

We had not made an Atlantic crossing an explicit part of our sailing plans. It had merely been an option. We had always said to ourselves that we would continue sailing for as long as we pleased. That was also the main reason we had not signed up for the ARC or any other rally. We always wanted to feel free, without any obligations or deadlines. Others we knew had decided to sail with the ARC for the sake of the obligation it brought. They wanted a something that would push them to do it. Without the deadline, the pre-paid entry fee and the group pressure by other participants, they said they might never set off.

Day 15

We had now been sailing for two weeks. There was still nothing but the sky and the ocean surrounding us.

The Atlantic felt infinitely huge and yet it counts for no more than 24% of the total ocean water on our planet. It is impossible to grasp how much sea there is. You can't really appreciate the distance from Europe to America by flying the Atlantic. The speed of the plane distorts distance and time. Sailing forces you to move at a speed better suited to human beings, more like the speed nature designed us for. Five, six, seven knots is the sort of speed men and women have been jogging along at for millions of years. It is only by travelling at this speed, that we can really experience the journey. That's why we walk, cycle or sail.

Over the SSB, the other boats further ahead had started to talk about when they would arrive in the Caribbean, what they would do and how great it would be to drop anchor. We listened to them talking about anchorages in sheltered bays, how they planned to jump into the clear water and how they would sleep a whole night through. I couldn't blame them... but for us it was still some way away.

It sounded appealing. And though we had bonded and worked together fantastically as a family, it would be good to meet some other people for a change. Plus there would be the break from worrying all the time about the boat, the weather and other ocean-users. Being at sea was all right for a time, but we were now not far off being ready for landfall.

Of course, most people who go to the Caribbean do so by plane and have a perfectly good time. Why didn't we travel by plane or car? The reason was that even if we saw the same places, we would not experience them in the same way. Cruising is a life-style and it's a life-style that appeals to us. We did it together and with like-minded friends, none of us worrying too much about where we were going. We had all the belongings we needed with us, including our home. For us, cruising is about growing as a human being, learning to cope with fear and uncertainty, living closely with the ones we care most about. It was about that sense of satisfaction that comes with reaching a new destination solely as a result of your own efforts. It is about comradeship and friends you meet and helping each other without the slightest thought of being compensated.

Day 17
"What - just five more days?" Jessica's voice sounded surprised and almost disappointed.

"We're almost there" Jonathan added, looking at the electronic chart.

I smiled. With just five days left, I felt like I had almost crossed the Atlantic. On the other hand, five days at sea is normally not considered a short passage. We still had some 700 miles to go. I remembered: crossing Biscay had been a matter of 536 miles and from Norway to Scotland had been a mere 280.

The weather had been gentle with us on our crossing so far, but for the whole of Day 17, we fought a succession of squalls. Each brought with it a towering cumulus cloud that grew into a cumulonimbus. These kept us busy with heavy rain and gale-force gusts of wind. One squall took us by surprise. It had been settled for a while so we had switched off the radar. I was doing some schooling in the cockpit with Jessica and Jonathan when suddenly it felt as though the boat had been picked up and thrown forward like a toy. My attention now drawn to the skies behind us, I could see a wall of dark rain approaching rapidly. "Quick! All schoolbooks inside! Let's reef the headsail!"

Karolina switched the radar on and took a look. The squalls that had hit us earlier in the day had been about a mile or so across. This one had a diameter of at least six miles. And we were right on its track.

The spinnaker pole, used to pole out the genoa, was, as usual, locked into position with a fore and aft guy as well as the topping lift. This way the pole is fixed and independent of the sheet. When reefing, the sheet slips easily through the end of the pole. The pole stays exactly where it needs to be for use after the squall. The system worked well and sometimes we left the pole up even when we had the headsail on the opposite side. It might not have looked very pretty but there was no one to see and it was practical. If the wind shifted a bit and we felt we could go back to running wing-and-wing, we could just pull the other sheet.

Best of all, it could all be done from the cockpit and, therefore, by one person on night watch. We had the rule that no one was allowed to leave the cockpit without another member of the crew watching. And leaving the cockpit at night should be avoided completely if possible. Of course, we always used a harness.

We also fixed the boom via the topping lift, main sheet and a preventer. The angle was fixed so that the main sail did not touch the spreaders or any other part of the rig when fully furled out. This meant we sailed slightly less quickly than we might have done but saved the sail from chafe. To use the in-mast furling, we would watch the swing of the mast and put a couple of turns in whenever the pressure on the sail was least. Half a dozen swings and the job was usually done. It was no harder to control than the headsail.

Last, but not least, was the cutter sail, which we hanked onto a removable stay just inside the genoa. If we sheeted that sail tight to leeward while the genoa was boomed to windward, the rolling was reduced quite significantly.

Our fourth sail, the gennaker, we used very little – partly because of the good trade winds and partly because it is quite a handful for a family crew.

As the rain approached from the stern, I quickly winched in the genoa. The rest of the crew did their best to get all cushions away, the schoolbooks inside and the hatches closed. We went below and let the autopilot take a wet and windy watch. After some 20 minutes, it was all over and we were left with fresh-water rinsed deck. The cushions came up again together with the pupils, and school continued until the next squall.

My thoughts were now firmly fixed on that moment in about five days' time when the rolling would be replaced by some gentle rocking at anchor in a quiet bay and Karolina and I could sleep in each other's arms, undisturbed, for an entire night.

Day 20

We were less than 24 hours away. We had had the most beautiful trade wind conditions during these last few days, with small waves and a good breeze of 15-20 knots pushing us rapidly towards our destination.

It was a strange to feel that we would soon leave our private little world out here on the Atlantic. Hadn't I been looking forward to landfall just a couple of days ago? Hadn't I wished our wild ride on the confused seas would soon end? And when squall after squall had gone through, had I not been wondering why we were out here at all?

But there was something limiting my pleasure at approaching dry land. The conflict went on deep inside. I felt a separation from what had become our home for these weeks. I was anxious about the land and the people who would be there. How did you behave in civilisation? Had I forgotten?

The Atlantic had become a home to us, a way of living - just the four of us and Regina. Never before had we spent so much time with just each other. For three weeks, our entire world had consisted of the 12 x 4 m boat and the ocean around us. Our world held everything we needed. We had shelter, food; we caught more fish than we could eat, generated our own water and more than enough power. And now, quite suddenly we were going to leave all this behind.

I wondered whether we could just anchor outside the bay and sit in the cockpit to watch land life from a distance for a while. This way, we could get used to civilisation slowly while still getting the main thing we wanted; a steady boat and a full night's sleep. After one night, we would be ready to go ashore.

After our last Atlantic dinner, all four of us sat in the cockpit, trying to sum up our ocean crossing. It had been our first. We could never do that again. We talked about what we thought of the crossing: if it had lived up to, or been different from, our expectations.

The children had not spent a lot of time thinking about all this. For them, Regina had become their natural home and they didn't seem to miss friends or land. "The Atlantic is great", Jonathan said. "We eat cookies and snacks during night watches!" Jessica liked the fact that we watched movies in the cockpit. I had never heard Jessica and Jonathan quarrel so little; they slept a lot, finding excitement in the fish we caught and the birds we saw. They had adapted completely to this life on an ocean.

I asked Karolina: "What had you not expected?"

Karolina immediately answered: "The lack of seasickness and the relative ease of sleep". Then she continued: "Of course, an ocean crossing is exhausting and I sometimes had difficulties in falling asleep at once, but, on the whole, it worked much better than I had thought."

She was right. After those first three days, we had all moved about without the slightest feeling of sickness. We cooked and baked, we cleaned, we read, we wrote, we carried on our lives. We did every normal task on our rolling home. Obviously, it was more of a challenge when nothing stood still, but we were not the slightest seasick.

Sleep actually worked better than we had expected. I had thought that Karolina and I would hardly meet for three weeks: when one went up, the other one would turn in, with a brief 'hello' in between. It actually worked much better than that. We slept quite well and had a reasonable amount of time together. The children often joined Karolina on the early night watch but otherwise got a good night's rest. During the day, they would take short watches, but always with one of us close at hand.

Karolina now asked me: "Leon, you were very keen on landfall not so long ago. Why was that?"

"The rolling" I replied. "I hate to hear the rig and sails slamming as the waves roll us from side to side. I get irritated when I take out something out of the fridge and everything else in there falls over. I don't like hearing things banging around in lockers or seeing loose things flying around inside the boat."

Squalls were also quite irritating. Our midnight efforts to reef the sails and stop things getting soaked could get tiring. The squalls were quite localised. While we were fighting frequent squalls, boats no more than a hundred miles away had steady winds. Squalls seemed to come in groups, so if you got one, you could almost be certain that this would be a busy night. On other days, we saw no squalls and wondered if the radar was still working.

The Atlantic is also much bigger than I had imagined. We went five days without seeing any other vessel at all. Every so often it felt as if it was never going to come to an end. Those could be anxious times. For Karolina, especially, the fact that the Atlantic is so huge and that help was so far away, was a concern. What if...thoughts could trigger the most horrifying pictures in your mind while you lay restlessly in your berth or when you were ghosting along into blackness on a moonless night. Every time Jonathan or Jessica had the slightest stomach ache, she was reminded of the fact that a hospital was about as accessible to us as it had been ashore during medieval times.

A consolation had always been the SSB radio. To speak with other sailors somewhere on the Atlantic, having similar thoughts, fears and feelings, helped a lot. Knowing that fellow ocean sailors were suffering from just the same confused seas, lack of wind or squalls, was a big reassurance. We were all out here doing our best in similar circumstances. Knowing that you are not alone and are able to speak to friends got us through the most frustrating days.

Karolina, Jessica, Jonathan and I broadly agreed on how we felt about our Atlantic crossing. At the end of our chat we all sat quietly in the cockpit for a long time, watching the Atlantic sunset one last time, looking up at the full moon, listening to the sound of breaking waves around us. The stars came out and it was just like any of the 19 preceding nights on the Atlantic. The only difference was that this was possibly the last.

"Well", I said, breaking the silence. "I better do the dishes and then turn in for our last night at sea." There was a hint of melancholy in my voice. And perhaps a bit of anxiety as well. Were we ready for landfall?

Luckily, the civilisation that seemed so daunting included many of our good friends. We had been missing our cruising friends and looked forward to meeting them again. All in all, I guess I was looking forward to landfall.

As they say on Bequia...

Chapter nineteen

In which we discover Bequia and look back at the crossing

NO COMPLAIN

I guess it was something to do with being at sea for all those weeks but, for the first few days ashore, we found it all a bit overwhelming. There seemed to be so much to do and see. We did not know where to start.

It is fair to say our expectations had not been high. We had heard so often about how the Caribbean had once been a paradise. More-experienced sailors told us how busy it had got over the past 10 years. Many of the books I had read described the deserted anchorages of the days before GPS became common. As it turned out, Bequia, our first proper stop-over, was delightful.

The islands of the eastern Caribbean are now, by and large, developed countries with proper economies based on tourism. We were tourists of a sort: we enjoyed going ashore for a beer in a local bar or to eat or to listen to a steel band. We wanted the services the tourist businesses supplied. We could not really complain about those businesses existing.

Of course, not all tourists are equal. We blue-water cruisers mixed, but did not merge, with people who had flown in and chartered yachts – and did our best not to mix at all with visitors from the big cruise liners. These would arrive and discharge their human cargo for a couple of hours. The visitors would walk slowly to the nearest souvenir shop, some of which only opened for the liners, before returning to the launches and so back to the air-conditioned isolation of their ship. Once night had fallen, the ship would up anchor and move on to the next island. They could visit a lot of islands that way. I wondered whether they really saw any of them.

If you came with higher expectations, of sandy-beached islands all to yourself, then you would need to keep sailing. But for plenty to do, some good service and a great sailing ground, these islands were not bad at all. I was impressed by the ease with which you could get gear for your boat, and by the skill shown by staff in the boatyards. Yes, the boat-boys who rowed up to you at anchor were keen to sell their services, but a polite and clear 'no, thank you' quickly had the desired effect – and a mutual, friendly respect was maintained. Sometimes their services suited us ideally. The laundry boat in Bequia did an excellent job, as did the boat that delivered fresh bread in time for breakfast. My mid-Atlantic fears about returning to civilisation were soon put to one side.

The climate, also, was more pleasant than I'd expected. I had feared it might be too hot and, even worse, too humid for a family from northern Europe. I had fretted about moaning children and the lack of air-conditioning. That turned out to be quite unnecessary. Yes, it did rain every day or, more accurately, every night. Closing hatches half asleep became a habit, as did re-opening them a couple of minutes later. But we soon got used to the regular temperature of just below 30°C (85F). The steady trade winds cooled our bodies, and if that was not enough, a quick splash overboard did the rest. We had no complaints about the climate.

After just a day or two on Bequia we knew we were going to be sad to leave. We were having at least as good a time as we had had since we left Sweden.

But not everybody felt like we did. There were cruisers who had been dreaming and planning and working on the single goal of crossing the Atlantic. Some of them now felt a sense of loss or anti-climax. Having achieved their big life goal, they felt an emptiness. They asked themselves: now what?

We also got to know sailors who had left home telling everyone they planned to sail around the world. After the Atlantic crossing some of them were no longer sure if several more, long ocean passages were what they wanted. What would they do now? How would they explain this change of plans to their friends and family? Or to themselves?

I was glad we had never boasted of plans to cross oceans or to stay away for a particular length of time. And we were not going to start talking about it now. For one thing, we did not know what we were going to do next. As we were, we could take each step at a time. Even if we stopped here and now, I would have been very pleased by what we had done. In some ways, I thought it was a miracle we had come as far as we had.

It was a miracle, but it was true. Six months before we had been just an ordinary family with a little experience sailing on our holidays and now we had reached the American continent. All we had done was take each step at a time. Even if you travel slowly, if you keep going, you will cover a long distance. We had been just like anyone with a dream but we had lived that dream.

Looking around among our fellow sailors, I realised that they were much like the people I knew at home. They were not eccentric adventurers who had broken all ties with society. They were normal people who just wanted to do something different with a little piece of their lives. They had cut one (or more) centimetres out of their life-tape and had gone looking for something new.

The Atlantic crossing had been the means by which we'd reached this place and this state of mind. It had been an adventure, and none of us regretted doing it. Having said that, none of us particularly wanted to go back to sea any time soon. We agreed the crossing had been hard work, both mentally and physically but, chiefly, mentally.

I was glad I had kept a diary during the crossing. Otherwise, the days would have merged in my memory. Karolina thought an ocean crossing was a bit like giving birth: you forget the hard parts and, eventually, you are ready to have another baby. After a while we might all be ready to go again – but not yet. We wanted to keep the anchor buried in the sand for a while longer.

Life on Bequia was very relaxed. We were all on 'island time' as it's called. Our Norwegian friend Trond from Coconut said the Caribbean islands were like the mañana countries but without the rush. I stopped wearing my watch. I didn't need it. The shops seldom stuck to their own opening hours. And the sun was enough to tell whether there was time for a jog or if it was already 'beer o'clock'.

Just now the sun told me it was time for a drink at the Frangipani. Getting together with fellow sailors, sipping on a rum punch and listening to a local band was Caribbean life at its best. I closed my eyes. The beat reached right into my heart. It wasn't easy to resist the call of those drums. Some of us were already dancing on the sand. I opened my eyes. I really was here.

The children were running around on the beach desperately trying to open a coconut they had found. Others had discovered some banana leaves and tried to plait with them. Friends were passing by, saying 'hello' or stopping for a drink, everyone talking about how lucky we were to be here. Only Steve was a bit quiet. He was thinking about the fact that he would soon be flying back to England.

"It's almost a pity it's so good..." Steve murmured. "The crossing and Bequia and all this were much more fun than I expected." He lifted his rum punch, holding it against the setting sun as if to check the match of the colours. "If it had been merely OK to crew across the Atlantic and spend a few days here, I might even have been looking forward to getting home by now. But this is not something I want to cut short. As soon as I get back, I will be dreaming about cruising the Caribbean."

We all felt sorry for Steve and grateful that we were staying. I wondered whether it might have been better for Steve if he had never had a taste of this life.

After a short pause listening to the steel band and watching the children playing on the beach, Sophie from Sarah Grace asked us how we felt our lives had been changed by going cruising. Karolina said she thought the lows were lower and the highs higher. And she wasn't sure if those ups and downs were better or worse than the relative stability of our old lives. Ever the mathematician, I asked her to average her net happiness over time and to arbitrate for sea or shore-based living. Everyone laughed, except Steve, who looked as if he were doing his own calculation.

The group went quiet and thoughtful again. The drums played on. I broke the silence: "The ups and downs you mention, Karolina, seem to me to be a good thing. Our days are no longer predictable. My old life was boring compared to this."

With the exception of one or two medical upsets, our old lives had been predictable. When I woke up in the morning I had a clear picture of what the day would offer. My meetings were planned, my calendar was full. There was hardly any room to do something spontaneous. Living was a matter of following the schedule. My watch, my Microsoft Outlook: these were my managers.

When unexpected things did happen, there was almost always a solution. If something needed repairing, we called an engineer. If we were ill, we called a doctor. Until someone close to us had a brush with cancer, I had lived my life as if I had known when I was going to die and could plan the whole of my three score years and ten. I learned in the oncology clinic that it could be too late, that you might not have a whole life-tape to enjoy. That was one of the things that made me snip the centimetre from the middle of the measuring tape. For me, one of the biggest dangers of a 'traditional' life is that it doesn't prepare you for the unpredictable. Better, I think, the ups and downs of cruising.

I looked around the gang seated on the veranda of the Frangipani. Some were smiling, some were not. Karolina was right about the highs and lows. This wasn't the perfect life. Perfection was not what we wanted. But it was good. We had no cause to complain.

Our Caribbean Christmas

SAILS FOR THE TRADES

The whole point of sailing in the trade wind zone is to get a steady downwind run. Non-stop downwind sailing can cause problems with chafe and rolling. It is also necessary to plan for squalls, especially at night.

One important thing to do is to make sure the boom you use to pole out the genoa is secured independent of the sheet. It should have a foreguy, aftguy and lift. The sheet simply runs through the eye. That way you will be able to roll the genoa without losing control of the pole.

The classic rig is two genoas, boomed on both sides with no main. Generally, this requires a second stay but some people manage with just a second slot in the furler foil. A little bit of main sheeted in tight can reduce rolling.

If you've only one genoa or a main that's large compared to your foresails, you will need to use the main. Setting up a preventer from the end of the boom to a block at the bow and back to the cockpit will allow you to lock the main boom in a position that's safe, right for the wind and avoids chafe on the shrouds. In this set-up, a storm jib or cutter sail sheeted tight will help reduce rolling.

Squalls tend to run in parallel lines so a small shift north or south can help you avoid them. If you are able to receive live routing advice onboard, this can help. Keep a watch out astern and, at night, if you have the battery power, use the radar. Reefing with furling sails should be straightforward. Reducing a slab-reef main or hanked foresails is going to require more crew on deck.

The strongest crews fly a gennaker or spinnaker. The winged type of spinnaker is becoming more popular but they are still quite rare on family boats.

Prepare for chafe by taping over anything likely to come in regular contact with a sail or sheet. You can temporarily stick strips of repair tape onto the sails themselves. And running rigging can be protected with tape or fabric tubing. You should have plenty of time, so experiment with different set-ups. That will also spread the wear.

A sister-ship off Bequia

A turtle off the Tobago Cays

Chapter twenty
In which we get very close to paradise

THE TROPICAL ARCHIPELAGO

I was holding the chart in my right hand. My thumb was strategically placed between two islands and a rock. This was Regina's current position. My left hand was holding the wheel and my eyes were eagerly scanning the vicinity, identifying the individual islands close by.

It was a lot like sailing back home in the Baltic. Navigating narrow channels, matching islands on the chart to those around us and finding a passage around various underwater hazards was nothing new. An incorrect identification, an uncertain bearing, a course just off the track, and we would literally be on the rocks. But we were confident in our eyeball navigation and it was good to have the added excitement after so much deep-sea sailing.

Though they may require quite similar pilotage skills, the Grenadines are, of course, very different from islands in the Baltic. Instead of underwater rocks, it is reefs you have to be wary of; pelicans take the place of sea gulls, and there are more palm trees than pines. "God must be a sailor," a friend once told me. "That's why He created the Caribbean."

We had fallen utterly in love with the Grenadines. These islands, which include Bequia, stretch from St Vincent in the north to Grenada in the south, with just a few miles of open water between each.

Our current island hopping consisted of passages of between five and twenty miles. Sailing days were between one and four hours - hardly worth getting the sails up. And when we did, it was mainly to enjoy the sailing for itself. We were taking it easy, just as the islanders did. Why rush? We found time for school, snorkelling and socialising with our ever-increasing circle of sailing friends.

The Grenadines is not a big archipelago but, if you have the right attitude and can settle properly into 'island time', you can easily spend a month here without feeling idle for a moment. After the Atlantic crossing, it is great to be able to relax somewhere like this. Enjoying the Grenadines at 'dead slow ahead' was just what we needed.

We approached from the north. I identified Mayreau, passed the Baleine Rocks to port and kept clear of One Fathom Bank, which, as the name suggests, is less than two metres deep. The colour of the sea faded from dark blue to a stunning light turquoise. We could clearly see the white-sand sea-floor beneath the boat. We weaved deeper and deeper into the group of islands called the Tobago Cays, making our way carefully between two beautiful islands called Petit Rameau and Petit Bateau and out into a wider stretch of water protected from the Atlantic by the half-submerged Horseshoe Reef. The anchor dug immediately into the clean sand, holding perfectly. The only sound was the gentle trade wind, whispering a welcoming tune.

There are no buildings on the palm-fringed islands. They looked as though they had been cut and pasted from a story book. I found it hard to believe that they were real.

Of course, Regina was not the only yacht now anchored in the lee of Horseshoe Reef. This was the twenty-first century Caribbean, after all. Never mind. I did not think it was any less beautiful for all the yachts moored around us. There were more than a couple of boats we recognised. Our friends, also, were taking their time to enjoy the Grenadines.

"Wouldn't it be a shame to leave the Caribbean now?" I said to Karolina as we both took in the incredible view. "If we were going to go on through the Panama Canal, it's about now that we would need to get moving."

"You're right", Karolina replied. "Let's do that next time. This time we can explore and enjoy the Caribbean. It's just too wonderful to hurry."

We stood holding hands on the foredeck with our bare feet feeling the warmth of the teak. The sun was just about to set over Petit Bateau and the full moon was rising over the Atlantic. It had certainly been a long and strenuous journey to get here from Europe but now we were here we realised the reward was worth it.

"Dad, Dad, look there!" Jonathan came rushing from the cockpit to join us. "I recognise this island." Jonathan pointed east, over Horseshoe Reef to the tiniest of all the palm-fringed islands. "It's the island where Jack Sparrow finds the rum in 'Pirates of the Caribbean', isn't it? I want to go there tomorrow with the dinghy to see if there is any rum left. I can see on the chart that there is a gap in the reef for the dinghy. Can we do that? Pleeeaaase!"

He was right. Petit Tabac, as the island is called, was the place where Johnny Depp's character was left to starve. Luckily, he found rum to keep him going. It was no surprise the island had been chosen by the movie-makers. It looked absolutely fabulous. I wondered whether we would find our own treasure trove.

"Regina, Regina this is Keoma, over". A familiar voice on the VHF interrupted our planning for the following day. "Welcome to the Cays, Regina. We wondered whether you would like to come over for a glass of wine before dinner? White Haven with their children Emma and Georgia will come as well. All the kids are keen to see Jessica and Jonathan again. And tomorrow they want to go snorkelling to show you the turtles and the fish! I'll call Koshlong, too, and see if they want to come. Over."

Of course we all wanted to go. Jonathan and eight girls gathered in the saloon, while the adults sat in the cockpit, enjoying a glass of wine. I don't think we had ever had such a busy social life. Saying 'goodbye' in one harbour before meeting again in some other anchorage was part of the routine of cruising life. And, of course, every time we met, we had to have a reunion and that meant a glass (or two) of wine.

The following day, none of the kids wanted to miss a swim with the turtles, or the chance of snorkelling on the coral reefs. We had a short school session in the morning and then dedicated the remainder of the day to underwater activities. We found turtles around and under the anchored boats, grazing on the seaweed that grew close to the islands. The children took it in turns to hold their breath and dive down to swim with a turtle. Some turtles appeared not even to notice but just carried on munching.

But the best snorkelling was out by the reef. Here there are small buoys to which you can tie up a dinghy so avoiding having to drop an anchor and damage the coral.

"Hey! This is like Finding Nemo." Jessica told me as I sat on the side of the dinghy pulling on my fins. "Look down here. It's Doris! Well, hundreds of Dorises, actually!" Jessica put her snorkel back into place and was gone, diving further and further down in the warm water. She was as excited as I was happy. Jonathan followed her with the underwater camera, looking to capture some of the magic of this new, undersea world. This was our first really great day's snorkelling and firmly established it as one of our favourite things to do.

Jonathan got his trip to Petit Tabac a couple of days later when the surf was low enough to let us dinghy through the reef. It was every bit as beautiful as in the film. But if there was any treasure or rum left, we did not find it.

Our next stop was quite a contrast to the unspoilt wilderness of the Tobago Cays. The privately owned island of Mustique is an example of what happens when people with money try to turn paradise into perfection. This highly-manicured island is kept in a state of pristine (and quite un-Caribbean) neatness by its extremely wealthy occupants. It was originally purchased by an eccentric Scotsman called Colin Tennant in 1958. He wanted somewhere that would appeal to his aristocratic friends. Today, there are about a hundred luxury homes, many owned by international celebrities.

Everything on Mustique is where it should be. There are benches perched where the view is best, there are shaded picnic tables with barbeques on the beaches; even the palm trees appear to have been carefully positioned. There are litterbins all over the island and plenty of neat, paved roads for the 'mules' (the sort of cross between a golf cart and a jeep that make up the only motorised transport). It's not to everybody's taste but we thought it was extraordinary. We liked Mustique for what it is.

Given the wealth and fame of the people who come here to holiday, it is surprising how welcome visitors are made to feel. No professional photographers are allowed on the island and no photographs are allowed of the houses or gardens but otherwise it's very relaxed. Particularly welcome are yachtsmen. We spent three days tied up to a mooring buoy a couple of hundred yards from the dock. In northern Europe, we often had to pay the top-rate harbour dues – those for yachts of over 40 feet. In Mustique, we were in the cheapest yacht category. Above us were rates for 71 to 85 feet, 86 to 100 feet and over 100 feet. You get a different sort of yacht visiting Mustique.

I put on my new island-style shirt and a pair of clean shorts so as to be suitably neat and tidy. Just up from the dinghy dock is Basil's Bar and Restaurant. Here, you can meet, drink, eat and look out for celebrities.

A bit further along is the bakery and a wine shop. The wine shop is impressive. There's an air-conditioned room filled with bottles of the world's finest wines, plus a big display of fine Swiss chocolate. Next along is a food store with a selection of groceries from the entire world, even Swedish meatballs. Clearly, only the best is good enough for Mustique people. In the fashion boutique, Karolina and I could not resist buying a new sun-hat each as a souvenir.

Higher up the street, you come to the school for families living and working on the island. Close to the school, is an impressive library and playground. There are stables for horses, a tennis club and, finally, at the northern tip of the island, an airstrip. All the gardens are beautifully kept. Each looks like a prize-winner.

Some of us visiting yachties could not resist trying to spot a celebrity or two. I did not play, as I would not recognise a celebrity if he or she walked up and shook my hand. Dan from Koshlong played a little joke on one group of island visitors. He was out jogging when he was passed by a group of visitors on an island tour in the back of a 'mule'. Dan quickly pulled his cap down low over his sunglasses and stared hard down at the pavement. As the 'mule' went by he heard a lot of excited whispering. When he looked up he saw it had stopped a hundred yards past him and the occupants were pointing and talking. Who Dan was meant to be, I don't know, but he certainly made the day for one group of sightseers.

We sailed on to nearby Mayreau and bought live lobsters from the boat boys. We gathered on Koshlong's aft deck to cook them on the barbeque. With garlic butter and lime, together with Karolina's freshly baked baguettes, they were delicious. We opened a bottle of Chablis we had brought from Sweden for an occasion like this. Best of all, perhaps, was the fact that we were sharing all this with our friends from Koshlong. We had grown close as we had sailed together since meeting on Porto Santo. Our children got along well and so did the adults. We made plans for the future – the sort of plans that have neither clear beginnings nor endings.

Sharing moments like these with our children was a particular joy. I was so pleased that they and their friends would have this time to look back on for the rest of their lives. The fact that Dan and Sue and Karolina and I had all taken the risks to make this possible bound us all the more closely.

I leant back, my belly filled with delicious lobster. We could hear the kids down below playing happily together. Jessica and Jonathan were by now almost fluent in English and had no problem communicating with their Canadian friends. They laughed and giggled while we adults moved on to the very serious subject of food. Wherever we cruised we tried to cook like the locals. After lobster, we decided, the next thing to try was conch or 'lambi' as it's usually called in the Caribbean. We had seen thousands of conch shells abandoned on the beaches. They were beautiful but a bit big to take home as souvenirs.

At our next stop, Union Island, the coolest place for a drink was a bar on a tiny island built out of thousands of conch shells piled on a submerged reef. You could only get to it by dinghy or swimming. The barkeeper had named it 'Happy Island'.

As far as we were concerned, these were all 'Happy Islands'.

DIESEL AND GAS

Sourcing, monitoring and looking after your diesel and gas supplies are some of the most important routine jobs while cruising.

Diesel that has been contaminated by water is one of the most common sources of engine trouble. Try to buy from places where the turn-over is high but, if you can, avoid buying just after a new delivery when the tanks will have been stirred up. Use a filter funnel designed to exclude water, if in any doubt. This will make filling up a slow process but is worth it in the long run and is especially important if you've bought from a barrel in an out-of-the-way part of the world.

To avoid having bacteria grow in your tanks, always add biocide after filling up. And, in case your fuel filter does get clogged up, always carry plenty of spares. A small hand pump will allow you to check the condition of the diesel at the bottom of your tanks. It should look clean with no water separating out below.

The main problems with gas are that different parts of the world tend to offer different types and some places will allow you to refill empty bottles while other countries insist on you exchanging an empty tank for a full one. The two main varieties are Butane and Propane. Sometimes you will get a mixture of both. Butane is stored at lower pressure, so you can put Butane in a Propane bottle but not the other way around.

In parts of Europe, Camping Gaz dominates the market. This is Butane. In Northern Europe and the Caribbean, Propane is more common. If you are starting from Europe heading for the Caribbean, therefore, it is probably better to search out some Propane bottles. If you're sailing for a while in the Mediterranean, you could buy an extra Camping Gaz bottle just for your stay there. Steel bottles will rust but you can get aluminum or GRP. GRP is both lightweight and allows you to see how much is left inside. The other way to monitor your supplies is by weighing. You should be able to do this with a fishing scale.

Gas is potentially dangerous so check the instructions on your stove and consult a registered dealer if in any doubt. Regularly check your gas alarm.

Carry plenty of gas if you can. Although you'll eat more salads in the tropics, you're also likely to bake more bread.

More watery fun off the Tobago Cays

Racing in Grenada

NOW FOR NOW

Two guys, up to their chests in water, held the boat in the surf about ten yards from the beach. They were waiting for their skipper, who had to run from the start down to the water and wade out to the boat, before they could begin the race. The boat — a classic wooden work-boat of about fifteen foot with a simple bamboo rig — was rocking wildly from side to side as the waves swept under it and up to the sand. As her mast tipped away from the beach, her starboard hull emerged from the bright blue water and flashed her name at me. 'Now for Now' was that name. "That's right," I whispered to myself. "Take now for now, Leon, don't worry so much about the future."

I didn't want to, but sometimes I just couldn't stop my thoughts drifting away from the present to the future and my worries about what would come after this adventure. We were in Grenada waiting for the Le Mans-style start of the annual regatta for local boats. The official shouted "go" and the skippers raced down the beach to their boats. As soon as each was on board, the crew jumped in too, and they all set off around the course out in the bay.

The reverse happened at the finish. The skipper had to jump into the water before the boat grounded and run up the beach to cross the finish-line. Some jumped too early and had to swim. First prize was $1000, and the runner-up claimed $500, so there was plenty at stake.

The crews raced hard, taking it all very seriously. And I, too, was in a serious frame of mind. I was thinking about jobs, challenges, the family, school, as well as home-water, holiday sailing. What would all that be like now that we had discovered the freedom of blue water sailing? I wondered how long we should and could carry on as we were. Our current plan was to head back to Europe in the coming spring. One year away ought to be enough, we now thought. We had already been away for eight months. We were nearer the end of our trip than the beginning.

Was I complaining about the fact that we had just six months left of sailing?

Who wouldn't be more than happy to have six *weeks* of sailing during their usual annual holiday?

But it wasn't the number of weeks or months to go that worried me. It was the whole business of going back to a new life ashore after we had spent so long cruising. We had forgotten what a normal life was all about. Either that or we no longer wanted to know.

This was odd. Before we set off we had had endless discussions about leaving our secure and well-regulated shore lives, always a bit fearful of making the leap into the uncertainty of cruising. Now we faced the same step but from the opposite side. And from Grenada's Grand Anse Beach, looking out at the racing work-boats and the ocean beyond, that step looked even bigger than it had at home in Sweden. Would we ever be able to make the goals of shore life our goals again? Would Karolina and I be able to find jobs that were interesting and stimulating but also gave us enough of the space and freedom we had tasted while away?

Earlier that day, I had gone to the locker for a clean T-shirt and had looked at all the fleece jackets stored at the back. I wondered why anyone would want to live somewhere where jackets like that were needed almost every day. I had thought about having to wear socks again and having my feet pressed into tight and uncomfortable shoes. I would no longer be able to wiggle my toes. Even more frightening was the thought of having a tie knotted around my neck. Worst of all, though, was the watch. The watch that would always be ready to remind me of the fact that I was running late for whatever I was doing, shouting at me to speed up, taking no notice of where I was or what I was doing or what I could do.

When the cruise was over, would I forget all I had learned about 'island time' and the Caribbean way to manage stress?

Shore life looked frightening. Just think of how an ordinary day started: An alarm clock would be ringing in the dark, shaking us out of our sweetest dreams, urging us to rouse the rest of the family and get breakfast eaten and cleared away by a fixed time. There it was again, that watch shouting at me. I wondered whether I would forget how it felt to wake up in the fore-peak of Regina shortly after sunrise? Would I remember the open hatch - fresh air all around us and a blue sky welcoming us to another sunny day?

What if we stopped, went back and then really, really regretted leaving the bright colours of the tropics? Would we then start dreaming about coming back or would we come to terms with our new shore lives? I didn't even know what I should hope for. Stopping cruising now felt every bit as risky as starting once had.

I looked at 'Now for Now' again. She was doing well but would have to pull something out of the bag on the downwind leg if she was going to finish among the prizes. She was right. I should stop worrying about the future.

Every afternoon, at five o'clock, the gang would assemble for 'happy hour' and half-price beers at the True Blue Bay Resort bar. More and more yachts joined, and soon our 'board meeting', as we called it, took in half a dozen boats every night. Here, we talked about the right time to sail back to Europe – or the possibility of not going. Some of our friends thought that a one-year plan was more than enough. Others felt that bringing the boat here was the big thing. They could now leave the boat and come back another year by plane. Others talked about living on the boat during the hurricane season, in somewhere like Venezuela, and spending the season learning Spanish. There were also boats planning to sail north to Maine or Canada. There was no lack of options.

One thing we all agreed on was that the way we currently lived could not be called a vacation. We had exchanged one full-time job for another. Instead of taking the car to the office every morning, we spent most of our days with home schooling and boat maintenance. The day ended a bit earlier than back home but it had started earlier, too. And though our 'board meetings' were more relaxed than their shore-based equivalents we rarely had more than a couple of beers, and the issues discussed were no less serious than any balance sheet.

Leaving tropical cruising would mean giving up something we had all worked hard to achieve and enjoyed a lot. But there were some things some of us would not be sad to leave behind. Simple tasks like grocery shopping, laundry, spare-part hunting or boat repairs could take days longer than they would at home. One director told the board that she was looking forward to a bit of time off from cruising. Everyone with children agreed that schooling was difficult and time-consuming. It would be a relief to hand the children back to professional teachers, at least for a few hours a day.

While cruising, getting time on your own either to do a job or just to get away and have time to think, took some organising. You couldn't just sneak off for a bit, especially if you were at anchor and going anywhere meant getting the dinghy out. "Where's Mum?" was often heard the minute mother disappeared, even if she had only gone to the stern cabin to stow something. If either of us was going ashore to get something, one of the children would always ask if they could come. It was wonderful to spend time together as a family, but now and again it could get a bit intense.

Another regular item on the directors' agenda was the question of when would be 'next time'. Cruising without children, we agreed, would be different. For a start, there was the question of what we would do all day. Rudy and Lilian from Switzerland, who were not sailing with children, just laughed. With their aluminium boat, they didn't even need to polish or paint to keep everything shipshape and shiny. They admitted that they were reading a lot of books and planned to learn to scuba dive. I wondered whether this would be how Karolina and I would cruise 'next time'.

A few things we were certain of. We would spend more time in northwest Spain. We would then head for Madeira and, from there, would go straight to the western isles of the Canaries, particularly La Gomera, which we had liked so much. 'Next time', we reckoned, we would stop in the Cape Verde islands and make landfall in Barbados. We might stay in the Caribbean for a year or two and then we could go to Venezuela, Los Roques in particular, and on to the ABC islands for scuba diving. This was what Rudy and Lilian were planning to do. Another director dreamed of San Blas in Panama. Cuba, Dan interjected, would be very interesting. Others talked about Costa Rica, Mexico and Belize. And then, of course, there was the big one: through the Panama Canal to the South Pacific.

As happy hour moved on, the more ambitious the future plans became. What remained difficult was 'this time'. What exactly would we do now and how would we feel about it?

The sun had already set and we were just about to break up and go back to our boats to prepare supper when we agreed an important resolution. We would not spend so much time worrying about the future. 'Now for Now' would be our mission statement. Our goal would be to enjoy the good fortune we had.

When we were there Grenada was still badly scarred by Hurricane Ivan. In five hours in September 2004, Ivan had ripped up much of what had been built or grown in five hurricane-free decades. The island had been transformed – and no one had had the slightest chance of affecting what had happened. Worrying about the future, I concluded, did not help. The challenge was to do what the Grenadans had done, and retain the strength and determination to start again – no matter what.

It was impressive to see how quickly some houses had been rebuilt. There were shiny, new roofs right next to houses that had been totally wrecked. Almost every building had lost its roof to Ivan and the trees had emerged from the storm with hardly a single leaf. I thought about the courage and strength it must have taken to re-build after that. Worrying had not helped, I thought. The Grenadans had acted.

Among the businesses that had got themselves back onto their feet was the well-known Spice Island Marina on the south side of the island. Everything in the yard was back to normal now. Thinking about the sea miles that lay ahead, we booked Regina in for a haul-out, two new coats of anti-fouling, some wax and polish on the hull and some new anodes.

We were very happy on Grenada and in no hurry to leave. The island was beautiful and the people were friendly. They had taken Ivan in their stride and didn't seem to worry about future hurricanes. They trusted it would all work out in one way or another. And so, we decided to go with 'now for now': to enjoy Grenada and to put off our worries about shore life until later.

I was not the only one of the family to find living in the present difficult. Jonathan would have done anything to speed up time to make him just a little bit older.

One morning, we heard an unfamiliar sound. It was only just audible and sounded like sobbing. Indeed, it was Jonathan lying in the saloon. Karolina put her arms around him and asked what was wrong. "Nothing", he said quietly. "Nothing". And then he asked quietly: "How old is Otti, Mummy?"

"Well, Otti is eleven, like Jessica", Karolina answered, and then Jonathan burst out in tears. "Why couldn't you have given birth to me just twenty days earlier?" he asked, desperately. Karolina smiled and explained to Jonathan that he had arrived ten days earlier than expected as it was.

Karolina began to understand. Otti from Sarah Grace had signed up for the Junior Open Water Diving course, something Jonathan had been dreaming about ever since he got his snorkel and fins. The sport's governing body, PADI, had recently reduced the minimum age for this course from twelve to ten so Otti could do it but Jonathan could not. He was too young by precisely 20 days.

We felt sorry for Jonathan. On the other hand, we both thought ten was quite young to be scuba diving in open water. And the theory test looked tough – even for Otti, who would be tackling it in her first language. But none of these arguments impressed Jonathan. He was desperately unhappy to miss out on the diving.

Nevertheless, we went to the True Blue Bay dive shop to find out more about the PADI courses for children. To our surprise, we found courses to suit both Jessica, who wanted something a bit simpler than the full agenda, and for Jonathan. Jessica could do a 'Discover scuba' programme and Jonathan could do something called the 'Bubblemaker', an introduction to diving for children of eight years or over. The main difference between the two was that 'Bubblemakers' went no lower than six feet or two metres while the 'Discover' students could go down 40 feet or twelve metres.

We decided the courses could be early birthday presents for Jonathan and Jessica. In the end, then, Otti from Sarah Grace, Emma from Koshlong and Jessica and

Jonathan went for a day's introduction to scuba diving. Otti and Emma both went on to complete successfully the whole Open Water Diver's Certificate.

As far as the children were concerned, diving was the coolest thing they had done for a long time. After a bit of school in the morning, they all went to the pool, tried on the scuba gear and practised safety measures. After lunch it was time to go out to the reef for a real dive. A launch took them out to the spot, which was said to be good for sea horses. Otti, Emma and Jessica all went down about twenty feet or seven metres, while Jonathan was happy diving in shallower water. He now had a taste of what it was all about and would put lots of effort into his English lessons to help him pass the Open Water certificate.

Grenada is quite mountainous and one of the best things to do away from the shore is to hike up to one of the many waterfalls and cool off with a dip under the cascading stream. With Sarah Grace and Koshlong, we hired a mini-bus taxi to take us up to start of one of the trails. The driver dropped us off, pointed in the direction of the trail and told us he would be back to pick us up at five. He roared away, reggae blasting out, and we were left in the quiet calm of the rain forest.

The path got steeper and steeper and, in places, was quite muddy. It was cooler up here but humid. Now and again the path fell away quite steeply and we had to hang onto the bamboo trees to stop us from slipping. After half an hour's walking we reached the Seven Sisters waterfall. It was more beautiful than I expected, with a pretty pool stretching out below the fall itself. There was nothing for it but to strip off and go swimming. The cool, refreshing water soon washed away my worries about the future.

After we'd done the anti-fouling and other jobs on Regina and she was back in the water, we took her to the next bay along from True Blue, to one of the quietest anchorages we ever found, tucked behind Hog Island. We had decided to leave Grenada in a day or two and begin to make our way back north. I stood on the foredeck and looked around at the other anchored boats, the mangroves and the reefs beyond. The wind had dropped as the sun had neared the horizon and there was now barely a ripple on the water. As the wind fell away, so did my cares. Batteries, engines, charging, oil-changes, laundry, schooling, even my worries about the future: it all faded away.

It had taken a full month of living on Grenada, but I had finally learned to take 'now for now'.

Seven Sisters waterfall, Grenada

GARBAGE

Dealing with garbage on a boat can be a problem. On passage, no right-minded sailor would ever throw anything that wouldn't decompose over the side and, at anchor, there is still the issue of taking bags ashore in the tender and finding a place that will deal with it responsibly. Most boat boys are honest but some may take your money and then dump your bags behind a bush. To be sure, deal with it yourself. On the more commercialised islands, such as the BVIs, it is not uncommon (or unreasonable) to be charged for dumping rubbish, especially if you're not paying marina or mooring fees.

But if you always think about garbage disposal when you buy, you can greatly reduce the amount of waste you generate. Leave any superfluous packaging ashore, especially thick cardboard, which may contain cockroach eggs. Look instead for thin, light containers, which can be washed, folded and stored after use. Some containers are conical and stow neatly within each other when empty. Aluminum cans should be crushed and plastic bottles cut up with scissors. At the end of our first Atlantic crossing we had collected only four medium-sized bags of garbage.

Hazardous items, such as alkaline batteries, are best kept on board until you get somewhere capable of dealing with them. Needless to say, old engine oil and boat batteries should both be properly recycled.

Traditional work boats, Grenada

Europe calling?

Chapter twenty two

*In which we visit a little bit of France and
get a feel for old England*

A FORETASTE OF OUR RETURN

"What do you think? Shall I pick it up?" There was something naughty in Charlie's voice. A telephone might be an everyday item for most people, but for a sailor used to VHF, SSB and Iridium, the ring of an ordinary land-line phone is something out-of-the-ordinary, especially when the ring emanates from a public booth. "Well, why not?" responded my generally well-mannered wife, Karolina.

I was walking behind Charlie and Karolina, talking to Charlie's wife, Juliet. Charlie ducked into the booth and picked up the handset. "Hello". We could hear chatter coming down the earpiece. "Oh, I don't speak French so well. I'm from England", Charlie said to the caller. Monsieur paid no attention. "Je...ne...parle...pas... bien.... le Français. Un moment s'il vous plaît.... Ici, un homme qui parle Français", and, with that, Charlie handed the receiver to me.

Somewhat taken aback, I had a go with the best of my school-boy French. "Allô?" I tried. Monsieur continued his monologue in French. I couldn't follow it all but I could make out that he wanted to know to whom he was talking and where in France we were. I tried to explain that he had actually called a public telephone in the Caribbean and not his aunt in Paris, or wherever.

"Ici, ce n'est pas la France", was the best I could manage even though I knew that this was in fact untrue. Technically, we were in France. The Iles des Saintes are not only technically a part of France but culturally and spiritually French, too. Everything was French: from the gendarmerie to the cars, from the cafés to the currency. If you look closely at a Euro note, you can see the French Caribbean islands in a little box of their own.

So, in a way, we had come home, and it felt rather odd.

The contrast with Grenada could not have been bigger. We had sailed north for just two days and two nights and had travelled from the most laid-back of Caribbean islands to modern France.

I was beginning to regret taking the handset. "Alors, ce n'est pas la France normale," I said, trying to be more precise. "Nous sommes aux Iles des Saintes. Ce sont des îles d'Antilles. En Amérique, vous savez? Et je suis dans une cabine téléphonique, et vous m'avez appelé, n'est-ce pas?" Charlie and Karolina were now laughing loudly.

The poor Monsieur told me - well, I think this is what he told me - that he had been given this number and was returning a call. He was convinced that I was the one who had called him. "Je ne crois pas, Monsieur. Je ne sais rien du tout!", which, again, was a bit of a fib, since I knew a few things he didn't, such as where I was. We ended the conversation, not entirely clear which of us was the more confused.

In many ways, it was good to be back in France. The restaurants all gave off that lovely smell of garlic and herbs. The shops stocked French wine and cheeses at what appeared to be subsidised prices. Without that, I guess, a Frenchman could not survive so far from his territoire. The words *liberté, égalité, fraternité* came to have a new meaning for me: the freedom to move to a wonderful climate, the same rights to enjoy good wine and cheese and fraternity with the French people at large. Every morning, I took the dinghy ashore and came back with fresh *baguettes*, with which we ate *brie* or *confiture* while sipping a large cup of *café au lait*. The coffee was actually the same as we always had but here, in the Iles des Saintes, it definitely tasted more like *café au lait*.

Less good was the fact that along with all this European-style sophistication came quite a lot of European-style stress. Staff in the cafés served us efficiently and quickly but with none of the happy faces we had got used to further south. 'Island time' was not something that applied to the French islands. Some of our gang found the islanders a bit unfriendly, but we did not. They were just lacking the laid-back, 'take-it-easy, man' attitude we had come to love so much.

From this little bit of France, we decided to head for Antigua, which, though independent, is still clearly marked by the many years it was a British colony. March 5th, which is both Jessica and Jonathan's birthday, was coming up and we wanted to be with as many of their friends as possible for the big day. So, we said *au revoir* to the Iles des Saintes and set off on the 85 miles north to Antigua.

Antigua is in many ways the sailing Mecca of the Caribbean. Antigua Week is the biggest race week of the season. There is also the Antigua Classic Week. The Blue Water Rally stops here and it was the finish for the Atlantic rowers. Remember those rowing boats getting ready for the off just as we too were stocking up in La Gomera in November? Well, we arrived in Antigua just in time to see one of them - Roz Savage - become the first solo woman ever to complete the race, after an amazing 103 days at sea.

I found it hard to imagine what it must be like to row for 103 days and nights on the Atlantic, alone. Roz's boat was 24 feet long. Storms broke or damaged all four oars on board. She lost her camping stove before Christmas and had not eaten a hot meal since. And her satellite phone had stopped working four weeks from the finish. This was some adventure.

As Roz rowed the last few miles into English Harbour, a flotilla of yachts and boats went out to meet her. Hundreds lined the quayside, including a choir of local schoolchildren. There was a huge cheer as she finally reached land, safety, glory and a hug from her mother. There were many inspiring moments on our trip but this was one of the best. When I last heard, Roz was planning to row the Pacific. I wish her all the luck in the world.

Roz's boat, once she had escaped it for a comfortable hotel, was berthed next to one of the enormous super-yachts that gather in English Harbour and the neighbouring Falmouth Harbour during the sailing season. It was smaller than many of the dinghies carried by these yachts. These dinghies are stored in lower-deck 'garages' and launched via hydraulic cranes or ramps. The really smart thing, we learned, was to have a whole separate 'shadow' boat just to carry these 'toys'.

This was the first time we had been really close to some of these palaces of the sea and it felt strange. One day Karolina was queuing up to pay our harbour dues. (You have to pay even just to anchor in English or Falmouth Harbours.) While she was counting her cash and making sure she had the necessary $50 for the week, the man in front paid his bill with a card. It was for $1,595. The charge, we were glad to learn, was a function of size.

Many of the large yachts come to Antigua not just for the regattas, scenery and chilled culture but also for the good-quality engineering and maintenance skills available on the island.

English Harbour is still dominated by the naval yard and facilities built in the first half of the 18th century and, for a time, commanded by Horatio Nelson. Many of the old buildings have been restored. You can still see the windlasses that were used to pull the boats ashore, the lofts where sails were made and mended and the hard-standing where boats were pulled onto their sides to have their hulls cleaned or repaired.

Nelson arrived in Antigua in 1784 and made himself unpopular with the islanders by banning trade with the United States. But he worked to improve the conditions for his own men and they liked him as a result. He particularly enjoyed being in Antigua, I read, as a consequence of his being 'very friendly' (whatever that might mean) with the dock commissioner's wife. I realise there are many reasons why Nelson is such a hero for Englishmen.

Today, the old buildings of Nelson's Dockyard once again host sail menders, carpenters and riggers and chandlers. It is like strolling through a living museum. While looking around or waiting for some boat work to get done, you get a feel for what it must have been like in Nelson's day.

The boat work is good but not always rapid. Spare parts, also, take time to arrive, so waiting is something you need to accept as part of life on Antigua. But we were used to taking it easy and there were lots of friendly people around with whom to share the time. Antigua is a place where many cruisers stay for longer than they planned. Lots make it their base for an annual return.

Yachts were being polished and varnished all day long. I have seldom seen so many shiny boats at once, not to mention so many big, shiny boats.

Some of the very biggest yachts in the harbour showed a red light at the top of their masts at night. I had seen it once or twice before and wondered what it meant but had never seen so many in one place. On one evening, I counted 19 such mast-top reds in Falmouth Harbour alone. The lamps reflected on the dark waters, making the whole place look like some sort of dodgy red-light district. I learned that the lights were not there for navigational purposes but for aircraft. Radio masts and tall buildings have to show a light — and these masts were at least as high as any building on Antigua. One yacht, we learned, had a mast of 90 metres or 300 feet. Regina's mast is 19 metres. That should give you some idea of the sort of boat we're talking about.

The island of Antigua is not a country on its own but is part of the two-island nation of Antigua and Barbuda. Barbuda is a few miles north east of Antigua and very different. It's still quite undeveloped and doesn't offer a lot more than frigate birds and endless, near-empty beaches.

We had a beautiful beam reach (sailing at 90 degrees to the wind, with the sails set at 45 degrees) up to Barbuda. You have to get quite close before you can see the island as it's very low in the water. Even quite close, it doesn't look much more than a sand-bank surrounded by reefs.

I stood on aft deck, holding onto the backstay with my face pointing into the warm wind. The water changed colour from dark blue to turquoise as we neared the island. By the time we were down to 10 metres, I could see the sandy ocean bottom. The sky was no less pretty — blue with some fluffy cumulus clouds being gently pushed across our track by the trade winds. Regina was doing a steady eight knots through flat seas. It was hard to believe that the entire Atlantic lay to the east. It was easy to understand why cruisers could stay in the Caribbean for years, returning each season for a bit more of the laid-back life of the Lesser Antilles.

One of our gang had already decided to stay in Antigua. Trond from Norway and his wife Lesley, and their children Camilla and Colin, had chosen to stay in Antigua through the hurricane season. The children would go to the island's international school. Next season, they would consider pressing on to the Pacific. It sounded so right!

Unlike most of the gang, Trond had kept contact with his work and had flown back a few times to Norway to complete short projects. He told us with a laugh that whenever he got off the plane in Oslo, it felt like he had been smacked in the face. The chaos of land-life hit him every time. Everybody was rushing around, yet no one seemed satisfied. "If you ask somebody at home how they are doing," he said, "the reply is - 'Yes, well, I'm busy. I'm on a new project at work which takes all my time and attention. I have to fetch my boy from soccer practice and to take him to a party and my daughter is waiting at a friend's house ready to be picked up for her dance class. My wife's at the gym, so, sorry, I can't talk. Got to go. See you later.'"

Trond shook his head and continued: "It's wonderful to come back to the boat here in the Caribbean. The lack of rush is just so refreshing – yet I still manage to get done all the work and boat maintenance I need to do. When you ask people around here how they are doing, you get a smile and the answer: 'Hey, I'm fine - I'm taking it eeeasy.' And then they put out their hand to knock knuckles. I just love it here."

Trond was right. One of my happiest memories of the entire trip is of the days spent on 'island time'.

After a couple of easy days on Barbuda, we came back to Antigua as several important parties were looming. With so many boats we knew coming and going, there was always something to celebrate. Most important for us, of course, was Jessica and Jonathan's party.

I had never much enjoyed organising their birthday parties at home. This was quite different. The venue was the beach. One dinghy pulled up on the sand became a table for cakes and, on another, we set out some drinks. We hung a quiz in the trees and the rest of the entertainment took the form of all their usual games in the sea or on the sand. Dozens of kids came from boats of all nationality. Jessica and Jonathan thought it was their best party ever.

Life can be easy. There is no need to make it complicated. I was beginning to see how the lessons we were learning on the trip would help us when returned to the real Europe.

COOKING

Cooking while cruising is not much different from cooking on board generally. But with a bit more time and a bit more variety of local produce available you should be able to make it a really enjoyable and inclusive activity. Take some broad-ranging recipe books with you. Look out for local specialities and ask how to cook them.

At anchor, make an event of a meal. Get everyone chopping or cleaning something. Use all the available space, including the saloon and chart tables. Put some music on and treat yourself to an apéritif.

Cooking on passage takes a bit more getting used to but isn't difficult while the seas are small. Make sure you have all the ingredients to hand before you start but don't put them out on the work surface until you need them. You should have a bar to stop you falling forward onto the cooker and a strap or backrest to stop you falling away. Anti-slip mats on the counter tops will make life easier. A pressure cooker will not only save gas and reduce temperatures in the galley but will also cut the risk of spills and burns from hot liquids. It is important to avoid burns. If you don't have a thick plastic apron, consider wearing your foul-weather trousers.

Cooking in bigger seas is more of a challenge. Always have some easy-to-cook meals ready for difficult occasions and for the beginning of a passage. Precooked meals that just need reheating are ideal. If you have a freezer, this is when it comes in most handy.

We all enjoyed cooking

Soufrière Hills, Montserrat

Chapter twenty three

In which we go beyond the standard Caribbean sailing circuit

ISLANDS OUT OF THE STREAM

Ahead lay a smoking volcano, rising up into the sky. On the island from which it grew, there was not a single sign of human habitation. Between us and the island, there was no sail or boat at anchor. If it had not been for Koshlong a couple of hundred metres behind Regina, it would have been easy to persuade ourselves that we had sailed through a time-portal to prehistory.

The picture in my head was one from Jonathan's book about volcanoes. Just a couple of dinosaurs walking about would have made Montserrat look exactly like one of the book's drawings. We had seen plenty of extinct or dormant volcanoes. To see a live one was quite something.

"Jessica! Jonathan! Quick! Come up and see this!"

In a flash, two blond heads appeared in the companionway. "Cooool! Is it erupting, Dad?"

"It does look a bit like it with all that smoke, doesn't it? But I don't think so. We've only come this close because the official website said no eruptions were predicted." The site had suggested it would be safe to approach from the north. The last eruption had taken place six weeks before.

"This is better than any firework I've ever seen" said Jessica.

We had sailed up the east side of Montserrat to keep clear of the smoke and ash that was still coming from the volcano's mouth. We had heard stories of hot ashes burning holes in sails. Once round the top of the island we sneaked carefully into an anchorage called 'Little Bay' on the northwest side of the volcano. Koshlong and Regina were the only yachts there, a very unusual sight in the Caribbean.

We had just about got the anchor sorted when a dinghy approached, driven by a man in jeans and a T-shirt. It was not until I saw his baseball cap that I understood his importance. In capital letters, it said 'P O L I C E'. Apart from his official headgear, he looked just like any other local guy. He welcomed us to Montserrat, told us about the registration procedure and that we should visit the Police Station if we wanted to stay for longer than one night.

We handed him a crew-list. He drove over to Koshlong – where the procedure was repeated – and then headed back towards the little dock, leaving our two boats alone and rolling uncomfortably in the poorly protected anchorage. As I watched him go, I wondered at the courage it must take to live under the constant threat of eruption.

Montserrat's Soufrière Hills volcano had been dormant for almost 400 years, longer than the volcanoes on Lanzarote in the Canaries. Then, suddenly, in 1992, seismographs recorded a growing number of minor earthquakes, finally leading to a major eruption in 1995, the first since 1632. The eruption destroyed most of the fertile land and the entire capital city of Plymouth. Overnight, Montserrat went from being an attractive and booming tourist island to a forbidding, prehistoric rock. Half of the 11,000 inhabitants were made homeless and many were forced to flee the island of their birth.

Some farmers stayed to work the small amount of fertile land that remained close to the mouth of the volcano. But on 25th June 1997, there was another major eruption. More than 50 people had to be plucked from the land by helicopter. 19 people died. After that, an exclusion zone was established extending out into the sea. We had sailed along its edge.

It seems it is only a matter of time before another major eruption takes place, and this time the entire island could be affected. Whether that will be this year, next year or a decade hence, no one can know for sure. But it was with a mix of fear, respect and excitement that we viewed Montserrat.

Unfortunately, the heavy swell and onshore winds made a trip ashore impossible. We didn't dare leave the boats swinging around on a lee shore.

I remembered the Little Prince in Antoine de Saint-Exupéry's book of the same name. He lived on a lonely little planet, not much bigger than a house. On the planet, there were three volcanoes, which the Prince brushed and cleaned every morning. Only one was active, so he used that as a stove for cooking. "But you never know…" he said, and continued to clean the other two just in case. As a kid, I had not understood the deeper meaning behind this. Now, at anchor off Montserrat, watching smoke slowly emerge from the crater of a volcano, I realized how important it is to prepare for even the unforeseeable threats.

Aren't we all living with a dormant volcano close by, or even inside us? Who among us is ready for an event that changes everything overnight? For the inhabitants of Montserrat it was the sudden outburst of Soufrière Hills. For the rest of us, it could be an illness or accident that throws all our plans and preconceptions up in the air. We just don't think about it, do we? Or do we secretly believe that we are immortal? How can you prepare yourself without getting depressed?

The Vikings believed it was the Norns, the female gods who ruled fate, who decided their destiny. We are left to work it out for ourselves.

Karolina, Jessica, Jonathan and I had decided that we wanted to fulfil our dream before some unforeseen eruption came along to make it forever impossible. It was that which had driven us all the way from our safe, familiar lives in Sweden across thousands of miles of ocean to where we were now. Looking at Montserrat and the devastation that had been wrought so suddenly, I was certain that if you want to do something, you must get on and do it. There is no time to lose.

The trick, I think, is to get the balance right between what you as an individual or family can achieve and what is determined by the forces of nature. It is, obviously, a very real dilemma for the people of Montserrat.

Another island which presents its occupants with some serious environmental challenges is Saba. Saba, which lies a few islands north of Montserrat, is like a single giant tooth thrust up from the gum of the sea. All around, its sides are steep. The only way onto it from a boat is via the 'Ladder' of 800 steps carved into the cliff-face.

We anchored in the appropriately named Ladder Bay, alongside only a few more boats than had kept us company off Montserrat. As a consequence of its shape, Saba has never been conquered by an invader. Before helicopters and the airport, the Ladder had been the only way to access the island. Ships had to anchor out in deep water, cargoes would be unloaded into smaller boats and then brought in to the steep and stony beach. Men standing waist-high in water would unload the packages and carry them up the Ladder.

Until the 1970s, everything had to come in this way. Among the bigger items lifted had been a piano and a bishop – not, I'm glad to say, at the same time.

We were lucky to have only a backpack and some water bottles to carry. It was still a major hike just to get up the Ladder to a village disappointingly called 'Bottom'. The name is apt, however, as Bottom, while being at the top of the cliff, is still the lowest habitation on the island.

To reach Saba, we had sailed a more westerly course, hopping between some smaller islands while sailors in more of a hurry took the usual route from Antigua to St Martin to the British Virgin Islands. After Montserrat, we had stopped at Nevis, then St Kitts, then Statia and then Saba.

Nevis is a fairly sleepy little Caribbean island; the old sugar plantations now turned into fancy hotels and the sandy, palm-fringed beaches dotted with tourist bars. St Kitts looked like a busy, commercial place with lots of new development around its cruise-ship dock. Statia was quieter than Nevis. There is an old Dutch fort at Oranjestad and an excellent hike up to the rim of the extinct volcano.

Statia and Saba belong to the Netherlands Antilles, together with St Martin to the north and Curaçao and Bonaire close to Venezuela in the south. St Martin and Curaçao have recently voted to become independent, while Bonaire, Statia and Saba are remaining part of Holland. At 877 metres above sea level, the top of Saba is the highest point in the Netherlands.

St Martin, Statia and Saba all get their share of financial support from Holland, but that money is clearly spent quite differently by each island. On Saba, a lot of effort appears to go into keeping the place neat and clean. Sabans are proud of their island. Each village is responsible for a part of the road network and the perfectly maintained roads are swept five days a week.

The roads are a relatively recent development. Until the 1940s, the only way to get from one village to the next was to walk along steep mountain paths. The Sabans wanted a road – and engineers were brought in from Holland. Perhaps because they were used to building roads only in their own country, the Dutch engineers said it couldn't be done; the island was too steep.

The Sabans did not accept this and a local man called Joseph Hassel put himself through a correspondence course on civil engineering and assembled a team of locals, who hand-built a series of roads up over a number of years.

The road from Bottom to the village of Windwardside is known to this day as The Road That Couldn't Be Built.

A lot of this we learned from Garvis Hassel, a descendant of Joseph, and a local taxi driver. Garvis is a fourth generation Saban and has lived on the island his whole life. To be a taxi driver on Saba is to be truly dedicated to customer service. Not only are the roads so steep that some cannot be attempted with all the passenger seats filled but some of the corners are absolutely terrifying.

There's a similar tale about the airport. Once again, Dutch engineers said there was no chance. To prove that a landing was possible, the Sabans asked the bravest pilot they could find on nearby St Barths to give it a try. They worked out which was the most likely spot and cleared the biggest boulders and filled the deepest holes. The pilot, Rémy de Haenen, got his plane down in one piece and, four years later, in 1963, a commercial airport was opened.

We carried on climbing to where most of the Sabans have their homes. The houses are beautifully maintained, all painted in the same off-white colour with green or ochre trim. Once built, the houses are handed down from generation to generation. The dead are generally buried in their own back gardens – very practical, we thought.

We met far fewer tourists and yachties on Saba than on most other islands. It has some excellent snorkelling and diving around its steep sides but, otherwise, manages pretty well on its own. Many Saban men are merchant seamen and only live on the island full-time after they retire. Because of this, during the 19th Century, Saba was known as the Island of Women.

I wondered what it must be like to live on Saba – one of the most remarkable places we had visited. It looked as though quite a high degree of conformity was required. If you want to paint your house pink or skip your daily road cleaning duties, this is probably not the place for you. But I was impressed by the Saban people's determination to build things like the roads and airport. 'Impossible' is not in their vocabulary. And they have a strong sense of community. There appeared to be no crime, and plenty of care for the sick and elderly. I could easily imagine being proud to live in such a society, taking pleasure from working for my little island.

We climbed back down the Ladder and dinghied out to Regina. A high proportion of the yachts moored around us were Dutch. It is an odd thing but true that European yachties tend to go more often to the islands that played some part in their country's colonial past. The only Caribbean island with any sort of Swedish connection is St Barths. It was a Swedish colony for almost 100 years. The French king, Louis XIV, gave it to the Swedes in 1784 in exchange for a trading post in Gothenburg. The Swedish king (in quite a contrast with contemporary policies) made it a tax-free port and it prospered as a peaceful alternative to the ever-warring French and British islands. The Swedes sold it back to France in 1878.

So, would we go to St Barths? This time, no. Today its reputation is as a place for super-yachts and Hollywood stars. By steering away from the crowds we had found some remarkable places and people. We were content with that. Now it was time to move on to our final Caribbean destination, the British Virgin Islands, and one very big party.

SECURITY

When you tell a landlubber that you're planning an extended cruise, it's not long before they mention storms, pirates or sharks. With confidence you can tell them that storms can generally be avoided by sailing at the right time, pirates by sailing to the right places and that sharks are mostly a lot less dangerous than people.

Piracy is nasty and every story flashes round the cruising community. But incidents are rare, particularly in traditional cruising grounds. Most are concentrated in just a handful of specific areas. Pilot books will contain warnings and more up-to-date news can be found on web sites like www.noonsite.com.

During our season in the Caribbean, we heard of one boat being boarded while at anchor at night. The husband and wife on board were threatened but not hurt. They were close to shore and away from other boats in a bay near a town with a rough reputation. Most cruisers don't lock hatches at night but do, for instance, arrange mosquito nets to make it difficult for anyone to get below without making a noise. A few people have motion-sensing lights in their cockpits. Just as you would lock your car at home, you should lock your dinghy and lift it up out of the water at night.

Being pick-pocketed during a run ashore in the main cruising grounds generally appears no more likely than in most European or American cities. When in a marina or alongside at a fuel-dock, it is obviously unwise to leave cameras and other valuables in view. And, again, apply common sense when walking back after a meal out in town. When leaving the boat at anchor, an LED light in the cabin should be some deterrence to potential thieves.

The Ladder up to Saba

Our cruising gang gathered in the BVIs

Chapter twenty four

In which we mix some happy times and sad

THE LAST BIG PARTY

We had been cruising together since Europe. Not constantly, but often. We met, partied and parted, and met again. We kept in contact via SSB, e-mail and VHF. Crossing an ocean together had forged a strong bond between us. We knew we could rely on each other. We had shared good times and bad. Saying good-bye but knowing we would soon meet again had become part of life. This time, however, it was different.

As we gathered in the British Virgin Islands for the last big party of our Caribbean season, we knew that many of the good-byes we said now would be for ever. It wasn't like saying good-bye to people we had met on holiday. It was more like the good-byes you say when you leave school or college or somewhere you've worked for many years. We all knew we would spread out across the world from here, possibly never seeing each other again. Strong feelings grew deep inside our hearts.

Some boats, we had already 'lost'. Friends had gone ahead. Others had decided to leave their boats in Trinidad, Grenada or Venezuela for the hurricane season and stay further south. A few lucky ones were on their way towards the Panama Canal and on to the South Pacific.

The rest of us had sailed north to leave the tropics before the hurricane season. The BVIs would be our last gathering. We all wanted to hold onto each other for as long as possible. But we knew as well that this would be the end of seven months of close comradeship. The day each individual boat left the BVIs, she and her crew would be heading off on their own.

I was by no means alone in feeling the strength of the bond. Many of us yachties admitted that we had not felt the same since leaving college. Yet we had not spent anything like that much time together. What made these friendships so special? Was it the fact that we had shared the dream of crossing an ocean? Was it to do with the way we had come so quickly to rely on and trust each other? Or was it the very practical fact that we had spent so much time helping each other?

Without the sailing friends we had made, where would we have found that vital length of diesel hose? Who would have explained how to take a water-maker apart? Who would be interested in talking about the best way to keep a marine toilet working or how to filter fuel? With whom could we compare experience of on-board yoghurt making or the unrefrigerated longevity of various fruit and vegetables? Together, we had been a strong team, with a good spread of specific skills. It was sad to see the team break up.

One reason the bonds become so strong, I guess, is that almost all these issues (maybe not the yoghurt) could have some bearing on our survival. Everyone in the gang knows why it is important to talk about things like engine problems or the weather and why it is important for us to work out the best way to deal with them. We all wanted to play our proper part in that process.

The BVIs are very popular with charter sailors. Somewhere like Grenada is mainly for live-aboard yachties but here, the charter boats are by far the most numerous. We watched them racing from place to place, trying to pack in as much as possible in their limited time. They got up and weighed anchor early in the morning, always keen to get to the next place on the recommended list before the best mooring spots were taken. They moved too fast, I thought, to even make holiday friendships. They must miss out on the whole of the comradeship experience that we had valued so much.

I do not criticise the charter boat people. If my time in the Caribbean had been as limited as theirs I would have done the same. I would have wanted to get value for my money and go sailing, sailing and sailing. I would be keen to see as many places as possible. And of all the Caribbean we had visited, the BVIs were the best suited to chartering. The waters are protected and clear, the islands beautiful and the distances between anchorages small. There are fantastic opportunities to explore exciting places, both above and below the water's surface.

For us, however, after six months of living in the Caribbean, and knowing that we were coming to the end of a major part of our adventure – and about to part from many of the people who were now most important in our lives –beaches and snorkelling were low priorities. It was much more important to us to make the most of these last couple of weeks together.

I thought back to what Karolina had said while sitting in the Frangipani in Bequia many months earlier. She had said that, while cruising, the highs were higher and the lows were lower. She was so right. Like an ocean swell, life's amplitude increases, while its frequency decreases. Never before had we felt as proud as we did after we had completed the Atlantic crossing. Our friends, who had done the same, could share that feeling and celebrate with us. And then, at other times, we had wondered why we were doing all this, asking ourselves why everything on the boat seemed to stop working at the same time or why trying to get the children to do their school work sometimes nearly broke your heart. Sharing this sense of ups and downs was another thing that bound us yachties together. And now, in the BVIs, it was all going to come to an end. This was as deep a trough as any on our trip.

My feelings about all this colour unfairly my memories of the BVIs. I did not like the omnipresent mooring buoys that made it so hard to anchor. And I found the local people less willing to chill and chat than they had been further south. But we still found some great places and things to do.

The Baths on Virgin Gorda was busy but fun. Giant granite rocks thrown up by a volcanic eruption lie piled on the beach forming caves and grottoes through which the waves crash and visitors can climb.

We crawled and climbed and squeezed our way through. We heard one holidaymaker asking whether what he called the "park" might be real. We smiled. I would love to have said "No way, buddy, this is all done by Disney. It's plastic. Looks great, doesn't it?" Fortunately for us all, I resisted.

We also had a great day diving on the wreck of the Rhone. This lies just off Salt Island south of Tortola. The RMS Rhone was a British cargo ship that plied routes between the UK, Central and South America and the Caribbean. One of the first iron-hulled ships, she was launched in 1865. Two years later, however, she was caught in a Caribbean hurricane and driven onto the rocks. More than a hundred people died.

Part of the wreck lies in not much more than 6m (20 feet) of water and was ideal for the children, who were by now really good at snorkelling. Some of them made it all the way down to touch the ribs and frames that still form a clear ship shape. Jessica and Jonathan thought it must be haunted. I told them ghosts did not walk underwater.

It happened that a lot of us had gone to investigate the wreck of the Rhone on the same day. I counted ten boats I knew, all within dinghy distance. When the diving was done and the sun started to drop, we gathered on a couple of the boats, the adults on one and the children on another nearby. After a couple of beers we decided to go back to our own boats to prepare a dish each and return to share and eat together. Karolina made a delicious egg mayonnaise. Some made salads. Others brought, cheese, cold meats and olives. I remember a couple of loaves but, strangely, no fishes. We ate and drank and talked and laughed together. There was plenty to go around, both good food and good feelings.

Another kids' favourite was the blow-hole on the eastern tip of Jost Van Dyke. From the anchorage between JVD and Little Jost Van Dyke, you take a ten minute walk past Foxy's Taboo bar to a bay enclosed by massive rocks with just a little opening to the sea. At high tide, waves beat against the stony shore on the windward side and break through and over the rocks. The spray bursts through with amazing power. Everyone sitting in the bay is tossed around between rocks, sand and sea.

It's a game that's not without its risks but all the yachty children were very sensible and had their fun without getting hurt. The same could not be said of some power-boat-driving youths who arrived just after us. Our kids warned them of the strength of some of the bigger waves but the newcomers paid no attention. They paid for their ignorance and arrogance with some fairly gruesome-looking cuts and bruises.

Fun though these days were they could not outweigh the hurt of saying good-bye to so many good friends. We did so one by one as each boat set off for the Bahamas or Bermuda or, in one case, back to Antigua. We took farewell pictures of each other, hugged and tried to hide our tears.

We all promised that we would communicate via SSB and e-mail and do our best to keep in touch.

A number of us have met since. Some have flown many thousands of miles to renew on-board friendships. I believe many of us will meet again, somewhere where the sea is blue and warm.

The Baths on Virgin Gorda

CARIBBEAN EXITS

Owing to the hurricane season, sailing in the Caribbean may become dangerous from June till November. Don't become over-confident.

Plan your Caribbean escape well in advance. Check with your insurance company, but always make your own decision having assessed the risks. Study cruising guide books and pilot charts. Prudent cruisers stay south of Grenada (approx. 12 deg N) or north of Chesapeake Bay (approx. 37 N) during the hurricane season.

You can either lay-up somewhere south of the hurricane belt, such as Trinidad, or leave the area through one of the traditional routes. The exit lines are typically towards Panama, to the United States via the Bahamas or Bermuda, or back to Europe via the Azores, with or without a stopover in Bermuda.

Sailors continuing into the Pacific leave westbound towards Panama and have to get started well before the end of the Caribbean season. This leg can be quite rolly. You will often encounter a stiff 15-25 knots trade against a countercurrent of up to a knot, which stirs up some uncomfortable waves at times. Stay further offshore for that reason and round the notorious capes not too closely.

Sailing northbound needs to be timed carefully: too early in the year, and you might sail into the cool 'northerly' of spring, giving temperatures down to freezing and gales on the nose. In other words, avoid sailing to Florida before the end of March and make landfall in North or South Carolina not until mid April. Obviously, leaving too late, you risk being in the hurricane belt.

The leg to Bermuda is often a pleasant sail due north, but wait until late May to continue from there towards the States or the Azores.

The traditional route via Bermuda to the Azores and back to Europe is to avoid the calms of the Azores High, which often lies on the direct route from the Caribbean to the Azores. These calms are less of a problem with today's good engines and ample diesel supplies, so you can well plan a direct route from Antigua or St Maarten directly to the Azores. On that direct course, don't leave before mid-May, so the risk of gales decreases significantly.

With some planning and timing you may find the Caribbean exit a pleasant one.

Jonathan diving on the wreck of the Rhone

Bermuda-bound, a flat sea stretches behind Regina

Chapter twenty five

In which we take a first, big step towards home

BERMUDA AND BEYOND

Imagine yourself gliding through deep space, surrounded by millions of stars. You are floating along like a spacecraft in a science fiction film. There is nothing to see all around you but blackness and stars.

There was no moon and it was flat calm. Ahead, I could make out Polaris. To our stern lay the Southern Cross. The glassy Atlantic acted like a mirror. There was no visible horizon. Stars twinkled all around us. They were above us, to our sides and deep, deep below us. It felt absolutely as if we were hanging freely in space.

The only evidence that we were still on planet Earth was the green glow of phosphorescence in Regina's wash. The millions of photoluminescent plankton almost within touching distance mingled brilliantly with the light of stars many millions of miles away. In the centre of it all was tiny Planet Regina.

I was standing my night-watch, positioned as I most like to be, leaning back against the binnacle, looking forward over the spray-hood and enjoying this extraordinary spectacle.

By this stage, we had been motoring for several days, and were making steady progress towards Bermuda. The engine was humming along at about 1450 rpm. The log showed 6 knots.

We had been gently pushed by our engine for four days and nights and still had half our 460 litres (120 US Gal) of diesel fuel. I imagined Regina's beautifully designed underwater body slipping through the black ocean virtually friction-free. I thanked her designer, Germán Frers, her builder, Hallberg-Rassy, as well as our two-geared Gori propeller and the Centaflex vibration damper for such economical progress.

What a fool, I thought, to be standing at the centre of all this beauty and to start thinking about propellers. But it wasn't so foolish. All the parts of a complex system were working together perfectly. It had the same sort of harmony and balance as the universe so strikingly visible all around me and, I thought, like us as a family, here in our tiny floating home. I felt happy and free.

The leg to Bermuda would take a week, which now felt just right for a passage. We would have time to get into a rhythm. Sea-sickness would go after the first day and tiredness after the second or third. We would have plenty of fresh fruit and vegetables for the whole voyage.

It had been sad to leave so many friends in the British Virgin Islands. And it was sad to leave the tropics. Had it only been Karolina and me, we would have stayed south and carried on cruising. Both children said they wanted to carry on, but Karolina and I decided that one year was right for us as a family. Jessica and Jonathan, we felt, would appreciate a 'real' school with teachers who were not their parents, whatever they said. Would there be times ahead when we would regret that decision? Yes. But we had made the best decision we could.

To the east, the sky was losing its inky blackness and acquiring a faint tinge of pink. Dawn was coming. To the west, the stars were still shining brightly. This magical night was coming to an end, just like our tropical interlude. But there would be more magical nights and more time for us in the tropics. In the meantime, there was still the matter of crossing the Atlantic for a second time. There were plenty of adventures still to come.

Setting off from the BVIs had been a much less stressful process than our departure from the Canaries. With check-lists from that first crossing, Karolina had gone to the supermarkets to stock up. In just a couple of visits she had filled the boat with enough fresh, frozen, tinned and dried food for weeks at sea. With an up-to-date spreadsheet, Karolina kept complete control over what was stowed where and how much was left of what.

With another tick-list in our hands, we had completed a full set of safety checks on the boat. It was Jonathan's job to go up the mast now. He inspected all the rigging, sheeves and lights. I changed the oil in the gearbox and the main engine, as well as the fuel filters and filters in the water-maker. I rigged the cutter stay and got the stay-sail ready to go whenever necessary.

Compared to our last Atlantic preparations back in the Canaries, this time was much less hectic. It might have helped, also, that we were not surrounded by hundreds of other boats doing the same thing at the same time. We were able to do just what we wanted at a pace that suited us.

Although we had confidence in the boat and ourselves, we still had to think carefully about the weather. This crossing would be at a higher latitude than our last. Statistics suggested we should prepare for at least one gale on our way to Europe.

Bermuda is a fish-hook-shaped archipelago of around 150 islands and islets. The largest are connected by bridges. The whole thing is surrounded by dangerous reefs.

It is no coincidence that the island's flag bears the image of a sinking ship. To help prevent wrecks, or indeed damage to the environment, all shipping movements are tightly controlled by a marine radio station. Ships and yachts alike have to call in and report a whole range of details concerning their equipment, crew and itinerary.

As required, we called Bermuda Radio when we were about 30 miles from the island. They checked our position and progress on the radar and gave us directions and clearance to enter St George's Harbour via the Town Cut. It felt more like flying a plane. But there are a lot of rocks about and the Town Cut is too narrow to want to be in it at the same time as a cruise liner.

Visitors to Bermuda, it seemed to us, were golfers, passengers on cruise liners or yachties. And there was maybe a fourth category – those who did not visit personally, but sent their money, instead. In Bermuda it is very clear why they call it 'offshore banking'.

For a golfer, Bermuda must be like El Dorado. There are nine courses within a total area of 13 by 2 miles (24 x 4 km). Anything not built on must be a golf course.

Many of the cruise liners come from New York. It's a 36-hour passage from there. The ships then spend two days in St George's before heading off for another 'cruise' to Bermuda's capital, Hamilton. After two days there, they go back to New York and the whole process starts over. You could, of course, take the bus from St George's to Hamilton. I don't think it would take more than an hour, even with plenty of stops.

The yachties are small in number compared with the cruise liner passengers but there are still more than a thousand sailing boats that call into Bermuda each year. In the early summer, many of these are on their way from the Caribbean, either to North America or to Europe via the Azores. A stop at Bermuda puts a welcome break into either trip.

"Welcome to the Bahamas!" joked the friendly customs officer as we came ashore in St George's. We asked for directions to a marina. He said these were hard to come by at this busy time of the year but that he would call his friend Bernie.

Bernie, who hails originally from Sweden, is the man to know on Bermuda. Zipping around on a moped with a white helmet covering his distinguished grey hair, he is always busy sorting out things like marina berths, repairs and discounted fuel for yachties.

Bernie managed to find us a place in Captain Smoke's Marina towards the west end of the harbour. This was partly because, sadly, the office and workshop of Captain Smoke's had recently gone up in it. Fortunately, the berths, the shower and a barbecue area had escaped the fire intact. We joined 5 other boats moored bow-on to the harbour wall.

Bermuda is quite a lot smarter than any island we had visited since leaving Europe, and Karolina thought we should put on some of our finer clothes before going ashore. After so long in T-shirt and shorts, I didn't really see why a change was necessary. But, as Karolina pointed out, if we didn't wear the smarter clothes we'd brought soon, we never would. Walking down the main street in St George's looking for a laundrette, I felt a bit strange in proper trousers and a long-sleeved shirt.

We spotted a man with a long beard, wearing old shorts and a stained T-shirt and carrying a can of engine oil. He was obviously a sailor. He would know the whereabouts of a laundrette. We asked and he peered sceptically back. "You are from a cruise-ship, aren't you?"

"No, no," we replied. "We live on a yacht. We just need some laundry done."

"Oh", said the man, still a bit wary. "You just don't look like yachties, you know. You're too smart! Anyway, I'm Jeff and I live on Indian Summer. I'm single-handing over to the Azores and then to England. Next winter, I will continue to the Caribbean and then to the South Pacific." We agreed to stay in contact via SSB during our crossing and to meet again in the Azores.

With our legs stretched and the location of the laundrette sorted, it was time to head back to Regina. Tonight we were going to be joined by our new crew member, Tom.

We had been talking ever since our first Atlantic crossing about finding an extra adult for longer passages. At that time, we had decided against it. We wanted to keep the experience within the family. We also wanted to avoid the responsibility of taking someone else on our first crossing. The crossing had gone well, however, and we now knew that we could complete a three-week passage on our own, if we wished. But we wanted to see what it was like to sail with company and we knew the next leg was the one most likely to involve some heavy weather.

Taking a guest on board can be tricky and the people we knew who had done it had had mixed experiences. A good friend can become quite the opposite when sharing the confined space of a cramped boat in the middle of the Atlantic. Private space is scarce. Everyone has to accept their share of the hardships. It's not easy to stay polite and forgiving when you are queasy and racked with tiredness. You need to trust each other's judgements. Everyone has to have faith in the boat and the rest of the crew.

There were not many friends we considered asking. And even fewer, we thought, who would see two weeks at sea as a holiday. On top of that, of course, there would be time needed at either end. We couldn't start the leg until the weather was right.

"Tom", Karolina had said, "Tom is a guy we could ask to do the leg to the Azores."

"Hmmm", I responded. "I don't know Tom very well." Tom and Karolina had sailed together, both as crew, on the Hallberg-Rassy 46 Mahina Tiare III a couple of years before. They had covered some 1600 miles between Tromsø in northern Norway and Gothenburg in Sweden.

"He's as solid as a rock when things get stressful," said Karolina. "We got on really well. I'm sure you'd love sailing with him."

I knew it was a good suggestion, but was still not certain Tom would enjoy joining a family of four on a boat of just 40 feet. The crossing to the Azores would take about two weeks. For the whole of that, if any of us felt like a little time off, there would be nowhere to go. If Tom agreed to come he was at least as brave as we were.

"We can always ask", Karolina continued, "He might not be able to come and then we can always sail by ourselves as we have done so far. But if he joins, I am sure it could be fun with Tom. And just think, you'll get twice as much sleep!"

That part sounded very tempting. Instead of three hours 'on' and three hours 'off', we could each stand a three-hour watch and then have as much as six hours of continuous sleep. There might even be time for reading, or fishing, or writing. And if some manoeuvre or sail change required two people on deck, the third could still carry on sleeping. And with three adults on board we might even get the gennaker up a bit more often. (Though I didn't mention this at the time.)

After some thinking, we sent off an e-mail to Tom asking him if he'd like to join us. This was five weeks before we planned to set off. That's not a lot of notice for the finance director of a US company. To our considerable surprise, he accepted 24 hours later. We were grateful to Tom's boss and wife for letting him come.

So, on 13th May, Tom stood in Captain Smoke's Marina with a big smile on his face, saying how happy he was and keen to get on board and off to sea. Unfortunately, it took a little longer for Tom's luggage to get to the island. But when it had, and with the weather looking good, we decided to go for it. A gale was forecast for Bermuda later in the week, so there was no time to lose.

ELECTRICAL POWER

Today's boats are much more power-hungry than they used to be and it is crucial that you get the balance right between what you're putting in and what you're taking out of the batteries.

First, think about your outgoings and estimate your power consumption per day; both at anchor and on passage. Remember that in the tropics you will use more power for light (darker and longer nights) and cooling (fridge and freezer). Do what you can to cut that consumption by installing LED lights and a water-cooled fridge or freezer with plenty of insulation.

Now design a charging system that will produce that many amp-hours plus a few to spare. Consider whether you want to run your engine or generator once or twice a day. Be cautious with the estimates provided by manufacturers of solar panels and wind generators. A less exciting but more productive investment than either of these can be a high-output alternator on your main engine. Another good value-option (though it presents safety issues) is a portable petrol generator placed on deck for charging at anchor.

On passage, tow generators can generate an amp a knot but can slow you down by up to half a knot.

Bear in mind when working out how long you can go between charges that batteries should never be discharged to less than 50% of their capacity. Without shore-power it's hard to charge them to more than to 80% so you'll generally have no more than 30% of your nominal battery capacity to use between charges.

For complete control, you can install an amp-hour monitor. Some of the cost can be offset against the fact that it will enable you better to look after your batteries and so keep them longer.

Tom takes his turn at catching supper

Tuning in to Herb

Chapter twenty six

In which a daunting passage turns out to be the perfect sail

MID-ATLANTIC AGAIN

Luckily, our red port navigation light was still hanging from its electric cable, but it was swinging wildly. One of the bigger waves must have pushed it upwards and out of its holder. Green water was running along the deck as Regina heeled to the freshening wind. We were close-hauled, heading east and well out into the Atlantic. The cockpit was dry but it was the deck that was the issue. I was going to have to crawl up it to fix the light.

Knowing that I would get wet, I did what I did on the west-bound crossing before going forward in a rough sea and stripped down to my life-jacket and shorts. I leant over the side of the cockpit and clipped on to the jack-stay, glancing forward in the hope of finding that the light had been washed back into its fitting. It continued to dangle.

I got Karolina up to the cockpit in case anything went wrong, and began to crawl forward. Slowly, I made my way from one strong-point to the next. I'd not got half-way to my destination when a big green wave smacked against the hull, covering me in spray. It was just like being back in the Baltic. I shook my head like a dog, promised myself I'd don full wet-weather gear for the next such outing, and carried on.

Finally, I got to the pulpit and was just about to grab the light when Regina dipped and a really big one sluiced over the bow. I must have said something unprintable. I fished up the light, which was, by now, filled with seawater. I unscrewed the fitting, let the water out, put it back together and tightened the screw holding it onto the pulpit. Then I turned and shouted above the wind to Karolina to switch on the navigation lights. To my surprise, they all worked.

I looked back from the bow at the sails. We were sailing with a double-reefed mainsail and our small stay-sail. Each had a beautiful shape. The whole boat felt perfectly balanced. We were flying along at 7 knots, despite being close-hauled. Regina was slicing through the waves. There was no slamming or any of that sickening sensation of falling off waves.

More green water washed over my feet and prompted me to get on with my return to the cockpit. I went below and had a hot shower. It was lovely. I checked the sea-water temperature on the indicator by the chart-table. It was actually 21°C (70F), which is a lot warmer than the Baltic in summer but still five or six degrees below what we'd become used to further south.

Karolina and Tom thought it was all very funny. When they had sailed together before, they had gone a long way north of the Arctic Circle. The water here was not what they would consider cold.

We were sailing along the edge of a low-pressure system. A bit further north and we would encounter very heavy headwinds. Sailing further south would not only mean going out of our way but would also mean no wind. Finding the balance between these two; sailing in a narrow corridor where the wind was just right, was the challenge. Fortunately, we had help from just the right man — a man called Herb.

Herb Hilgenberg is something of a legend among Atlantic sailors. Born in Braunschweig in Germany, Herb emigrated with his parents to Nova Scotia, Canada, in 1953, when he was 15 years old. In 1982, he and his Swiss wife Brigitte, together with their two small children, went cruising on their 39-foot double ender, Southbound II.

In those days, weather forecasts were scarce and unreliable. On a passage from North Carolina to the Virgin Islands they ran into bad weather and Herb broke his arm. It took them a further ten days until finally making landfall in the Virgin Islands. From then on, Herb became increasingly interested in weather forecasting.

In 1984, the Hilgenberg family sailed into Bermuda and stayed for about ten years. One of Herb's daughters still lives on the island, as far as I can discover, and his boat, now renamed, can be found in an island marina. It was from the boat that Herb started to help friends with weather reports, first on VHF and then via SSB. In 1994, Herb and Brigitte retired to Canada, but his nightly forecasts continue, as does his call-sign of Southbound II.

Each evening, from 1930 UTC, almost every day of the year, Herb broadcasts on 12.359 kHz. As many as 70 boats try to call in and sign on before 2000 UTC. From 2000, Herb calls each boat that has managed to sign on and talks them through a detailed weather forecast and routing advice. He works his way across the entire Atlantic from the approaches to Falmouth to the approaches to Colon. And sometimes even further. To give each boat an individual three day weather forecast can take up to two hours. And you better pay attention. If you miss your turn, you will not be called again. Many boats don't try to sign on but just listen, waiting for a forecast for a boat near them.

"How do you pay Herb?" is a question a lot of first-time Atlantic sailors ask. And the answer is that you don't. The service is totally free and, in my opinion, provides better guidance than any computer model.

Over the years, Herb has developed a variety of data sources and models. He compares all these and checks them against the first-hand reports he gets from each yacht. Armed with a bunch of coloured pens, Herb corrects standard weather charts, moving the highs and lows and increasing or decreasing wind speeds. After twenty years of his doing this, it is not surprising that Herb's forecasts are so accurate.

With his highly organised systems, Herb knows exactly where 'his' boats are, or should be. He's not afraid to comment on a boat's speed or lack thereof. When yachts report their current weather observations, Herb often says "Yes, that's about right..." If it's not the weather he's expecting, Herb doesn't hesitate to ask the sailors to check their instruments.

In our case, it was not hard to understand why Herb had routed us well to the south of the classic track from Bermuda to the Azores. The Azores High had been pushed a long way south, allowing east-bound low-pressure systems and their accompanying cold fronts to pass much further south than usual. What makes Herb so special is that he can find that really quite small and ever-moving corridor of optimal wind. All we have to do is aim for the way-point he gives us each evening. Apart from a first couple of days of 20-25 knot headwinds, the weather for our crossing to the Azores was perfect.

I can only hope that Herb is aware of the profound gratitude thousands of yachts feel for him and Southbound II. Having Herb onboard gives you a great sense of confidence. On this passage, we did our best 24-hour distance to date of 169 miles or an average of over 7 knots. Many days we managed around 160 miles.

Not everyone was so lucky, however. We heard how boats further north had faced really heavy winds. I was almost embarrassed by the comfort of our passage. As I had hoped when we signed on Tom, we got the gennaker out on quite a few days. The seas were generally flat. It was hard to believe we were back in the middle of the Atlantic. I was a bit worried Tom might think this was what ocean sailing was always like. I won't disillusion him. I'd like him to come again.

The perfect weather did not make it an uneventful passage. I had just gone below decks when I heard Jessica shout from the cockpit: "Oh, what's that?" I rushed up the companionway and followed Jessica's shaking hand. She was pointing down, into the sea below the boat. Through the clear water we could see something steel-blue, almost turquoise, right underneath Regina. My first thought was that we must be sailing over an iceberg. Our echo sounder showed a mere 0.9 metres of water beneath the keel. Jessica was jumping up and down with excitement. "It's a fish. A huge fish! Is it a dolphin? No, it's a whale. It's a whale. Daddy, look! A whale!" And she was right.

Without touching Regina, the whale turned to parallel our track and rose just enough for its back to break the surface. "It's a sperm whale!" said Jonathan, who had also rushed to the cockpit. The head shape looked right and the back was wrinkled like the picture in our wildlife book. The whale was not much more than 2 metres (6 feet) way from the boat and was easily keeping up with our 7 knots. It was at least the same size as Regina, if not bigger. It stayed in that position for only a few seconds and then dipped and slowed to move slightly aft of the boat. I was glad we had no fishing line out. After another couple of minutes, it moved slowly away, blowing two or three times before it disappeared back down to the ocean depths.

I had heard people talk about 'spaghetti legs' before, but did not realise quite what they meant. I did now. My legs felt as weak as well-cooked pasta. Of our whole cruise to date, this had been the most breathtaking moment. The whale was so close; we could almost have touched it. Why had it come to see us? Was it looking for a bit of company out here in the great, wide ocean? The engine had been running to charge the batteries; we were in gear and the propeller was turning, so the whale must have heard us. It could not have come across us accidentally.

I was glad the whale had not chosen to rub its back on Regina's hull. We were aware of at least four boats that had been involved in collisions with whales on the westbound Atlantic crossing. One had had her propeller shaft bent so her crew could only use the engine in neutral for charging batteries until they got the chance to change the shaft in St Lucia.

It took us 13 days to get from Bermuda to Faial and, thanks both to Tom and to Herb, it remains our most enjoyable ocean passage. Landfall in the harbour at Horta was straightforward. Tom flew home a happy man. Herb promised to join us again for the next and final leg.

When we arrived in St Lucia we had been one of many crews completing their first ocean crossing and the mood was one of almost hysterical relief and delight. The crews that stop at the Azores are almost all experienced ocean sailors. They are either completing a north Atlantic circuit as we were or are on their way to just about anywhere. It gives the marinas a different feel. It's all a bit calmer and more serious. I liked it.

The passing yachties still find time to make their marks on the harbour walls. Horta is where this tradition started and the paintings are everywhere around the harbour. Many are real pieces of art. Many, also, bear witness to repeated visits.

We made one for Regina, using a similar design to the one we had used in Porto Santo some nine months earlier, carefully leaving space for us to add further visits in future years. I wondered whether we would ever come again.

I walked around the harbour looking at the pictures just as I would in an art gallery. I looked for friends' boats and famous boats. Every one fired something in my imagination. Some were old and fading away, like memories. Some were still wet. All the great sailors come to Horta. Joshua Slocom did. So did Tristan Jones and Bernard Moitessier, and many more. I felt very proud to be part of that tradition.

No proper sailor leaves Horta without putting his mark on the harbour wall and nor does he go without at least one drink in Peter's Café Sport. The café, which overlooks the harbour and opened in 1918, is now run by a third generation of the founding family. Jose Azevedo, who had been known as 'Peter', had died the year before we arrived and his son, Jose Henrique, was now the patron. It felt a bit like entering a church. I thought of all the sailors who had gone before me and how they would wish me luck at sea and I wished the same for those who came in our wake.

The Café is always full and everyone looks up when you enter, checking to see if it's someone they know or someone due to come in from the sea. Ensigns and sailing club pennants hang from the roof and along the walls. Each tells its own windswept story. Together they represent a thousand far-flung ports the world over.

I had dreamt of walking into Peter's Sport Café many times. I was proud and happy at the same time. I was among like-minded men. I was with my family and my fellow sailors. And I was in a place that had been shared by all my heroes from the past.

The talk in the café when we were there was all about the recent storms. One yacht was still missing. All sorts of alerts had been raised but nothing had been heard. It turned out their engine was broken and they had switched off their radio in order to save power. They were towed into Horta a couple of days later. Another boat that limped in while we were there was a British yacht that had lost its mast. It had come down about a hundred miles west of Faial, apparently as a result of a shroud wearing through at deck level. They had had to cut the mast away but still managed to find a pole to fly the appropriate courtesy flags when they came into Horta. Very British!

Many of the sailors who had arrived in the last couple of days spoke of very heavy weather. There were reports of winds of up to 50 knots. In total, it seemed four boats had lost their masts and one crew had abandoned ship and been rescued by a freighter. Fortunately, no lives were lost. Despite the beer, it was sobering talk.

I was grateful for our good luck and good guidance from Herb.

BUREAUCRACY AND IMMIGRATION

Cruising from one country to another is fun and not particularly complicated. Immigration officers are often friendly and helpful; if you treat them with respect. Bear in mind that their forefathers may not have been treated very well by your forefathers and that their role embodies independence and nationhood.

Some countries require you to fly the yellow quarantine flag until immigration procedures are complete but many don't. The pilot book will usually say, but, if you are uncertain, it is never wrong to fly it.

Allow plenty of time for immigration. Customs and health clearance, if required, can often be sorted in the same or adjacent offices. Dress in something smarter than your scruffiest shorts. Bring your boat papers, passports and a photo-copied crew list complete with name, passport number, date and place of birth and nationality. Often the official will want to see exit papers from your last port to make sure no one has joined or left the crew.

If you plan to take on crew in one country and drop them in another, send your crew-member a letter explaining this and he or she will be able to use that should questions arise regarding their lack of a return ticket.

Some countries, notably the USA and its territories (such as the US Virgin Islands, Spanish Virgin Islands etc), require a visa issued in person at a US embassy before you can arrive by yacht. This is not a good thing to discover the night before you are due to sail from Tortola to St John to pick up some incoming guests.

Peter's Café Sport, Horta

Terceira, Azores

Chapter twenty seven

In which we leave the Azores, but promise to return

THE LAST ATLANTIC LEG

"It's only twelve hundred miles, after all…" Penny, from the British boat Tamarisk, was sounding confident. We were all sitting in Regina's cockpit enjoying a glass of Azorean Pico wine. "Well, you know," she continued, "it should only take us nine or ten days. The only thing left on my to-do list is to go and get some fresh vegetables and fruit from the market tomorrow. Then we are ready to go."

It had taken Tamarisk and her crew three weeks to reach the Azores from Bermuda. On the advice of Herb, they had slowed down and even stopped, hove-to, to avoid the storms further east. Having not seen them for more than a month, we had a lot to talk about: they about their long passage from Bermuda, and we about these wonderful islands and their people. We'd visited four of the nine Azorean islands and were already talking about returning to visit the remainder in years to come.

There is so much to enjoy in the Azores. Just take the wine. The bottle we were drinking had been grown in the stony vineyards on the island Pico, now protected by UNESCO as a 'world heritage site'. The stones thrown up by the old volcano had been moved to give access to the fertile soil beneath. Where did all the stones to go? They were simply piled up to form walls around each little plot of vines. Only later was it discovered that the stone walls actually protected the vines from the salty winds and held the warmth of the day long into the night.

We were moored on Terceira, which we liked best of the islands we visited. The main town of Angra Do Heroísmo is packed with beautifully preserved buildings. It is a flourishing little city, with small businesses, shops and restaurants, all busy and ready to welcome visitors. Most of these seemed to be Portuguese. That surprised us. Why didn't holidaymakers from further afield come to the Azores? Was it the lack of sandy beaches? I would happily give up sandy beaches for the fantastic atmosphere and friendly people of Terceira.

The island is trying to develop a business around yachting – not just passing visitors but people who want to base their yachts on the Azores. The islanders have invested heavily in a new marina, and there is a full-service yard specialising in winter lay-ups. Karolina suggested to Penny that we should both come back one summer to spend more time exploring the Azores. "After all", she said, "it is only 1200 miles!" They both laughed.

There are lots of things to enjoy on the Azores. The people are as welcoming as any we met on our whole trip. You can go whale and dolphin watching. The islands themselves are varied and attractive, with lush green mountain slopes and fantastic flowers. Plus there are some spectacular volcanoes – the last of our Atlantic island tour.

Imagine you are standing at the sea's edge, next to a lighthouse, on a fine day. Suddenly, you see something happening beneath the water a little way out from the beach. Bubbles and then smoke come to the surface; finally you can see rocks poking up: a new piece of land has emerged. Incredibly, that is exactly what happened at Ponta das Capelinhos on the western tip of Faial no more than 50 years ago. The lighthouse is still there but is now well inshore and unused.

Terceira has Furnas do Enxofre. Visiting its crater, we were told to watch our step and keep a close eye on the children. This was easier said than done. Jonathan thought it was really exciting. The sides of the volcano were pock-marked with holes that looked like large rabbit burrows, but from which blasts of hot, sulphurous gas emerged. There were no guardrails, paths, entrance fees or other tourists. It was lovely to have it all to ourselves. I suspect, however, that soon such exploration will be impossible. We could see several signs of planned building work.

There were plenty more Azorean sites to explore, but the days were racing by. We wanted to get back to Sweden and have a bit of time before school restarted. That meant being back in home waters in five weeks' time. We were still in the middle of the Atlantic. We had only been in the Azores for a month but it was time to get moving.

As usual, I read a range of pilot books and guides to our planned passage. One of them was World Cruising Routes by Jimmy Cornell, the founder of the ARC (Atlantic Rally for Cruisers). He is a very experienced sailor and his book covers every corner of the cruising world. What I read did not sound too cheerful: "All passages from the Azores to Northern Europe are usually close hauled… With the exception of the odd sunny day at the start, the weather along this route is invariably grey, wet and cold."

Regina and Tamarisk left on the same day. Tamarisk was headed for Falmouth. We would go to Ireland. We said our good byes and wished each other luck. For two sunny, calm and warm days we motored out of the Azores northbound. Finally, we found some wind, head wind, just as Jimmy Cornell had predicted. We carried on close-hauled in a north-easterly direction. These north winds must have had started in the Arctic, they felt so cold. The temperature of the water was now down to 14°C (57F). The chilliness of the air prompted us to switch the diesel heater on for the first time in nearly a year.

Jessica was freezing. Jonathan was complaining. Karolina was putting on socks, boots, long pants, a fleece and a jacket. I was looking for my cold-weather sailing hat, which I could not find any longer after a year in the tropics. It had to be somewhere!

Our barometer shows pressure, temperature and humidity, and offers a couple of words by way of a weather forecast. So, if the pressure drops quickly, it flashes STORM. This time, as if it was teasing us, the barometer told us in big letters that the meteorological situation was currently WET and COLD. At the same time, it showed a little cloud symbol. It certainly was cloudy. I wondered whether the man who programmed the barometer had read Jimmy Cornell's book.

Jonathan curled up like a dog in front of the hot air heater. And if he wasn't there, he was in his berth, spending days reading Harry Potter in English. Jessica was getting more and more involved in the sailing, taking her own watches and proving an excellent look-out for ships. She had grown so much during our cruising year. We had sailed away with two children and returned with two crewmembers. It was wonderful to see our children grow and take responsibility, becoming not just a son or daughter but also a reliable part of the team.

The weather forecast was talking about an active cold front and several low pressure systems heading for Ireland. We had better hurry up and get into port before the gales arrived. Again, I was pleased with Regina's upwind performance. The hull, the deep keel, the rudder and the fully battened furling mainsail all worked well together to give us a succession of fast days. Our best was 176 miles in 24 hours. The 1200 miles from the Azores to Ireland took us eight days. But, after the first two, every one was grey, wet and cold.

Long before we sighted land, we were dreaming of a pint of Guinness in a warm, cosy Irish pub.

WEATHER

There are three reasons for feeling fairly confident that you will be able to avoid storms. First, weather forecasting is a lot more accurate than it used to be. Second, in open sea and with no pressing hurry to reach a destination, you have a lot of scope to get away from bad weather. And third, seasonal weather patterns are now well-documented and, even with global warming, fairly reliable.

To make use of weather forecasts you will need to be able to receive them and that means either some sort of satellite communications or short-wave radio. You can buy bespoke routing advice via email from a company such as Commander's Weather. Or you can get automatically generated GRIB-files sent via email and use them to do your own routing. Or you can sign on with a radio amateur like the legendary Herb. Any of these should be able to predict bad weather at least three days ahead. That gives you time to move several hundred miles, if necessary, in the opposite direction.

You'll also greatly reduce the risks you face by picking the right time of year for each passage. Books like Jimmy Cornell's World Cruising Routes offer a wealth of information about where to sail when.

Before you get away from the coast, get used to using websites for short-term forecasts. Find ones you like and check their reliability over time. Be careful not to check a number of forecasts and extract the most favourable predictions from each.

Finally, don't forget the actual weather around you. Learn to read the clouds. Watch for squalls and always keep an eye on your barometer.

The Fastnet Rock

Ross's Bay near Aran Island

Chapter twenty eight

In which we go the harder way around

THE WILD WEST

We were anchored close to the old fort on the island of Inishbofin about seven miles off the Galway coast. The island is reputed to have once been a base for Ireland's pirate queen, Grace O'Malley. But it wasn't pirates that worried us now. We had put out our two biggest anchors in tandem, one in front of the other. We had let out a lot of chain and positioned ourselves to cope with wind from any direction. On the back-stay, we had set the small anchor-sail to keep Regina's bow into the wind. A snubber with a rubber spring had been hooked onto the chain to take the shock loads. Now we could only wait. And hope.

The Atlantic gale arrived as predicted, gusting to 40 knots, even inside the bay. The west coast of Ireland is a rugged but charming place, just like the people. Many still speak Gaelic – or Irish, as they prefer to call it. All have grown used to the Atlantic waves that roll and crash onto the lee shore of Europe's most westerly outpost. Even the Vikings generally steered clear of this coast. They came a couple of times, but preferred the safer and easier east coast and made what is now Dublin their main trading post and boat-building centre.

Why had we chosen to go round the outside of Ireland? Sitting waiting for the gale off Inishbofin, this was not an easy question to answer.

The low-pressure system of 990 hPa must have passed extremely close to us, as our barometer dropped rapidly from 1010 hPa to 992 hPa in just a couple of hours.

Four yachts were anchored alongside Regina. Four is a crowd on this coast. Two had problems with their anchors and started to drag. Their crews worked hard in the freezing wind and rain to re-set their anchors in the weedy bottom. One succeeded quite quickly. The other was not so lucky and drifted closer and closer to Regina. Over the roaring wind, we could hear the crew yelling at each other. More people came up on deck to help raise the anchor. The boat continued to get closer. If she hit us the shock might dislodge our anchor and cause us both to drift back towards the rocks.

243

I pulled my hood down to shield my face, grabbed our biggest fender and went up to the foredeck. The other yacht was veering from side to side but always moving back towards Regina. I stood ready with the fender. She got closer and closer until, at the last moment, the anchor snagged on something and she swung and missed us by no more than a boat's length.

"Stop!", was all I could think of to shout.

The boat carried on moving back across the choppy water towards the rocks. In my head, I could already see her smashing into them, her hull punctured and crew jumping for their lives. It was not until the very last moment that they managed to lift their anchor and use their engine properly to drive them away from impending doom.

"That was close!" I said to Karolina, as I slipped back down the companionway and into the warmth of Regina.

The experience was in stark contrast to the previous evening spent enjoying a pleasant couple of pints of Guinness in the local pub. We chatted with the locals and were asked the usual questions about our trip and what we thought of Ireland. One of the regulars wanted to know how long it had taken us to sail all the way from Sweden to the west coast of Ireland. Our answer of one year and one month prompted a raised eyebrow. So we explained. Of course, more questions followed and soon we were entertaining the whole pub with our tales of maritime adventure.

Having spent much of the last year in the company of fellow cruisers, the questions now put to us made us feel as though we were back in the days before we left. That was the last time people had thought of us as different, daring and maybe a bit irresponsible. Here they came again: Did we really sleep on board? Did we always anchor at night? What did the children think? What would happen to their schooling? How could we quit our jobs? Were we not afraid? Had we encountered any storms? And so on.

"Well," I responded "the worst weather we've encountered on the whole trip is what's forecast for here tomorrow night. The wind is meant to go up to Force 9 and veer from south-east to north-west." I took a long draught of Guinness and continued. "I know that you think this is just a summer gale and will soon be over. I have read about your winter weather and have nothing but respect for your ability to survive and prosper out here. On the trade-wind routes we sailed you don't get anything like this."

Why, then, had we chosen the wild west coast of Ireland? If we had known about the weather that would hit us off Inishbofin, we would definitely have gone east.

But that would have been a pity. This is a beautiful cruising ground. The scenery is fantastic, the people are friendly and the Guinness is poured perfectly.

We had approached Ireland via the famous Fastnet Rock, making landfall in a tiny village called Crookhaven. It has 35 inhabitants... or possibly 36. The lady we asked was not too sure, since a baby was about due. Despite being so small, the town had no fewer than two pubs and a restaurant. Just the sort of place to make landfall!

It was in Crookhaven that we discussed the west or east issue. Going west would mean we would have circumnavigated Ireland in the course of our trip – the only island of which that would be true. But going east would be quicker and safer.

Time was getting short and I didn't want an accident so close to home to spoil what had been such a trouble-free trip. We had sailed some 16,000 miles – but had no illusions about being invulnerable. We were still the ordinary family on a somewhat longer cruise than usual. We were not adventure heroes.

What swung the decision in the end was our desire to carry on exploring. We had come to love finding new places and meeting new people. To retrace our steps any sooner than absolutely necessary just felt wrong. It would feel like our adventure was ending already. We were also impressed by things we heard from people who had sailed Ireland's west coast. They were all emphatic in their belief that west was best.

The west coast of Ireland is like nowhere else we had been. From Crookhaven on, it was one extraordinary place after another. One of the first was The Great Skellig, or as it's also known, Skellig Michael. This barren rock eight miles offshore was, for many hundreds of years, home to religious hermits. You can still see the beehive-shaped stone huts dating back 1400 years in which some of them lived. Those who found even that too sociable, could retire to a cell right at the top of the island. Here, their devotions would be interrupted only by the wind and wildlife.

If Great Skellig had been quiet, Little Skellig was the opposite. When it first appeared over the horizon, it looked as though it had white cliffs. But as we neared we realised the white was not rock but some of the 40,000 gannets our guidebook told us nested on the island. As we got nearer still, the sky began to fill with birds. Jessica questioned why they all chose to nest on this one island. I didn't know the answer but wondered whether it might be for many of the same reasons as we humans gather together in cities.

From Crookhaven, we sailed to Ballycastle. This small harbour described itself as "a sleepy, drinking village with a fishing problem". And, indeed, as well as an impressive fleet of fishing vessels there was a no-less numerous selection of pubs.

Our next port, Dingle, had so many pubs we couldn't have got round them all in a week. Its main attraction, however, was not the pubs but a dolphin called Funji, who has lived in the bay outside Dingle for more than 20 years. Funji is free to swim out to the Atlantic to rejoin the rest of his species but chooses to stay in Dingle. We took the dinghy out to find him, and it wasn't long before he bobbed up to say 'hello'.

On the Aran Islands, we visited the pre-historic Dun Aonghasa, an enormous D-shaped fortification built on a 100m (300ft) high cliff during the Bronze Age. As usual, we took the dinghy in and set about tying up alongside the town pier. Politely, we were asked not to park there today. The local school was to have its swimming lesson there later in the afternoon. The water temperature was around 15°C (60F). These children must be tough. Later, at anchor, as we sat under the sprayhood extension waiting for one of the frequent rain showers to pass, we heard voices. We thought a dinghy had come alongside without our noticing. I climbed out of the tent and found no dinghy but two women, swimming. "Do you need help?" I asked, wondering if they wanted to come aboard. We were, after all, several hundred metres from the shore. "Oh, no, thank you. We're just out for a little swim." And off they swam, giggling and talking to each other.

We didn't leave Inishbofin until the storm had gone through completely. The next leg started calmly enough. The wind was forecast to rise but to no more than Force 6. The forecast, however, did not include squalls. We could see the cold front approaching and, on the radar, pick out the squalls embedded within it. By this stage, it was already blowing a steady Force 7 with gusts well over 30 knots.

Karolina, sensible as ever, suggested reefing. The mainsail was already down and we were running with about half the genoa. Now we rolled up all but about six feet. I cleated off and ducked back under the spray-hood. Then it hit us. The rain cut the visibility to little more than the length of the boat and beat down the waves to leave an almost flat sea. The wind measured 45 knots, more than we had ever seen before at sea.

How would you feel under such circumstances? What would you have thought and prayed for? I think I probably know the answer and that is why I think I must have gone just a bit crazy.

I enjoyed it. It was beautiful. Regina was just flying along, sailing at a steady 9 knots. And everything was fine. The boat did not feel over-pressed. Regina was loving it. The autopilot carried on steering. My wet-weather gear kept me warm and dry. What did I have to complain about? Jessica and Jonathan didn't even notice the squall. Not until long after the front had passed and the sun was shining again, did they stick their heads out of the companionway to ask why everything was so wet.

Entering the harbour at Broadhaven, we found two familiar boats already anchored. We had seen no more than half a dozen different yachts in the whole of our west coast voyage and it made a pleasant change to do a bit of socialising. Tom and Dorothy on the American boat, Joyant, had been living on board for six years and had covered more than 45,000 miles. Only once, they said, had they experienced stronger winds than we had come through this afternoon. We were doubly reassured; getting caught in such strong winds was a rare thing. And now we were confident Regina and her crew could cope with such squalls.

The next leg, to Aranmore, was straightforward. We anchored, thinking our Irish adventure was coming to an end. That turned out not to be the case.

As we were tidying up we noticed an impressive swell beginning to build up in the bay, breaking over the nearby islets. It was the result of a storm out in the Atlantic. A nearby weather buoy was reporting a 5m (15 ft) swell. We would have a rolly, sleepless night, I thought. But it could have been worse.

"PanPan – PanPan – PanPan," said the voice on the VHF. "Man in water in heavy swell. This is Clifton Coastguard. Over."

We sat listening for a response. Barely a couple of minutes later, we saw two men still in their work clothes dinghying out to the moored lifeboat. Quicker than you could say "Full Speed Ahead", the boat was roaring out of the anchorage. Like angels of the sea, they flew over the breaking waves. My British and Irish friends, I think, don't always realise how lucky they are to have the Royal National Lifeboat Institution. The RNLI has saved more than 135,000 people. There are more than 200 lifeboat stations around Britain and over a thousand trained volunteers in Ireland alone. It's a service unmatched anywhere in the world.

The following morning, after an uncomfortable night, the swell had dropped enough to continue. We were due to round Bloody Foreland. I was glad to read that its name comes from the colour of the rocks, not its propensity to sink ships.

The swell was still big enough for nearby fishing boats to disappear completely in the troughs, but the seas were long and we were able to make progress. Then the radio went off again.

"PanPan – PanPan – PanPan, this is Malin Head Coastguard. A windsurfer in difficulties off Melmore Head. Any vessel in vicinity, please report to Malin Head Coastguard. Over."

Silence. More silence. No rescue boat this time? Time seemed to stand still. I grabbed the microphone:

"Malin Head Coastguard, this is the Swedish sailing yacht Regina, position one mile north-east of Melmore Head on easterly course."

I mentioned our easterly course, to announce that we actually had already passed Melmore Head. I also wanted to stress that we were a yacht and possibly not the best suited to save windsurfers in difficulties close to land.

"Yacht Regina, this is Malin Head Coastguard, thank you. What is your ETA to Claddaghanillian Bay?"

We got the sails down, turned round and started motoring back into the swell and wind towards Melmore Head. The water temperature was 13 deg C (55 F). I knew that if I had been in water that cold I would hope someone was coming to get me as fast as possible.

- "8 minutes", I responded and pushed the throttle up to the maximum.

I looked for Claddaghanillian Bay on the chart. There were rocks all around it. As we motored we talked quickly about launching the dinghy and trying to use that to rescue the man.

To my considerable relief, there then came another voice on the radio:

- "Malin Head Coastguard, this is Melmore Rescue Boat, we are on our way. ETA 4 minutes."

They were going to get there before us.

We circled and watched and listened as the coastguard coordinated the rescue. It became obvious that is was very difficult for the Melmore Resuce craft to find the surfer in the swell. One time, it even passed the casualty by no more than 100 yards and still they could not see him.

Minutes passed like hours. Finally, relief came.

- "Malin Head Coastguard, this is Melmore Rescue, casualty found, taking him aboard at this moment. He is breathing with difficulty."

- "Melmore Rescue, copy that. Confirm you have him in thermo blankets and proceed with first aid. An ambulance is waiting for you ashore."

They left in high speed and we all hoped that there would be many more windsurfing afternoons for the man now lying in thermo blankets inside the rescue boat.

Regina was finally released from her backup mission and we went on to Lough Swilly. The rescue had left us all feeling a bit sombre. It had reminded us how dangerous the sea can be. But, as we anchored, three bottlenose dolphins swam up to the boat. They dived under the hull and swam around us, sometimes lifting their heads above the surface, as if to get a better look at us. It was the closest we had got to dolphins on the whole of our trip. "They are cheering us up", Jessica said, "I think they want to tell us that everything is fine with the windsurfer."

The west coast of Ireland can be dangerous. But it can be delightful, too.

Little Skellig, home to many thousand gannets

CREW

Who you sail with depends entirely on your personal circumstances. I was lucky to have Karolina, Jessica and Jonathan (and Tom) for our trip but all sorts of variations can work, including going alone.

It's important both you and your passenger are clear about the difference between 'crew' and 'visitor'. The latter can lie back and enjoy themselves, 'crew' are there to play an active role, stand watches, do their share of the washing up and help move the boat from one cruising ground to the next. They should, of course, also enjoy themselves.

For couples, the question is usually whether to do the long passages alone or with one or two extra crew, or for the weaker sailor to go by air and for friends of the skipper to take his or her place.

I was very pleased to complete our first ocean crossing alone as a family. Others we met found the addition of one extra crew made the night watches easier and everyone behave with a little more civility. Others fell out with their crew, spoiling what should have been a golden time. You will know what is best for you.

If you decide to look for additional crew, start early and pay more attention to compatibility than to sailing expertise. You will know your boat by the time you get to a longer passage and should have plenty of time to teach sufficient basics in the first few days at sea.

Give each other as much space as possible. At sea, leave someone who has gone to the foredeck alone with their thoughts. At anchor, let your spouse sometimes go off in the dinghy on his or her own. Everyone on board must have their own locker where their stuff is findable when they want it. And don't insist that everything on the boat be perfect all the time. If a member of the crew feels like a bath, some crisp linen and a meal cooked by someone else, book the odd night in a hotel.

Most importantly, stay honest with each other and respect each other's needs. Learning to do that well will be one of the biggest benefits of your time away.

Jonathan and dolphins in Lough Swilly

Helping us home

Chapter twenty nine

In which we reflect and return

THE LIST

On a night watch somewhere on the North Sea, I found The List. The List had been written years earlier, long before we left home for our sailing adventure. It had been part of the process through which we had put ourselves before making our decision. On it were listed all the points for going and all the points against.

I had forgotten about The List and read it eagerly. Had our hopes been met, I wondered? Had our fears proved groundless?

These are the points we had listed as reasons for going:

Meeting exciting new people
Becoming better sailors
Finding time to write and to take photographs
Doing exciting hikes
Reading many good books
Seeing new countries and cultures
Swimming and snorkelling
Spending time in a warm climate
The chance to try something new
Learning and practising new languages
Filling life with adventures and something to remember
Being able to concentrate on one thing at a time
Achieving the satisfaction of reaching a goal and a dream
Finding the 'meaning of life'
Finding quietness and time to think
Living a more healthy life-style
Feeling self-sufficient
Welding the family together

Our fears were summarised in the following points against going:

Frequently being far from medical care
Living on a tight budget
No jobs to return to
Uncertainty about life after the cruise
Living without our old friends or family close by
A year away from professional teaching for the children
No car – having to walk and carry everything
Doing the laundry and washing-up by hand
Sharing a room with your sibling
Not being able to have all your things with you
Frequently having to part from friends
Not being able to keep up hobbies like tennis, dancing, and music
Living without a high-speed internet connection

The List was compiled by all four of us as a family, and in no specific order. The important thing is not the exact contents of The List but that it is honest. If one member of the crew is looking for an adventure on storm-tossed seas and another is after sunshine and relaxation, some re-thinking is probably necessary.

After talking to many cruisers, we have reached the conclusion that it is important for each member of the crew to have their own positive reason for going. If the best they can think of is "because my spouse wants me to" or "because my parents say we have to", the voyage is unlikely to be a success. Some single-handed sailors go that way from choice. Many do not.

All sorts of things can provide that meaning. We met happy cruisers who had taken up art and couldn't wait until they got to a new place to paint. Others collected recipes and yet more were bird watchers. We met a French couple on a catamaran, who held small concerts in marinas, playing *chansons* for whoever wanted to listen. Others were divers, using sailing as a means to reach new underwater worlds and many children collected courtesy flags, postcards, stamps or shells.

Some items on The List now made us laugh. One in particular was our worry about having to live without a car. Since returning, we have really questioned the need for a car. We try to take the bus or walk whenever we can.

Although we had recognised that schooling would be a challenge, we hadn't realised just how much time and emotional effort it would entail. We found it difficult to be our own kids' teachers, at least when it came to persuading them to get on with some of the less-exciting stuff. We did our best to focus on the basic subjects of reading, writing, maths and English. We did skip bits of the curriculum: Jessica and Jonathan could not list all the major rivers in Sweden, but did know the nine Azorean and most Caribbean islands from north to south. They had missed out on playing in sports teams but had learned how to get along with children from all over the world. They didn't know the Swedish kings, but did know a lot about the colonial history of the British and French. They couldn't name Swedish politicians, but could distinguish between species of dolphins. In other words, they learned different, but equally valid, things.

It had been difficult to keep up with hobbies, something we would take up again, once at home. For a year new hobbies, such as snorkelling, cooking and hiking, had replaced our old ones. These had given us just as much pleasure.

What our children did miss was Swedish food! We were all really looking forward to Swedish meatballs and lingonberries when we got home. But, at the same time, we also missed the fresh tuna and mahi-mahi we had enjoyed so much in the tropics.

Surprisingly, Jessica and Jonathan did not complain about sharing a cabin and did not miss any material possession for which there had not been room. They played a lot with each other and very seldom quarreled. In fact, most boat kids we met seemed to be pretty good with each other. The care and concern they showed when appropriate was quite touching. There was no bullying. No one got excluded from a game. No one was looked down on for lacking the latest trendy gear. Boys and girls, younger and older children all mixed together happily.

What was the best thing about our trip? I would say the people we spent time with; starting with our own children, and rippling out to all the amazing individuals we came across along the way. We made a lot of wonderful new friends for life and built confidence in our ability to make new friends and to keep them despite frequent partings. Jessica and Jonathan became completely fluent in English.

I personally also enjoyed being able to deal with one issue at a time, concentrating on the task I was working on, instead of having millions of projects on the go simultaneously. Karolina just laughs when I say this, believing a failure to multi-task is a typical male problem.

What have we learned during the year? Well, an important thing I learned was that there is usually more than one way to achieve something. The English have a rather revolting saying: 'there is more than one way to skin a cat'. I didn't skin any cats, but seeing how things are done differently yet successfully in different countries and by different sailors I truly learned the importance of flexibility. Whatever is going on, the important thing is to remain focused, look for work-arounds if necessary, stay innovative, see possibilities where others might see problems and constantly work on improving your system or situation.

We learnt also to distinguish between issues we could influence and things we could not. If the bus was late or the customs office had closed for the day, there was nothing we could do about it. The best thing to do was to take it easy. And we learned that we could achieve more than we ever had imagined. Even huge obstacles, such as an ocean, could be overcome by taking one step at a time and using common sense. Nowadays we are less frightened by change. We are looking forward to new challenges, whatever they might be.

So, there are all those reasons for going. But there are also practical things that hold you back. Often people have suggested that it was easy for us because we had the money, or the boat, or the experience, or the confidence in our children managing without settled schooling. The list goes on. But, of course, it's not really about us. It's about them and their excuse for not going.

I can admit today that I used to think a bit like that. If only I had more money, I would be able to go. But I was wrong. We met cruisers with all sorts of backgrounds and all of them had made sacrifices of some sort to get away. And so have we. It might take as many as ten years to re-build the savings that we spent during this one year. We sold our house. We passed on our business. But money can be earned again. The chance to experience what we experienced, especially with your family, might never return.

Living your dream is one thing, but living after you've achieved your dream is another challenge altogether. How do you live with no more goals or dreams? Do you become like the Olympic champion, who gets depressed after winning the medal he has worked for all his life. I have heard from other cruisers that it helps to have a new project to work on once you get back: a new house, a new job, or preparation for another cruise. It is best not to spend your whole time regretting the fact that you've returned.

We had moved on from our old lives to build something new. It took us a year to understand this. Slowly, things that had previously seemed important acquired new meanings. By taking our sabbatical cruising year, we had learnt how to open up and be prepared for new things, not just on our return but for the rest of our lives. We hadn't rejected our old lives. There was still much we valued there. But it was experience on which we would build, not a set of habits in which we would stay trapped.

I went back up into the cockpit and looked around for lights, checked the course and the sails. Within a few hours, we would make landfall in Norway, our home waters, and from there, it would just be a short distance to Regina's home in Sweden.

I looked forward to our adventures at sea continuing ashore.

Regina under gennaker

Väderöarna on the west coast of Sweden

Chapter thirty
In which we open a new chapter in our lives

THE COMPASS BOXED

Yet another box, still to be opened, sat in front of me. It was numbered '62'. What did that signify? I opened it. It was full of old shoes. Didn't I open a box full of old shoes yesterday? I moved on to the next; clothes. Where would we put them?

Our new flat was a lot bigger than Regina but a lot smaller than our old house. Today it looked like there was going to be less space for us in it than there had been on the boat.

I continued to another box-filled corner of the room. Would there be something more interesting in these? I opened one and found cables, another contained videotapes, another lamps, and several were full of filed documents. I opened a file: invoices. Why?

Slowly, we began to remember why. Why all these things had been important to us. I remembered my fear of missing these essentials. They felt more like an encumbrance now. Why had we needed so many things?

Having worn shorts and T-shirts for a year, there was something a bit sad about opening a box of heavy, winter clothes. It was as if they were saying 'you don't want us, but you'll need us. It's going to get cold, you know.' As for the big, grey, ugly TV, who had missed that? Not us when watching a DVD on a laptop under the stars with friends, that was for sure.

So, here we were, unpacking our old lives. I felt a stark sense that we had changed a lot since we had put this lot into the boxes.

Instead of collecting possessions, time for each other and time for adventure were what we valued now. Time is the big thing people seem to lack these days. I thought back to the Time Management courses for busy businessmen I had been on, and smiled. What use were they compared to the Island Time lesson taught in the Caribbean?

Everything suddenly seemed to move so fast. And most frightening of all was the ease with which we were drawn back into our old ways. It did not take long until we were part of the time-lacking, money-making world once more.

Money can be earned, saved, distributed and grow and does not age. With time, it's different. Contrary to its monetary counterpart, time is equally spread among people; everyone is granted 24 hours every morning, as a gift. The same amount every day, neither less nor more. It's up to you to invest these 24 hours wisely – you will never get them back. You can't put time into a bank account, saving it for later. Similarly, you can't get time on credit. Time, we now felt, was more valuable to us than money.

With Island Time left back on the boat, we all accelerated back into our 21st century, multi-tasking environment. No longer was there time to stand still, to pause, or just to think over a situation before taking action. So many things are to be organised, so many tasks to complete, and all simultaneously.

Of course, we managed. It didn't take long until we also began to enjoy the various luxuries life ashore could offer. Our 14 months of cruising began to fade in our memories. Had we really gone away sailing for a year or had it all been a dream?

I carried on poking through the opened boxes. One, hidden behind some kitchen appliances, looked familiar. When I opened it, a scent of freedom welcomed me in. I dug deep. There were several heavy layers of magazines and brochures collected over decades. Information about good marinas along the west coast of Europe, cruising boats brochures, tips on provisioning, ideas on equipment and other essentials for a sabbatical year on a boat. It was the box of my dreams. These had kept me company through many a night, while I dreamt of going cruising. And now? Quicker than I could ever have imagined, we had gone and come back.

I looked at my treasures from the past. Since I last had them in my hands, we had grown to be like the experienced sailors described in the magazine pages. I smiled and nodded in approval as I browsed through the bundle. Yes, this was how it had been; this was what we had experienced, too. This had been our life. And now? Do we feel boxed in? Is it all over?

I think you could feel like that after a trip like ours. But we decided that was not what we were going to do. We were now in a new chapter of our lives and, like the last, we would make the most of it. We don't know what this chapter will contain. It won't be the same sort of adventure as crossing an ocean, but it will be an adventure. That is for sure.

Moving on does not mean pretending the past has not happened, however. There is nothing wrong with looking back a bit. I put the cruising files into a convenient bookshelf. Maybe they would be useful again one day? I knew we would not go long-term cruising again until Jessica and Jonathan had finished school. But that time would come.

While I was dreaming, Karolina was doing some serious work, sorting through a pile of papers on our kitchen table. "Bills", she said and got out the laptop to log in and start organizing online payments. Living on shore certainly involves spending a lot more money than had been the case while cruising. We needed money for rent, electricity, water, heating, car insurance, petrol, health insurance, TV-licence fees and taxes. We bought new bikes for Jessica and Jonathan and our trips to Ikea meant not only more furniture and stuff to fit into the flat but also more bills. "The boat had all the furniture we needed…" I grumbled. Karolina ignored me.

But it is a new chapter. It has been fun to move house and start afresh. It wasn't long before we started to enjoy ourselves. Every morning, when Jessica and Jonathan happily scampered away to school, I felt gratitude for their professional teachers. I wonder how many families really understand how fortunate they are to have a school for their children?

Jessica and Jonathan love their new school and, I am proud to say, had no difficulties whatsoever going back in after a year away. They were actually quite a bit ahead of their schoolmates and not just in obvious subjects like English. Somehow, despite the frequent heart-ache, schooling on the boat seems to have worked. So, dear blue-water-dreamer-with-children, don't blame your hesitation on your kids. Don't postpone your cruising adventures, just because of your children. Just be prepared to become a semi-professional teacher. And forget about spending your mornings at anchor reading or learning the guitar.

I needed a rest from unpacking boxes and Karolina had paid the bills. The children were still at school, so she suggested we go grocery shopping before they got home. Before we went sailing we had never realized what a luxury it is just to be able to stroll to a shop and buy food or pretty much anything else. There are no backpacks and no checking for cockroaches. Once home, the fridge opens at the front and you put things in and take things out. There's no standing bent over the top-loaded boat fridge, having to take everything out before getting anything in.

And it's so easy to get rid of rubbish. Having spent so long reducing and reducing the amount of rubbish we produced, it felt strange to just throw things into bins. Where does it all go? Unrestricted fresh water is another treat we have difficulties getting used to. We can enjoy a long, luxurious shower without having to worry about the water level in our tanks. It just keeps coming out of the wall. The same goes for electricity. As long as we pay for it, it comes as soon as we throw the switch. No more do we have to wash our clothes with our feet. And the dishwasher does its job much better and more quietly than I ever could.

Despite all this and despite our determination to make the most of this new chapter, many of the people around us still seem unhappy and unsatisfied. Is it just the lack of time? All too well could I remember how I felt before we went. Every morning felt like Monday morning. We had found a track, which did not seem to lead anywhere particular. Just straight on. "Ha!" I said out loud. Karolina looked at me, wondering what was going on in my head. "Remember how difficult we felt it was to actually take the decision to 'give up everything' and go cruising?" I said.

Karolina laughed. "Yes, that is true! And now we are already back again. But next time, we know just how possible it is to go. All you need is the courage to drop those mooring lines."

She was right, both literally and spiritually. The actual decision to go cruising had been the single most difficult part of our whole sailing adventure. Why? We had been afraid of change, of course. We were doubtful how much our children would enjoy it. We didn't want to leave family and friends. We were worried about our financial situation. And our plans were questioned by others.

Knowing how easy it is to switch – in both directions – gives us a sense of freedom that is now one of our biggest sources of happiness. We can look at our current shore-life with all its possibilities and luxuries as an opportunity. But we know that, should we, once again, wish to find a life beyond roads, shopping malls and dishwashers, the decision to go will not be difficult.

Of course, there are times we miss the cruising life. If I was totally honest, I would rather still be out there. Some of our friends went on. They got to places like Venezuela, Cuba, Mexico, San Blas and Galapagos and some are still going. It hurts a bit, to think that as I write families new to cruising are on their way to the Canaries for their first Atlantic crossing. I wonder whether these families and couples are having the same fantastic time as we had? Who are they? Have they found each other, yet? A little bit of emptiness creeps into my heart when I realise that I am not a part of it anymore.

I went back to my cruising files and picked out an old blue-water sailing magazine. I had read it many times before. It was still a delight but I read it now with new eyes. I knew this wasn't just dreams. This could be true. And we could be part of it again.

And we might go again, one day, when the time is right to cut another centimetre out of our lives!

Karolina, Leon, Jessica and Jonathan on Bequia

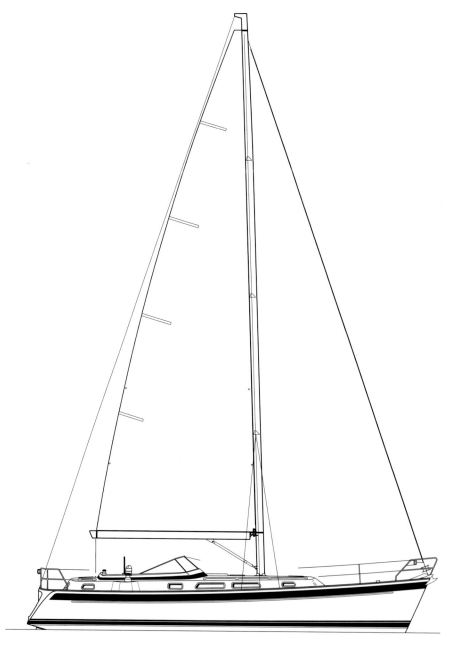

Hallberg-Rassy 40. Courtesy of Hallberg-Rassy ©

THE BOAT

We equipped the boat for a variety of waters and future possibilities. Safety was our top priority.

Hallberg-Rassy 40	Hull No 6
Designer	Germán Frers
Hull Length	12,40m / 40'8"
Max Sailing Waterline	11,52m / 37'10"
Waterline at Rest	10,60m / 34'9"
Beam	3,82m / 12'6"
Draft	1,99m / 6'7"
Displacement	10t / 22 000 lbs
Lead Keel	4,1t / 9 100 lbs
Sail Area with Working Jib	80,8 m2 / 869 ft2
Sail Area with Furling Genoa	93,5 m2 / 1006 ft2
LYS handicap, approx	1.24
Water Tanks	(2) 353 l / 93USG
Hot Water Tank	(1) 40 l / 11 USG
Mast over Water incl. Antennas	19,8 m / 65 ft

RIG AND SAILS

Mast	Seldén 19/20, cutter, with double spreaders and manual in-mast furling	www.seldenmast.com
Mast steps	2 foldable steps at top of mast	
Granny bars	Pulpit around mast ("granny bars") for safe and comfortable work at mast	
Furling	by Seldén: Furlex genoa furling	www.seldenmast.com
Boom	1 spinnakerboom stowed along mast	www.seldenmast.com
Halyards	2 mainsail, 2 genoa, 1 gennaker, 1 cutter	www.seldenmast.com
Vang	by Seldén: Rodkick with gas spring	www.seldenmast.com
Mast trim	by Seldén: manual backstay tensioner with winch handle	www.seldenmast.com
Winches	by Lewmar, genoa: 50CEST electrical (2), mainsail: 30CST manual (2), on mast: additional 2	www.lewmar.com
Main Sail	by Elvström Furling Main EMS4V, 41.9 m2, vertical battens, Gitterspectra, 380 oz	www.elvstromsails.com
Genoa	by Elvström Gitterspectra, 51.6 m2, 380 oz	www.elvstromsails.com
Jib	by Elvström, standard, 38.9 m2	www.elvstromsails.com
Staysail	by Elvström, apprx 17 m2 on cutter stay	www.elvstromsails.com
Gennaker	by Elvström, 125 m2,	www.elvstromsails.com
Anchor Sail	by Sydsegel	www.sydsegel.se

PROPULSION

Engine	by Volvo Penta, D2-55 , 55 hp	www.penta.volvo.se
Impellerseal	by TrueMarine: Speedseal Impeller cover	www.speedseal.com
Ventilation	electrical engine room fan	
Propeller	by Gori, 3 blade foldable with overdrive, fixed as reserve	www.gori-propeller.dk
Coupling	by Centa: Centaflex M 160K 3,2 35mm flexible shaft coupling	www.centa.info
Thruster	by Sleipner: SP95T, 8 hp, 12V	www.sleipner.no
Rope Cutter	by Ambassador, 3 blade	www.ropestripper.com
Diesel	475 ltrs in 2 stainless steel tanks	
Fuel Filter	by Racor: 500MAM10	www.racor.com
Oil Filter	by FilterMag: Magnetic Oil Filtration fitted onto standard oil filter	www.filtermag.com
Funnel	by Mr Funnel for safe tanking in addition to the two diesel filters in series and draining pump of main tank	www.mrfunnel.com
Additives	by Parker: Racor Diesel Biocide, to eliminate bacteria growth,	www.racor.com
	by Soltron: Enzyme Solutions, to burn off contaminated fuel	www.soltron.co.uk

ELECTRICS

Batteries	Service Bat. by Trojan: 8 x T105, 12V 900 Ah	www.trojanbattery.com
	Batteries for SSB: by Tudor 24V, 62Ah	www.tudor.se
	Engine Start Batteries by Tudor: 12V, 62 Ah	www.tudor.se
Shore Power	by Mastervolt: Isolation Transformer (110V and 230V), Ivet-C16, 3.5kW	www.mastervolt.com
Charging	by Volvo-Penta: Standard 60A on main engine	www.penta.volvo.se
	by Amptech: 160A High Output Alternator (HOA) on main engine	
	by Mastervolt: Alpha Pro 3-step regulator	www.mastervolt.com
	by Electromarine: HOA brackets for Volvo Penta D2-55	www.electromarine.no
	by Mastervolt: Shore Power MASS 12/60 from 230V to 12V, 60A	www.mastervolt.com
	by Thrane&Thrane: CH4656, from 230V to 24V	www.thrane.com
	by DuoGen: Combined Wind & Water generator	www.duogen.co.uk
Inverter	by Mastervolt: Mass Sine 12/2000, from 12V to 230V, 2kW	www.mastervolt.com
Instruments	by Volvo-Penta: 12V instrument for engine battery	www.penta.volvo.se
	by WEMA: 12V instrument for house battery	www.wema.no
	DCC 4000 Ah and charging supervision	www.odelco.se

STEERING

Helm	by Whitlock: Wheel steering by wire	www.lewmar.com
Emergency	Tiller steering, direct from aft cabin	
Autopilot	by Raymarine:	www.raymarine.com
	Main control unit at helm: ST7001	www.raymarine.com
	Secondary control unit at hatch: ST6001	www.raymarine.com
	Computer: 400G with rate gyro and AST ("Advanced Steering Techn.")	www.raymarine.com
	Drive unit: Typ II, electrical, liniar	www.raymarine.com

NAVIGATION

Compass	At helm: by Suunto	www.suunto.com
	Electronic: by Raymarine, high speed fluxgate	www.raymarine.com
Nav.System	by Raymarine:	www.raymarine.com
	In cockpit: RL70C colour Radar/MARPA/Plotter with Radar Overlay	www.raymarine.com
	On radar pole on aft deck: 2 kW Radome antenna	www.raymarine.com
	In cockpit: ST60 Logg + ST60 Sounder + ST60 Wind	www.raymarine.com
	In cockpit: ST6001+ Auto Pilot Control Unit	www.raymarine.com
	At chart table: RL70RC b&w Radar/MARPA/Plotter	
	At chart table: ST60 Multi	
Interface	by Raymarine: NMEA/RS232C with serial PC connection	
Radar Refl.	by Blipper: Passive 210 Radar reflector on mast	
	by Jotron: Active Radar Reflector ARR	www.jotron.no
GPS	by Raymarine: Raystar125 (WAAS)	www.raymarine.com
	by FURUNO: GP-32 (WAAS)	www.furuno.com
	by Garmin: Handheld GPS eTrex	www.garmin.com
	by Magallan: eXplorist200	
AIS (added later)	by True Heading: AIS-CTRX Class B Transponder	www.trueheading.se
	by Y-Tronic: Yacht AIS Transponder Software	www.y-tronic.com
Binoculars	by Steiner: 7x50AC Commander III w/compass	www.steiner.de
Sextant	by Celestair: Astra III B Delux with WH Mirror	www.celestaire.com
Barograph	by Vion: Electronic "Weatherstation" A4000	www.vion-marine.com
Software	by MaxSea on PC: "Yacht" includ. weather module for GRIB-files	www.maxsea.com
	by Pangolin: TideComp 2000 for Tidal Calculations	www.pangolin.co.nz
	by Pangolin: Nautical Almanac	www.pangolin.co.nz
	by Pangolin: Astro Calculator for Celectical Navigation	www.pangolin.co.nz
Charts	by C-Map: NT+	www.c-map.no
	Paper Charts	

Liferaft	by bfa-marine: 6 person	www.zodiacmarine.com
Fire-fighting	1 x 6 kg and 3 x 2 kg fire-extinguisher, one in each cabin plus in cockpit locker	
	Fire blanket in galley	
Pumps	Manual bilge pump operated from under deck	
	Electrical emergency pump	
	by Robota: mobile 230V high capacity pump "Best One Automatic" 150 l/min, also useful as fire extinguisher	www.robota.se
	by Jotron: TRON40GPS, 400MHz, GMDSS, with Hammar H20 hydrostatic release.	www.jotron.no www.cmhammar.com
EPIRB	by Jotron: TRON45S, 400 MHz in grab-bag	www.jotron.no
	by SeaMarshall: 4 personal mini-EPIRBs,	www.seamarshall.com
	by SeaMarshall: homing device for personal EPIRBs	
SART	by Jotron: Search And Recue Transponder SART	www.jotron.no
Watermaker	by Katadyn: Survivor 06 Manual (previoulsy "PUR")	www.katadyn.com
Life buoys	by Plastimo: one standard life buoy	
	by Swebuoy: man-overboard life sling/buoy	
	by Hansa: "Hansa-Linan Båt" throwing line	
Dan buoy	by Plastimo: Dan Buoy with light	www.plastimo.com
Ladder	by Plastimo: Safety ladder with 5 steps for bow or midship	www.plastimo.com
Strobe lights	by Jotron: Life buoy strobe light TRON5F	www.jotron.no
	by Jotron: one AQ4 strobe light	www.jotron.no
Life vests	by Jotron: four AQ5 strobe lights	www.jotron.no
	by Kadematic: 15ALR-DW incl spraycap, light, harness (2)	www.kadematic.de
	by Kadematic: 15 Bebe AL incl light, harness (2)	www.kadematic.de
	by Secumar: X-treme harness (2)	www.secumar.com
	additional harnesses (3)	
	by Baltic: 3 sailing vests Offshore with harnesses	www.baltic-sweden.com
Jack Stays	by Baltic: 2 children sized vests	www.baltic-sweden.com
	2 lifelines of woven ribbon along decks for safety harness	
Flares	by Wichard: 3 x W06505 fittings for harnesses in cockpit	www.wichard.com
	by Hansson PyroTech: 8 parachute, 8 red, 4 white,	
Lightning	2 smoke	
	Lightning protection by connection of mast, stays and shrouds with lead keel	
Cable Cutter		
Drogue	Felco C16 for emergency demasting	www.felco.ch
Grab-bag	by Hathaway: Galerider Storm, 36"	www.hathaways.com
	by Pelican: 1520 (watertight)	www.pelican.com

COMMUNICATIONS

VHF	Main by Sailor at chart table: A1 with DSC, GMDSS	www.thrane.com
	Secondary handset in cockpit: C4951WP, waterproof IP67	www.thrane.com
	Working handheld by Jotron: TRON TR20+, splashproof	www.jotron.no
	Emergency handheld by Jotron: TRON VHF GMDSS, waterproof, floating	www.jotron.no
MF/HF	SSB by Sailor: System 4000, 150W, with DSC, GMDSS for Area A2	www.thrane.com www.thrane.com
Sat-C	by Thrane&Thrane: TT 3026L/M, Inmarsat Mini-C	www.thrane.com
Iridium	by Sailor: SC4000, fixed marine, with data and external antenna	
NAVTEX	by FURUNO: Navtex NX-300	www.furuno.com
Antennas	by Comrod:	www.comrod.com
	VHF Main in masttop: AV51P	www.comrod.com
	VHF DSC on Radar Pole: AV51BI	www.comrod.com
	MAS1 Multifunctional on radar pole: SSB DSC + AM/FM Stereo + NAVTEX	www.comrod.com
	AC15 on radar pole: GSM, triband 800MHz + 900MHz + 1800MHz	www.comrod.com
	by Sailor: Automatic Antenna Tuning Unit HA4615 and Back Stay	www.thrane.com
	by Ronstan: Antenna isolator on backstay	www.ronstan.com
	Earth plates (3) and Bonding	
Software	by Mailasail: Iridium Compression	www.mailasail.com
	by Thrane&Thrane: EasyMail for Mini-C	www.thrane.com
	by Pangolin: HF Propagation predictor for SSB	www.pangolin.co.nz
	by Xaxero: Weatherfax 2000	www.xaxero.com
	by Xaxero: WindPlot GRIB-file Viewer	www.xaxero.com
	by Grib.us: Grib file reader	www.grib.us

ANCHOR AND MOORING

Main	Delta, 20kg, stowed at bow	www.lewmar.com
Chain	60m 3/8" chain for main anchor	
Windlass	by Lewmar: Ocean 1	www.lewmar.com
Controls	from fore deck and remotely from helm	
Stopper	Chain hook and separate line	www.hr-parts.com
Second	Bruce, 15kg, 10m chain + 70m woven "ribbon" Ankarolina, stowed on pushpit.	www.bruceanchor.co.uk
Third	Breeze, 15kg	
Davit	by Noa on stern pushpit for Bruce/Breeze	www.noa.se
Light	On masttop plus Sure-A-Light by Suremitron	www.suremitron.com
Cables/Ropes	3 x 50 m (150' "Panama-chanel size")	
	2 x 30 m	
	numerous x 10 m for mooring	
Compensators	by Aronowitsch&Lyth AB: Mooring Compensator "Bungy"	www.arolyth.se

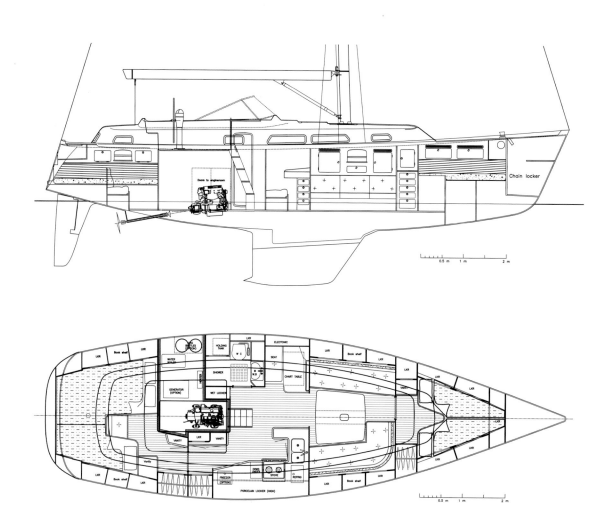

Hallberg-Rassy 40. Courtesy of Hallberg-Rassy ©

GALLEY, HEAD, WATER AND COMFORT

Stove	by ENO: Gascogne model 0823	www.eno.fr
Gas	2 x 6kg Swedish bottles with Propane	
Gas valve	by Truma: GS8 Gas Remote Switch, operated from galley	www.truma.com
Gas adapter	by Fogas: Part No 12-6022 to fill up Gas in other countries	www.fogas.se
Watermaker	by Spectra: Newport 400, 12V, 60 l/hour	
	(in Grab-Bag for Safety by Katadyn: Survivor 06 Manual)	www.katadyn.com
Water filter	active coal filter in central water system	
Hot Water	by Isotherm: 40 l, heated by engine and/or shore power	www.isotherm.com
Heater	by Webasto: AirTop 3500, 3,5 kW	www.webasto.com
Pumps	by Whale: Gulper 220 shower discharge pump	www.whalepumps.com
	by Jabsco: PAR MAX3 fresh water pump	www.jabsco.com
	by Flojet: R4325-145 deck flush pump, 13 l/min	
Fridge	Isotherm with Danfoss compressor, SP-system, water cooled	www.isotherm.com
Freezer	Isotherm with double thermostat (thus also usable as fridge)	www.isotherm.com
Toilet	by Jabsco: PAR with holding tank	www.jabsco.com
Ventilation	by Lewmar: 3 skylights	www.lewmar.com
	10 opening port holes	
	Electrolux vent over V-cabin	
	4 dorade vents (2 in saloon and 2 in aft cabin)	
	6 Hella Turbo fans (V-cabin, galley, nav-station, aft cabin)	
	Original Mosquito Net by Lewmar for Hatches	www.lewmar.com
	Mosquito Net for baby trolley over hatch	
Lee cloths	2 in saloon and 2 in aft cabin	www.hr-parts.com
Water Treatment	By DTI, Sweden: XINIX FreeBact-20	

AUXILIARIES

Dinghy	by Achilles: LSR96	www.achillesusa.com
Outboard	by Yamaha: 8C 2-stroke, 8 hp	www.yamaha.com